FOXTON
INCLINED PLANE

A HISTORY OF THE 'THOMAS' CANAL BARGE LIFT

A boat outing mainly for children circa 1901, the highlight of which was a journey up the inclined plane.
Taken from a lantern slide, this is most probably a Sunday School trip, because there are a number of adults present as well. The good condition of the caisson's paintwork suggests an early date. It is ascending the inclined plane having just come out of the lower canal basin, as evidenced by the water pouring from the wheel assemblies. Note the relatively minor leakage from the bottom of the guillotine gate.

The top of the Foxton Inclined Plane in winter, as photographed from the upper canal arm, possibly soon after the inclined plane was closed in November 1910 but before it was finally abandoned with the caissons midway down the plane. COURTESY THE FOXTON INCLINED PLANE TRUST

The reasons for suggesting this dating are the poor condition of the paintwork on the winding house; the lack of smoke from the chimney even though the caisson is clearly partly down the plane; the lack of any visible human activity and the fact that the stoplogs are missing from the the gable ended structure which housed them, sited to the right of the coal chute from the left hand aqueduct.

FOXTON
INCLINED PLANE

A HISTORY OF THE 'THOMAS' CANAL BARGE LIFT

DAVID CARDEN

Black Dwarf
Publications

CANAL AND FOXTON LOCKS, NEAR MARKET HARBOROUGH.

A circa 1905 picture postcard of the Grand Union Canal, inclined plane and locks at Foxton. PARKHOUSE/POPE ARCHIVE

FOREWORD

Over the last forty years, there have been a number of books about the Foxton Inclined Plane and Foxton Locks. As Keeper of the Foxton Inclined Plane Trust's Museum, I have read all of them and have been personally involved in the production of several. Of particular note is the work by Peter Gardner and Frank Foden, the first to produce a modern book, and also that by Dave Goodwin. During the years since, no one has gone back to the primary sources and reviewed all of the evidence so thoroughly. This book does just that.

Historical research involves being just like a detective or a scientist. You must go to the original evidence, in this case documents and photographs, evaluate the witness statements and the existing publications, weigh up the evidence and come to conclusions. As an author, you then have to present the results in a readable and interesting way. This book does all of this and gives you, the reader, the opportunity to evaluate the evidence for yourselves.

I could not have written this book. I am passionate about the lift, why it was built, why it declined and why it should be rebuilt. I cannot, however, provide a detached evaluation of the evidence. To me, the lift and its history are simply wonderful.

I became Chairman of the Foxton Inclined Plane Trust at its first meeting in 1980 and, for the last twenty years, have been employed as the full time Keeper of the Foxton Canal Museum. I hope that you enjoy this book as much as I have but, be warned, the locks and the Foxton Inclined Plane boat lift get under your skin; you too could become an enthusiast, perhaps even a member of the Trust.

Michael G. Beech, Foxton 2012

So far, although much has been written about the wider Foxton Locks site, few have focussed as closely as David Carden has within these pages on the fascinating detail of the boat lift, which was its centre piece at the beginning of the 20th century.

Lest we forget, the boat lift was intended to replace the double staircase of locks, which was creating a huge bottleneck, hampering competition against the railways. Sadly, the expected trade did not emerge and, despite being an industrial masterpiece, the structure was mothballed, only to be sold for scrap a decade later, with the locks re-emerging as the only route up or down the hill for boats. Lying dormant, the site became overgrown and the remains largely ignored, apart from the active Foxton Inclined Plane Trust which has worked tirelessly to recognise their importance and campaigning for restoration

On the positive side, around a century after it was first opened, the Foxton Locks Partnership raised almost £3 million towards partial restoration, including rewatering the upper arm, dredging the bottom basin and clearing the plane of vegetation, together with interpretation and access improvements.

Completion of this phase of work led to commissioning of a masterplan to guide the full restoration, including supporting visitor facilities. Unfortunately, the current economic climate makes it unlikely that external funding can be found to carry out full restoration to working condition. Much, however, is still to be done and I believe that David is the one who will be able to tell it. It has been said that the only certain thing about the future is uncertainty.

James Clifton, Regeneration Manager, British Waterways & Chairman of the Foxton Locks Partnership, 2012

CONTENTS

© Black Dwarf Publications & David Carden 2012
Designed by Neil Parkhouse

British Library Cataloguing-in-Publication Data.
A catalogue record for this book is available from the British Library

ISBN: 9781903599 20 4

BLACK DWARF PUBLICATIONS

**Unit 144B, Lydney Trading Estate, Harbour Road,
Lydney, Gloucestershire GL15 5EJ**
www.lightmoor.co.uk

BLACK DWARF PUBLICATIONS is an imprint of
BLACK DWARF LIGHTMOOR PUBLICATIONS LTD

Printed by
Berforts Information Press, Eynsham, Oxford

A picturesque summer view of Foxton Junction, circa 1905. COURTESY THE FOXTON INCLINED PLANE TRUST

The junction at the bottom of Foxton Locks, nicely framed by the arch of the turnover bridge carrying the towpath from one side of the canal to the other. The buildings of the inclined plane on the skyline appear to be in good condition, although neither of the caissons are in view which suggests that they are in operation on the plane or that they have been parked up halfway down the plane. The bottom lock is under the bridge, middle right, whilst the building that is today the Foxton Locks Inn is visible behind the trees on the left.

INTRODUCTION

'Such a concentration of narrow locks [at Foxton] *takes some time to negotiate, and constitutes a serious hindrance to traffic, because boats are unable to pass each other except between the groups of 'risers'. It was with the object of obviating this delay that the Foxton Inclined Plane Lift was constructed and opened for traffic in the spring of 1900. Of all the many strange freaks that the mechanical age has produced, this was one of the strangest, and the photographs of the extraordinary contrivance which hang in the bar of the 'Black Horse' in Foxton are well worth inspection.'*
Extract from Narrow Boat *by L.T.C Rolt*

These words, by the famous 20th century canal enthusiast and celebrated industrial author, Tom Rolt, provide a wonderfully quirky opening to this book. I opened my first book on the Anderton Boat Lift with a similarly disparaging quote, in that case taken from a letter by Mr G. Davies to the *New Civil Engineer* magazine on 7th March 1996, which referred to British Waterways' proposal to restore the historic boat lift as *'rebuilding a monster'*. As we now know, the so-called 'monster' was successfully rebuilt, or more accurately restored, to full operation and was formally re-opened to traffic on 26th March 2002.

Let me say at the outset that I admire and am humbled by the work of the Victorian engineers who designed and constructed these extraordinary structures, and I cannot agree with the suggestion that the Anderton Boat Lift is a monster nor that the Foxton Inclined Plane is one of the strangest freaks of the mechanical age. Presumably English Heritage wouldn't agree either, as it scheduled both of these canal structures as Ancient Monuments.

It is worthwhile continuing this comparison between the Anderton Boat Lift and the Foxton Inclined Plane a little further. Both structures were built on a grand scale at the end of the Victorian era, when civil engineers, such as Brunel and Telford, were not just professionals but were celebrities, carrying out audacious construction works with few of the tools available to modern-day engineers. Consider, for example, Brunel's Clifton suspension bridge or his Great Western Railway, or perhaps Telford's majestic Chirk and Pontcysyllte aqueducts on the Llangollen Canal, or the second Harecastle Tunnel on the Trent & Mersey Canal.

The needs that led to the construction of the Anderton Boat Lift and the Foxton Inclined Plane were the same; namely to overcome serious bottlenecks in Britain's canal system at a time when the commercial future of the canals was under serious threat. As early as the middle of the 19th century, engineers were predicting the demise of the country's canal system in the face of competition from the up and coming railways. For example:

'MR. BIDDER, V.P., said … with their [narrow canals] *present dimensions, he was convinced that they must eventually be superseded by railways. He therefore thought that all the different schemes of lifts and inclined planes could never, hereafter, be of practical utility.'*
Extract from the Proceedings of the Institution of Civil Engineers, 24th January 1854

With the threat from the railways even more of a reality, there must have been severe doubts regarding the wisdom of building the Anderton Boat Lift in 1875 and then the Foxton Inclined Plane in 1900, but both of these structures *were* built. The driving force behind them was the survival of the canals against the onslaught of the railways.

Both structures overcame major differences in height; in the case of the Anderton Boat Lift, 50ft 4ins between the Trent & Mersey Canal and the Weaver Navigation, whilst in the case of the Foxton Inclined Plane, it was 75ft 2ins on what is now referred to as the Leicester Arm of the Grand Union Canal, originally the Leicester Section of the Grand Junction Canal.

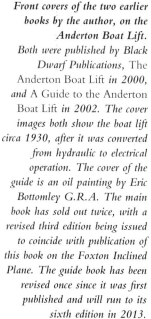

Front covers of the two earlier books by the author, on the Anderton Boat Lift. Both were published by Black Dwarf Publications, The Anderton Boat Lift *in 2000, and* A Guide to the Anderton Boat Lift *in 2002. The cover images both show the boat lift circa 1930, after it was converted from hydraulic to electrical operation. The cover of the guide is an oil painting by Eric Bottomley G.R.A. The main book has sold out twice, with a revised third edition being issued to coincide with publication of this book on the Foxton Inclined Plane. The guide book has been revised once since it was first published and will run to its sixth edition in 2013.*

The two structures, however, differed in two distinct ways. Firstly, the engineers responsible for the designs, namely Edwin Clark for the Anderton Boat Lift and Gordon Thomas for the Foxton Inclined Plane, adopted radically different solutions to the problem of conveying laden narrowboats and barges from one level to another. Secondly, the boat lift was undoubtedly a commercial success, in spite of the rush to rail, in that it operated over a period of eighty-eight years between 1875 and 1983, whereas the inclined plane was, by comparison, a commercial failure, with an operating life of just ten years between 1900 and 1910. Would it be fair to conclude that the decision by the Weaver Navigation Trustees to proceed with the construction of the Anderton Boat Lift was a stroke of genius, whilst that taken by the Board of the Grand Junction Canal Company to construct the Foxton Inclined Plane was ill-considered and reckless? This conclusion, however, would be rather too simplistic, as many other factors come into play in defining the success or failure of such projects, as hopefully will be made clear in this book.

Notwithstanding the above, I consider that, under different circumstances, the Foxton Inclined Plane could have been listed by Robert Aickman, co-founder of the Inland Waterways Association, among such structures as the Anderton Boat Lift, Barton swing bridge aqueduct and the Pontcysyllte aqueduct as one of the 'Seven Wonders of the Waterways'. The fact that it is not is most likely a function of the case that it was built in the wrong place and at the wrong time, and as such was a commercial failure. Added to this, when the list of the 'Seven Wonders of the Waterways' was compiled over fifty years ago, the Foxton Inclined Plane had been, to all intents and purposes, lost and forgotten.

★ ★ ★ ★ ★

My intention in writing this book is to try to provide a complete written and pictorial history of the Foxton Inclined Plane, commencing at the beginning of the 19th century, when the Grand Junction Canal came into being during the 'canal mania' period, and ending at the present day. The motivation for writing this book is similar to that which drove me to write my first book on the Anderton Boat Lift – to feed the increased public interest in the Foxton Inclined Plane, now that the Foxton Locks Partnership, which includes British Waterways and the Foxton Inclined Plane Trust, is actively planning the restoration of one of the strangest freaks of the mechanical age, to use Rolt's words.

In writing *The Anderton Boat Lift*, I endeavoured to fill an obvious gap on the library shelves, as there were no previous publications dedicated to this fantastic canal structure. Although I started the research for this book on the Foxton Inclined Plane assuming that there was a similar dearth of published material, I very soon realised that this was far from the case. Almost without exception, each time during my researches when I examined original source material, it soon became apparent that someone else had been there before me.

The challenge in writing this book, therefore, is to pull all the relevant information together, whether previously published or not, into a readable document that tells the full story of the Foxton Inclined Plane in a new and refreshing way that makes you, the reader, want to read on and to make you feel that your money has been well spent!

I have deliberately used the format that I adopted for my first book; that is to say, the chapters are generally in chronological order beginning the story well before the construction of the Foxton Inclined Plane and completing it in the present day with a brief glimpse of the future plans. I have chosen to start each chapter with a pertinent extract from an original record or previous publication, and then have liberally used other extracts within the text to give diversity of presentation and to let the original records speak for themselves.

Wherever possible, I have referred back to original sources rather than rely on secondary sources for my information. This is entirely the approach I took, for example, in writing Chapter 11 – 'The Downfall of the Engineer'. In this case, I carried out detailed research at the National Archives at Kew, making extensive use of the original Minute Books of the Grand Junction Canal Company and other historical records. Despite this, the end result is text that is not dissimilar to an article that was written by David Heathcote entitled 'The Thomas Affair'. However, I have been able to provide significantly more detail that, in

The top of the Foxton Inclined Plane circa 1901, looking northwards from the towpath along the upper canal arm. COURTESY THE WATERWAYS TRUST
This photograph is one of six which accompanied a paper entitled 'The 'Thomas' Lift constructed at Foxton Leicestershire by the Grand Junction Canal Company', written by Gordon Thomas circa 1904; Thomas was the Engineer to the canal company and the lead designer of the Foxton Inclined Plane. The accumulator house, the winding house, the chimney and the two aqueducts are all clearly visible. A caisson is connected to the right hand aqueduct, and both the aqueduct gate and the guillotine caisson gate are in the raised position, thereby allowing a barge carrying mechanical equipment to be moved out, presumably after having ascended the inclined plane. A lift attendant can just be made out in the control cabin, whilst two boys are standing behind watching proceedings.

A spectacular view up the Foxton flight of locks with the winding house, the boiler house chimney and one of the aqueduct gate frames of the newly constructed inclined plane in the left background, circa 1904. NEIL PARKHOUSE COLLECTION

The locks were, by this time, generally in poor condition, having been neglected for several years by the Grand Junction Canal Company pending the opening of the inclined plane. They are seemingly no longer in use as all the paddles are raised and some of the gates have swung open.

FOXTON LOCKS.

W.P.

my humble opinion, makes my attempt to tell the story of the ruin of Gordon Thomas, the Engineer to the GJCC and lead designer of the inclined plane, more complete and, hopefully, more interesting.

Furthermore, I have tried to make each chapter self-contained, so that each can be read in its own right without the need for cross-referencing to other chapters. This objective, however, often requires a brief introduction at the beginning of each chapter to summarise earlier events and to set the scene for what is to follow.

★ ★ ★ ★ ★

In the sleeve notes to *The Anderton Boat Lift*, published in 2000, it is written that '*David has not written any previous books – and may well not write another!*' Well, it has to be said that the completion of this, my second book, was a close run thing. New authors often say that the hardest thing to do is to follow up their first book and the same can be said for me.

I am not a professional author; I am a practising civil engineer with a job, a family, several hobbies and consequently, a busy and often hectic lifestyle. Furthermore, whilst I am a waterways enthusiast and part-owner of a 58ft narrowboat, I do not consider myself to be a canal historian. As a result, finding the time, let alone the gumption, to write this book has at times been a struggle. I hope that you, the reader, think it has been worth the effort.

★ ★ ★ ★ ★

An artist's impression of the Foxton Inclined Plane in operation.
From The Story of Our Canals, *Ladybird Achievements Book Series 601, 1975.*

Although my name appears on the front cover, as always, a book like this is never just the work of one person. It is therefore incumbent upon me to acknowledge the efforts of those, otherwise hidden people and organisations. So, I wish to express my thanks, once again, to all those who contributed in some way or other to the writing of this book, whether by

BOTTOM
DOCK.

A view of the lower canal basin and one of the caissons at the base of the Foxton Inclined Plane, circa 1905. COURTESY THE FOXTON INCLINED PLANE TRUST
The plane looks to be in generally good working condition, although there is significant shrub and tree growth on the excavated banks which suggests the photograph was taken several years after the inclined plane was opened in 1900.

words of encouragement, practical assistance or by allowing me the use of documents and photographs. I need to give particular thanks to the following:

Mike Beech, for his tireless support and advice, for proof reading the text for historical accuracy and for contributing a Foreword to this book
Marian Carden, my wife and constant supporter during the years that it has taken me to complete this book
James Clifton, for his enthusiastic support and for contributing a Foreword to this book
Mike Cooper, for his support, advice and intricate proof reading of the text for grammatical accuracy and continuity
Lesley Jennings, friend and assistant researcher
Gill Milmo, friend and assistant researcher
Ross Norville, friend, ex-colleague and CAD draftsman, for the diagrams in the book
Neil Parkhouse, friend and publisher

I also wish to acknowledge the organisations listed below, whose records have been essential in providing the information that has enabled me to write this book. In particular, I would like to thank the Foxton Inclined Plane Trust, who have given me free and ready access to all their archived documents:

Black Dwarf Lightmoor Publications Ltd; **British Waterways** (James Clifton – Regeneration Manager South); **Chard Museum**; **Foxton Inclined Plane Trust** (Mike Beech – Museum Keeper & Company Secretary; Mike Cooper – Assistant Museum Keeper); **Institution of Civil Engineers** (Archivist – Caroline Morgan); **Ironbridge Gorge Museum Trust**, Coalbrookdale (Archivist – John Powell); **Leicestershire Records Office**; **National Archives, Kew**; **National Library of Scotland**; **Northamptonshire Records Office**; **Somerset Heritage & Libraries Service**; **Warwickshire Records Office**; **Waterways Archive – Ellesmere Port** (Archivist – Linda Barley); **Waterways Archive – Gloucester** (Archivist – Caroline Jones)

★ ★ ★ ★ ★

I dedicate this book, firstly, to the memory of my mother, **Margaret Rosemary Carden,** who died on 15th October 2009, aged 89. She supported and proof read for me during the writing of my first book on the Anderton Boat Lift and encouraged me with this book.

I also dedicate this book to two of my friends and fellow engineers, **Jason Brett** and **Brian Haskins**, both of whom have died in recent years.

Jason was a fellow colleague at Lewin, Fryer & Partners, a consulting engineering company based in Hampton, Middlesex, where we both worked on a project for British Waterways to restore the Anderton Boat Lift. Jason was a young and lively person who was seemingly a friend to everyone and an enemy of no-one – he had a natural joy for life that was infectious. In 2004, Jason and his wife, Lucinda, went to live and work in Bahrain but Jason and I continued to keep in touch by phone and meetings on his occasional returns to England. The last time that we spoke was when he rang me unexpectedly at home on a Saturday evening to chew the cud on some subject or other. With hindsight, it is a regret of mine that I cut the conversation short on the basis that he would ring again in the next few days but he never did. Not long after that, Jason and Lucinda were amongst the sixty or so people who tragically died when a private trip boat sank in the Gulf of Bahrain off the coast of Dubai on 4th April 2006. Jason was in his early thirties.

Brian died in 2002 at the age of 79. I only really got to know Brian when I was writing my first book on the Anderton Boat Lift. Brian, at that stage, had retired from British Waterways, with whom he had a distinguished career ending up as Chief Engineer for the North West Region. It was because of his time in this role that I first got to meet him, as I was in the process of interviewing current and retired members of British Waterways' staff who had been involved with the boat lift. Prior to then, I have to admit to being a little intimidated at the mention of his name by his ex-colleagues, as he was evidently highly regarded. However, my views changed almost the moment I met Brian. He was quiet, patient and encouraging, and I rapidly gained a respect and liking for him. On his own suggestion, he became a key member of the production team for the Anderton book, not only with valuable inputs on the text but also as a proof reader and adviser on the accuracy of what I had written. My main regret is that Brian died before the new friendship between us could be developed further.

★ ★ ★ ★ ★

To close this Introduction, here is an extract from *Foxton; Locks and Barge Lift* by Peter Gardner & Frank Foden, which rather appropriately links the Anderton Boat Lift with the Foxton Inclined Plane:

> '*Thus Foxton retained its importance as a place of special interest to canal people, and reinforced its reputation by becoming the site for one of the oddest, most technologically ingenious pieces of engineering in the whole canal system. The Anderton Lift, constructed in 1875 and reconstructed in 1908, on the Weaver Canal was, indeed, most spectacular – and still is – but not one whit more ingenious than the lift at Foxton.*'

I hope that this extract and the one at the beginning of this Introduction are sufficient to arouse your interest in the history of the extraordinary canal structure that is the Foxton Inclined Plane and to make you want to read on.

Sources For This Chapter
Narrow Boat, L.T.C. Rolt, Eyre Methuen, 1944
The Anderton Boat Lift, David Carden, Black Dwarf Publications 2000
The Proceedings of the Institution of Civil Engineers, 24th Jan. 1854

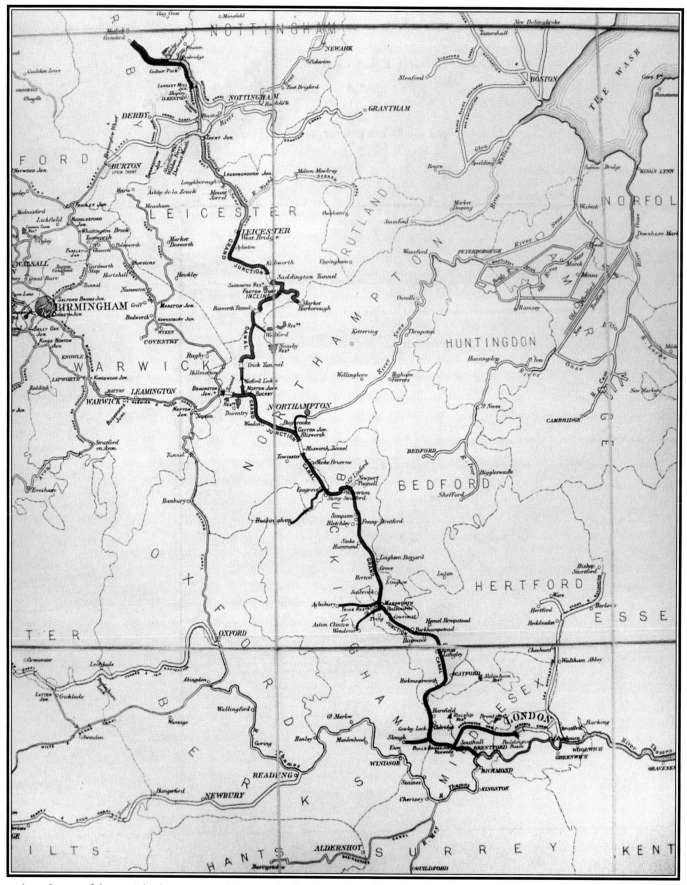

An early map of the new inland waterway route between the East Midlands and London. COURTESY THE FOXTON INCLINED PLANE TRUST *Southwards, the route was via the Loughborough Navigation, the Leicester Navigation, the Leicestershire & Northamptonshire Union Canal, the Grand Union Canal and the Grand Junction Canal. This new route between the River Trent near Nottingham and the Thames at Brentford in London was nominally 80 miles shorter than the original route along the Thames and then via the Oxford, the Coventry and the Trent & Mersey canals.*

CHAPTER 1

1793 TO 1814
ROUTES TO LONDON FROM THE EAST MIDLANDS

'By the 1790s early canals were proving profitable and the inland waterway network impressive, with London joined to Birmingham via Oxford and Fazeley and the Thames & Severn providing a route to Bristol. Moreover, after the disastrous American War, the administration of the Younger Pitt had restored the economy. Only one canal was authorised in 1790, but in 1791 seven received their Acts, in 1793 twenty, and in 1794 ten. In 1795 it was only four, and by 1797 the canal boom was over.'
From The Illustrated History of Canal & River Navigations *by Edward Paget-Tomlinson*

The above extract relates to the relatively short period of history at the end of the 18th century, when there was a rush to invest money in the up and coming inland waterway system, which provides the backdrop to the story on which I am about to embark, that relating to the Foxton Inclined Plane.

In order to tell the full story of the extraordinary structure that is the Foxton Inclined Plane, it is necessary to deal with the reasons for the development of the inland waterway route between the East Midlands and London immediately after this so-called 'Canal Mania' period. It is my intention, therefore, to describe first the waterways between the East Midlands and London at the end of the 18th century and then to give more detailed accounts of the development of the three canals constructed at the beginning of the 19th century, which provided the physical conditions that eventually led to the construction of the Foxton Inclined Plane around 100 years later. The three canals I refer to are the Grand Junction Canal, the Leicestershire & Northamptonshire Union Canal and the Grand Union Canal. The latter two canals are often referred to jointly as the Old Union Canals.

By way of clarification, it should be noted that the three canals no longer exist as single entities. The original Grand Union Canal and the Leicestershire & Northamptonshire Union Canal, together with the Loughborough Navigation and the Leicester Navigation, are jointly known today as the Leicester Line of the present-day Grand Union Canal. The Leicester Line runs from Norton Junction near Braunston, northwards through Leicester and Loughborough to Trent Junction, on the River Trent near Long Eaton. Notwithstanding this, please note that, in this and the following chapters, any references to the Grand Junction Canal or the Grand Union Canal will be with respect to the original canals.

★ ★ ★ ★ ★

Before I focus on the development of the three canals above, it might be helpful to summarise the essential facts concerning the overall waterway network between London and the East Midlands. By reference to the excellent book by Edward Paget-Tomlinson and other documents, I have tabulated what I consider to be the most relevant details of the key navigations, as best as possible in chronological order of date of construction (see **Table 1**).

Most of the waterways identified in this table, especially the later ones, were built with the principal objective of transporting coal to urban centres, whether from the Derbyshire, Nottinghamshire or the Warwickshire coalfields. This is, to some extent, borne out by Simon Winchester, in his book about the development of the science of geology during the 18th and 19th centuries:

'And for the ordinary public too canals became immediate sources of betterment; no longer did coal

WATERWAY	START & FINISH (APPROX. LENGTH)	LOCK WIDTH*	APPROX. PERIOD OF CONSTRUCTION
River Thames Navigation	London to Oxford (and beyond) (101 miles)	'Flash' and broad locks	1605-1795
Coventry Canal	Coventry to the Trent & Mersey Canal, at Fradley Junction (33 miles)	Narrow	1768-1790
Oxford Canal	The River Thames at Oxford to the Coventry Canal at Longford (91 miles)	Narrow	1770-1790
Loughborough Navigation	The River Trent near Long Eaton to Loughborough (9 miles)	Broad	1776-1778
Erewash Canal	The River Trent near Long Eaton to Langley Mill (12 miles)	Broad	1777-1779
Cromford Canal	The Erewash Canal, at Langley Mill, to Cromford (15 miles)	Broad (with narrow tunnels)	1789-1794
Leicester Navigation	The Loughborough Navigation at Loughborough to Leicester (16 miles)	Broad	1791-1794
Warwick & Birmingham Canal	Warwick to Birmingham (23 miles)	Narrow (until 1930)	1793-1799
Grand Junction Canal	The River Thames at Brentford to the Oxford Canal at Braunston (93 miles)	Broad	1793-1805
Leicestershire & Northamptonshire Union Canal (Old Union Canal)	The Leicester Navigation at Leicester to Market Harborough (24 miles)	Broad	1793-1809
Warwick & Napton Canal	The Warwick & Birmingham Canal at Budbrooke, to the Oxford Canal at Napton (15 miles)	Narrow (until 1930)	1795-1800
Grand Union Canal	The Leicestershire & Northamptonshire Union Canal at Foxton to the Grand Junction Canal at Norton Junction (23 miles)	Narrow locks but with wide bridges and tunnels	1810-1814

TABLE 1.1: THE INLAND WATERWAYS BETWEEN LONDON AND THE MIDLANDS AT THE BEGINNING OF 19TH CENTURY

* The width of a 'wide' lock is nominally 15ft whilst the width of a 'narrow' lock is nominally 7ft 6ins

double in price in the aftermath of heavy rains – now it was always cheap, and, except in times of thick canal-choking ice, bad weather scarcely ever affected its price or the speed of its delivery again.

The Duke [of Bridgewater] was quite right to foresee that indeed in those early, heady days the greatest canal cargo of all was to be coal. One horse, plodding quietly along ahead of a fully-laden coal barge, could haul 80 times more than if he were leading a wagon down a muddy road and could take 400 times as much as a single pack-horse. All of a sudden, anyone with a coal mine, anywhere in England, now wanted a canal – so that his anthracite and his steam-coal could be carried quickly and cheaply into the furnaces of the Industrial Revolution.'
The Map That Changed The World *by Simon Winchester*

A fact that is especially pertinent to the story of the Foxton Inclined Plane, and one that over 200 years later is very easy to overlook, is that, in general, the waterways listed in the table above were originally promoted as separate companies, very often in direct competition with each other. This point has been well made by Charles Hadfield in his book *British Canals – An Illustrated History*, published in 1950:

'We are nowadays so used to thinking of all matters of trade in national terms that it is difficult for us to realize that both the canals in their day and the railways in theirs began as essentially local affairs. The canals had indeed grown into a national system by the fact of joining up with one another, but they had never got over the stage of being small, independent and jealous units, often competing with each other as well with other rival methods of transport such as roads, the coastal ships and the horse railways; they were constructed of all sizes and shapes, and traffic passed from one to another with difficulty, and on the whole without encouragement.'

This disjointed development and lack of co-operation is evidenced by the failure of the individual companies to agree on a standard canal size, with the majority being built with narrow locks but others with wide locks. Whilst the locks tended to be built to one of these two standard widths, their lengths varied significantly throughout the national network, from 57 feet up to 72 feet.

★ ★ ★ ★ ★

The situation towards the end of the 18th century, over 100 years before the building of the Foxton Inclined Plane, was that the canal network in the Midlands, as we know it today, was only partly in place, with the remainder either under construction or being planned. By 1793, the Oxford, the Coventry and the Trent & Mersey canals were open, which together with the River Thames, provided the first inland waterway link between the industrial Midlands and London. In addition, the Erewash Canal was complete, thereby providing a route from the Nottinghamshire and Derbyshire coalfields to the River Trent and the Trent & Mersey Canal, whilst the Cromford Canal, which was to extend the Erewash Canal northwards to other coalfields, was under construction. Finally, for this part of the East Midlands at least, the Loughborough Navigation, the first stage of linking the mining areas to Leicester, was open, whilst the Leicester Navigation, the second stage, was close to completion (**Figure 1**). The remainder of the canals that would make up the final network were soon to be constructed.

In 1793, construction work was started on two of the canals that are central to the story of the Foxton Inclined Plane; namely the Grand Junction Canal between Brentford and Braunston, and the Leicestershire & Northamptonshire Union Canal, which was intended to

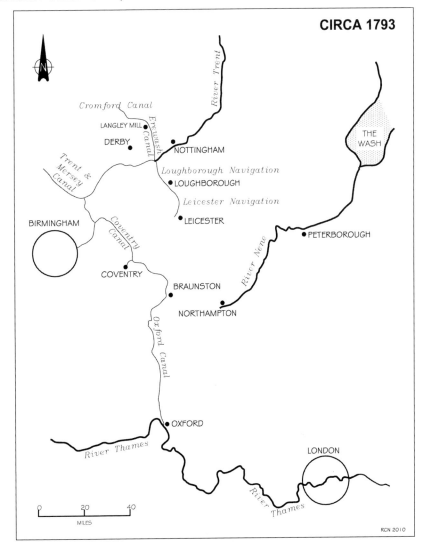

Figure 1: The inland navigation system between the East Midlands and London, circa 1793, prior to the building of the Grand Junction Canal. DRAWING PREPARED BY THE AUTHOR & ROSS NORVILLE *At that time, the only inland waterway link between the coalfields of the East Midlands and London was rather circuitous and unreliable, being via the Erewash Canal, Trent & Mersey Canal, the Coventry Canal, the Oxford Canal and the River Thames.*

link Leicester with the Grand Junction Canal arm at Northampton. By 1809, the inland navigation system between the Midlands and London was close to completion. However, due to financial difficulties, the Leicestershire & Northamptonshire Union Canal had been terminated prematurely, initially at Debdale Wharf, which is approximately one mile north of the village of Foxton. Eventually, the canal was extended to Market Harborough (see **Figure 2**, page 21).

As can be seen, the failure to complete the full route of the Leicestershire & Northamptonshire Union Canal between Leicester and Braunston resulted in a missing link between Market Harborough and the Grand Junction Canal, a gap that would eventually be filled by the construction of the aptly named Grand Union Canal (see **Figure 3**, page 24).

★ ★ ★ ★ ★

I will now attempt to address the development of each of the three canals that are central to the background of the Foxton Inclined Plane, which is to say those that were constructed in the early 19th century and provided the route between London and Leicester and, by means of other waterways already constructed, the coalfields of the East Midlands.

The Grand Junction Canal

'With the completion of the Midland canals it became necessary to cut a waterway to London in order to link the great trade centres of the country. The Oxford Canal was not satisfactory owing to the distance and cost of sending goods to London via the Thames from Oxford.'
Extract from British Waterways Inland Cruising Booklet 8 – Cruising on the Grand Union Canal Part 1: Regent's Canal Dock and Brentford to Braunston Junction

In 1790, the only waterway link between the industrial heartland of England and London was by means of the Oxford Canal and the River Thames; a route that included a mixture of broad locks and 'flash' locks on the Thames and narrow locks on the Oxford Canal. 'Flash' locks are no longer in use but at the end of the 18th century they were quite common, being located at man-made weirs across the river, which held back water for milling or navigation purposes. When boats wanted to pass through, gates were raised in a short section of the weir and those boats travelling downstream were flushed through on the surge of water, whilst afterwards, those travelling upstream would be hauled up against the flow through the gap left by the raised gates.

The problem with the Thames and Oxford Canal route was that it was relatively indirect and the journey time was long and unpredictable. This would have been due to a number of reasons, including the time needed to negotiate the 'flash' locks on the Thames; the risk of delays caused by flooding of the Thames; the need to transship goods between barges and narrowboats at Oxford; and the risk of congestion caused by the thirty-eight narrow locks on the Oxford Canal.

The establishment of a more direct and more reliable route was a very attractive proposition for potential investors in those years of 'Canal Mania'. Not surprisingly, manufacturers and transport companies were also generally in favour of a new canal on the basis that it would introduce competition for the Oxford Canal Company, which in turn would, they hoped, bring down the cost of transporting goods.

Consequently, in 1791, preliminary investigations were started for a canal link from London northwards, to meet the Oxford Canal at either Aynho or Braunston. This, in turn, aroused several complementary proposals, which included a new canal to link Leicester with the proposed Grand Junction Canal near Northampton (the Leicestershire & Northamptonshire Union Canal), and also new canals to provide a more direct link between the Oxford Canal at Napton and Birmingham, hence the Warwick & Birmingham and the Warwick & Napton canals.

According to Charles Hadfield in *The Canals of the East Midlands*, the Oxford Canal Company responded to the obvious threat posed by the proposed Grand Junction Canal. Samuel Simcock and Samuel Weston were appointed to survey a route for an alternative canal southwards from the Oxford Canal at Hampton Gay, six miles north of Oxford, to the River Thames at Isleworth. This was referred to as the London & Western Canal. If it had been constructed, the canal would have been approximately 60 miles in length and would have eliminated the greater part of the Thames Navigation from the Oxford Canal route between the Midlands and London:

'In 1792 a preliminary survey was made for a canal from Hampton Gay on the Oxford Canal to Isleworth on the Thames. The scheme was abandoned in favour of a cut from higher up the Oxford Canal at Braunston, to Brentford on the Thames.'
Extract from British Waterways Inland Cruising Booklet 8 – Cruising on the Grand Union Canal Part 1: Regent's Canal Dock and Brentford to Braunston Junction,

For some reason, most likely due to financial inducements made to the Oxford Canal Company by the promoters of the Grand Junction Canal, the proposed London & Western Canal was not taken forward.

In 1791, James Barnes was commissioned by the Grand Junction Canal promoters to survey possible routes for the new canal between Brentford and Braunston. Soon after, William Jessop was commissioned to re-survey Barnes' proposed route. The result was that the greater part of the route proposed by Barnes was adopted but south of Watford the alignment of the proposed London & Western Canal was selected. The chosen route was generally westwards from the River Thames at Brentford to Uxbridge, then northwards through Rickmansworth, Watford, Berkhamsted, Leighton Buzzard and Bletchley to link up with the Oxford Canal at Braunston. The new canal would need to overcome two summits, one over the Chilterns at Tring and the other over part of the Northampton Uplands at Daventry. Tunnels were required at Blisworth and Braunston. A number of branches from this main route were considered but several, including those to Daventry and Watford, were never built. Others, to the urban centres of Northampton, Paddington and Buckingham, however, were eventually constructed.

The Act of Parliament for the Grand Junction Canal received the Royal Assent in April 1793, most likely against vociferous opposition from landowners and other affected parties, including the proprietors of the Thames Navigation and the Oxford Canal Company, who viewed the proposed Grand Junction as a threat to their commercial interests. After lengthy and protracted negotiations, the Oxford Canal Company's opposition was eventually bought off by the Grand Junction promoters by a guarantee of £10,000 income per year. In addition, as would have been common practice at that time, the promoters of the Grand Junction solicited support for the Act from other canal companies, as evidenced by the following extract from *The Canal Builders* by Anthony Burton:

> 'When the Grand Junction Canal Company was going to Parliament, they naturally sought the support of other canal companies, including the Lancaster. Since these two canals were at opposite ends of the country, there was no possibility of any conflict of economic interest. But before agreeing, the Lancaster Committee had to check with their Parliamentary supporters to see how such a move would fit into the political pattern.'

Work began on the construction of the canal soon after the passing of the Act, with William Jessop, who had previously acted as the Engineer for the Leicester Navigation, appointed as Engineer and James Barnes as his Resident Engineer. A prominent canal engineer such as Jessop would most likely have had several simultaneous commissions as Engineer and therefore could not be expected to be on site on a day-to-day basis, hence the need for the appointment of a resident engineer to supervise the works in his absence. The construction of the canal was not without its difficulties:

> 'From the start in 1793 to its completion in 1805 the Grand Junction offered almost insuperable difficulties to William Jessop, the engineer, and his assistant James Barnes in cutting and locking at Braunston Hill, Blisworth Hill and the Chilterns. Two tunnels had to be cut through the intractable ironstone outcrops at Braunston and Blisworth which ate up time and money. The Blisworth Tunnel held up completion for several years. A plate tramway was used to carry goods over the hill to connect the two parts of the uncompleted cut.'
> *Extract from* British Waterways Inland Cruising Booklet 8 – Cruising on the Grand Union Canal Part 1: Regent's Canal Dock and Brentford to Braunston Junction,

Although the greater part of the canal was navigable by 1800, seven years after construction had begun, flooding problems on the original alignment of the Blisworth Tunnel necessitated the construction of a replacement tunnel. As a consequence, the Grand Junction Canal could not be opened along its whole length until 1805. With the expected volume of traffic in mind, the promoters elected to include wide locks for 70-ton barges, which could safely navigate the tidal part of the River Thames from Brentford into central London.

With the completion of the Grand Junction Canal, traffic routes between the Midlands and London were markedly improved. The extract below suggests that, with the opening of the Grand Junction Canal, long distance traffic on the Oxford Canal was significantly reduced:

> 'By 1805, therefore, a great change had taken place. The Birmingham trade to London was

now via Warwick, Braunston and the Grand Junction, while the Midlands trade, once it had passed by Fradley and Hawkesbury to Braunston, also took the Grand Junction route, so that the Oxford Canal south of Napton became used only for local traffic.'
From the British Waterways Inland Cruising Booklet 9 – Cruising on the Grand Union Canal Part 2: Braunston Junction to Birmingham, and adjoining canals

★ ★ ★ ★ ★

The Leicestershire & Northamptonshire Union Canal

'When therefore an extension, the Leicestershire & Northamptonshire Union, was authorised on the same day in 1793 as the Grand Junction (itself a broad canal), to connect with its Northampton branch and the River Nene, that also was planned for barges. It only got as far as Debdale near Foxton in 1797, and there it stopped for lack of funds, except for the opening of the Market Harborough branch in 1809.'
Extract from British Waterways Inland Cruising Booklet 10 – Cruising on the Grand Union Canal Part 3: Norton Junction to Trent Lock

In parallel with the preparations for the promotion of the Grand Junction Canal, plans were being put in place for the extension of the Leicester Navigation southwards. The original intention of the promoters of this proposed extension was to terminate the canal at Market Harborough, with the canal being called the Harborough Navigation. This plan, however, was soon rejected in favour of taking the canal further southwards to meet the proposed Grand Junction Canal near Northampton, thereby completing the inland canal navigation between the coalfields of the East Midlands and London.

William Jessop, the Engineer to the Grand Junction Canal, was also appointed as Engineer for the Leicestershire & Northamptonshire Union Canal, whilst Christopher Stavely, who had been his assistant during the construction of the Leicester Navigation, was commissioned to survey the route. An Act of Parliament for the new canal received Royal Assent in April 1793, the same day as the Grand Junction Canal, and construction began soon after. The route originally approved by Parliament was from Leicester southwards along the Soar Valley, then generally south east following the River Sence past Blaby, then Foxton to Market Harborough. From there it was to curve southwards past Theddingworth, East Farndon, Great Oxenden, Kelmarsh, Maidwell and, eventually, Northampton, via the Nene Valley and the proposed branch of the Grand Junction Canal. The total length of the proposed canal was 43 miles.

Not untypically for canal promotions, the cost of construction of the new cut was seriously underestimated. Partly due to major increases in material costs and partly due to construction problems on the Saddington Tunnel, the available funds rapidly diminished. As a consequence, in April 1797, just four years after being started, the works were forced to a premature end with the termination of the canal at Debdale Wharf near Gumley, a mile or so north of Foxton village. At that stage, only 17 miles of the route from Leicester had been completed.

The promoters had clearly not given up on the venture as, in 1802, James Barnes was commissioned to review the originally proposed route to Northampton. Barnes subsequently recommended that an alternative route from that defined in the Act should be adopted, which would take the canal southwards from Foxton over the Northampton Uplands to meet the Grand Junction between Long Buckby and Braunston. It would seem, however, that the promoters were not convinced, possibly due to concerns about water supplies; they subsequently appointed Thomas Telford to carry out his own review of the possible routes. This resulted in Telford advising that a more easterly alignment, similar to the original parliamentary route, should be adopted, taking the canal through Market Harborough and into the Welland Valley before linking up with the Grand Junction, again near Long Buckby. Telford's route was significantly longer and more arduous but would have had the benefit of fewer locks and a better supply of water.

Although the construction of the Grand Junction was, by that time, well advanced, the decision was taken, presumably due to the lack of funding, to abandon the proposed link to the Grand Junction Canal and only extend the Leicestershire & Northamptonshire Union Canal by a further 7 miles or so along Telford's route through Foxton and into Market Harborough. An Act for this limited extension was granted in 1805 and the works were completed four years later, at an additional cost of £40,500. Thomas Newbold acted as Engineer for this extension. The Leicestershire & Northamptonshire Union Canal was formally opened on 13th October 1809 (**Figure 2**), with celebrations on the day culminating with a dinner for invited dignitaries at the Angel Hotel in Market Harborough.

To be compatible with the Loughborough Navigation, the Leicester Navigation and the Grand Junction Canal, the twenty-three locks on the shortened Leicestershire & Northamptonshire Union Canal were built to a wide gauge.

Overall, the new canal took sixteen years to build and even then fell well short of its original objective of Northampton and the Grand Junction Canal. As a consequence, certainly during the early years of its existence until the opening of the Grand Union Canal in 1814, it would only have carried local traffic. It must, therefore, have been a financial disappointment as far as the original investors were concerned. Furthermore, the Grand Junction Canal Company (GJCC) would also have been bitterly disappointed by this turn of events. It can be assumed that the GJCC had hoped to draw lucrative trade from the Leicestershire navigations on to its canal from the Nottinghamshire and Derbyshire coalfields.

★ ★ ★ ★ ★

The Grand Union Canal

'Eventually a group of promoters drawn both from Leicester and the Grand Junction company formed the (old) Grand Union to make the remaining and difficult portion of line that would connect Leicester by water with London, this time a new route between Debdale and Norton Junction. It was opened in 1814.'
Extract from British Waterways Inland Cruising Booklet 10 – Cruising on the Grand Union Canal Part 3: Norton Junction to Trent Lock

Finally, and significantly with the full backing of the GJCC, the decision was taken to finish off what the Leicestershire & Northamptonshire Union Canal had failed to do; namely to complete a waterway connection between the East Midlands and London that did not rely on the vagaries of a river navigation.

Benjamin Bevan, who had previously worked on the Grand Junction Canal, was appointed as Engineer for the new canal. He was apparently influential in the decision to adopt Barnes' rather than Telford's route, presumably on cost grounds – Telford's route

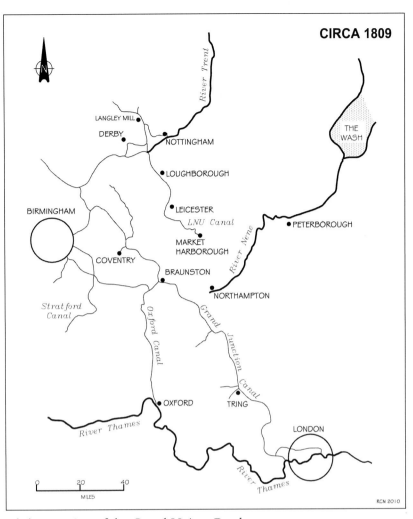

FIGURE 2: The inland navigation system between the East Midlands and London, circa 1809, showing a gap between Market Harborough and the Grand Junction Canal to the south and no link to the River Nene. DRAWING PREPARED BY THE AUTHOR & ROSS NORVILLE
With the completion of the Grand Junction Canal between London and Braunston, and the partial completion of the Leicestershire & Northamptonshire Union Canal between Leicester and Market Harborough, the stage was set for the construction of the Grand Union Canal to complete the more direct waterway link between the East Midlands and London.

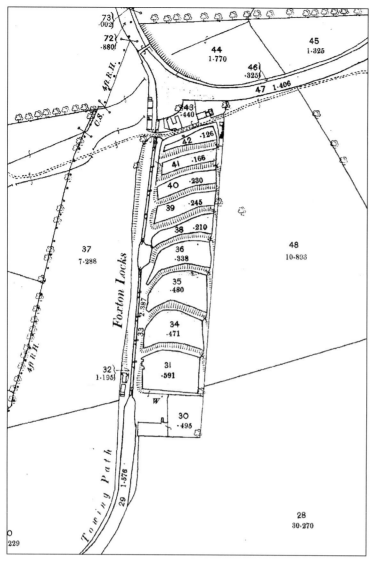

Detail from the 25 inch OS map for 1886, showing the Foxton Locks. COURTESY, WWW.OLD-MAPS.CO.UK The building of the locks took two years and was completed circa 1814. The Leicestershire & Northamptonshire Union Canal is at the top of the map and the summit section of the Grand Union Canal leads away from the locks at the bottom. By 1886, the canals in question had been in the ownership of the Grand Junction Canal Company for just two years, the whole being referred to as the Leicester Section. In total, there are ten locks in two staircases of five, separated by a short pound. The overall height overcome by the locks is 75 feet.

was nominally 9 miles longer than that proposed by Barnes and would have necessitated the construction of several expensive cuttings, embankments and aqueducts. The adopted route left the Leicestershire & Northamptonshire Union Canal at Foxton and then went generally southwards via Lubenham, Husbands Bosworth, North Kilworth, Yelvertoft and Crick, to connect to the Grand Junction Canal at Norton Junction near Long Buckby.

The Act of Parliament was granted in 1810, although not without opposition. Amongst the objectors were businessmen in Northampton, who presumably disliked that fact that the new route of the canal did not have a link to the River Nene. As a consequence, the GJCC were forced to make a concession by agreeing to construct a branch from the Grand Junction Canal to Northampton within the next three years.

Somewhat curiously, the decision was taken to adopt narrow locks on the Grand Union Canal, which contrasted with the wide locks on the connecting canals both to the north and south. Edward Paget-Tomlinson, in his *Illustrated History of Canal & River Navigations*, suggests this was because the GJCC wanted to discourage further wide barges along their canal, due to the delays already being caused by one-way working through the Blisworth and Braunston tunnels. This is generally confirmed in *The Old Union Canals of Leicestershire and Northamptonshire*, a document published by the Old Union Canals Society in 1990, which suggests that the GJCC would only allow narrowboats through the Blisworth Tunnel so that there could be two-way working, which in their view was a more effective procedure than one-way working by wide barges. However, there is an alternative explanation:

'Because by that time other canals with narrow locks had joined the Grand Junction, it had become clear to that company that the extra expense of building broad locks on the (old) Grand Union was not justified.'
Extract from British Waterways Inland Cruising Booklet 10 – Cruising on the Grand Union Canal Part 3 – Norton Junction to Trent Lock

Overall, the reason for the adoption of narrow locks on the Grand Union Canal was most likely a combination of the poor water supply on the chosen route of the Grand Union Canal; the ease of working narrowboats through the tunnels on the Grand Junction and Grand Union canals; and the cost saving associated with constructing narrow locks rather than wide locks.

Whatever the reason for the choice of narrow locks, the decision would lead to major difficulties for the GJCC in later years, when faster travelling times were being investigated in order to compete better with the railways. The narrow staircase locks at Foxton and Watford would prove to be major bottlenecks on the Leicester route, between the Nottinghamshire and Derbyshire coalfields and London.

It is of interest to note that *The Old Union Canals of Leicestershire and Northamptonshire* states that a clause in the Act for the Grand Union Canal allowed for the widening of the locks at any time in the future, presumably on the basis that the economic conditions were favourable

*A view up the Foxton Locks circa 1898. COURTESY THE WATERWAYS TRUST
This photograph has been entitled 'Misery at the Locks', which no doubt reflects the cheerless wintry scene. A laden narrowboat is descending the flight of locks, with the family crew and towing horse all posed for the camera. The father appears to be in uniform and is tending the horse, which is being fed while temporarily off duty. The mother is on the left holding a rope, whilst the daughter is sitting on the tailgate balance arm; both are heavily dressed against the winter weather. Both lock cottages are just visible in the mist on the horizon and the locks are generally in poor repair. The earthworks for the construction of the Foxton Inclined Plane are just visible in the left background*

and that the GJCC changed its policy on wide boats using its tunnels. Furthermore, with amazing foresight, the Act also contained a clause allowing for the locks at Foxton and Watford to be replaced, sometime in the future, with inclined planes – a clause that would be used ninety years later to facilitate the construction of the Foxton Incline Plane.

It also seems likely that the original plan may have been to build standard flights of locks at Foxton and Watford, that is to say locks with short lengths of canal or pounds between, but following recommendations from Benjamin Bevan, the decision was taken to build sets of staircase locks. The reasons for this were primarily due to the need to minimise water losses from the summit pound, to maximise the speed of working and to reduce construction costs. In addition, however, the steepness of the escarpment at Foxton may have militated against the adoption of standard locks.

Construction began in 1810, with the locks at Foxton and the summit section of the canal southwards. By June 1812, about five miles of the summit section from the top lock was complete and by October the same year the flight of locks was finished. Geological problems were encountered during the works on the Crick Tunnel, to the extent that, in 1812, the line of the first tunnel had to be abandoned with a new tunnel being constructed on a completely different alignment. Overall, the Grand Union Canal took four years to complete.

As stated above, the locks at Foxton were built narrow and configured as two sets of five staircase locks, in which the tail gate of the top lock forms the head gate of the next lock down and so on, with no intervening pounds for boats to pass. Each lock had a side pond to conserve water. Only single-way working was possible through each staircase, although a relatively short central pound was provided for boats to pass each other between the two flights. The total rise provided by the ten locks is 75 feet.

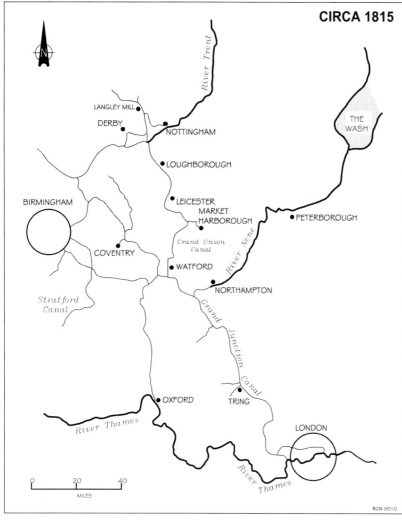

CIRCA 1815

FIGURE 3: The inland navigation system between the East Midlands and London, circa 1815, with the gap between Market Harborough and Braunston filled by the Grand Union Canal. DRAWING PREPARED BY THE AUTHOR & ROSS NORVILLE
This is effectively the inland waterway network that exists today, albeit the 'Grand Junction Canal' is referred to today as the Grand Union Canal, with the 'Grand Union Canal' now being part of the Leicester Line of the Grand Union Canal.

It is worthy of note that the design of the staircases at Foxton and Watford by Benjamin Bevan is amazingly economic in water usage terms and is thought to be unique in Britain. The use of side ponds to each of the locks results in the loss of only one lock of water from the summit section of the canal for the cycle of one boat up and one boat down. With a line of boats moving in one direction, the water loss increases to one lock per boat. Another benefit of the side ponds is that there is no need for lengthy preparation of water levels in the locks prior to the movement of boats. This contrasts starkly with the situation at the Bingley Five Rise staircase on the Leeds Liverpool Canal, which does not have side ponds. At Bingley, all but the top lock have to be empty prior to a boat beginning to descend the staircase, whereas all but the bottom lock needs to be full prior to a boat beginning to ascend the staircase. This situation leads to several locks of water being drawn off the summit.

The summit section of the canal leading southwards away from the top of the Foxton Locks is nominally 20 miles long and 412 feet above sea level, making it one of the highest in the country. It includes two lengthy tunnels, at Husbands Bosworth (1,166 yards) and Crick (1,528 yards).

At the southern end of the summit, the canal descends at Watford near Long Buckby, firstly by means of a single lock, then a staircase of four locks, followed by two more single locks. The total rise provided by the seven locks is 52ft 6ins.

★ ★ ★ ★ ★

The Grand Union Canal was officially opened on 9th August 1814 (**Figure 3**), with much pomp and ceremony, which was customary for such events. On the day, a convoy of boats travelled north from the southern limit of the canal at Norton Junction, up the recently completed Watford Locks, and through the Crick and Husband Bosworth tunnels, before descending the locks at Foxton. An excellent article from the *Leicester Journal*, 20th October 1809 edition, that describes the occasion in very colourful terms is given in full below:

'On Tuesday morning last, a deputation from London was met by a deputation from the OLD UNION CANAL COMPANY at Long Buckby, in Northamptonshire, for the purpose of opening the GRAND UNION CANAL, where it unites with the GRAND JUNCTION – thus forming a direct communication by water from the Metropolis through Leicester to Nottingham and Cromford. – The first boat was fitted up in an elegant style, with an excellent band of music, the flags of the different companies – and a beautiful banner, the gift of Mrs Cradock, of Gumley, with a large assemblage of beauty and fashion aboard, followed by two other boats fitted up for the reception of such ladies and gentlemen who chose to be of the party – the rear being brought up by two of Messrs. Pickfords fly-boats, on their passage from London, proceeded down the line to Welford, when another boat from the Welford branch amply supplied with refreshments was brought to, and moored alongside, into which the company went and partook of abundance of

good things – this was a necessary precaution, as the boats had shortly to pass the long and dark tunnel which forms the communication in that neighbourhood; strong symptoms of fear were first evinced by some of the ladies – which were at last surmounted by the gallantry and polite attention of the gentlemen – a close package, great hilarity and good humour during the interval of darkness – brought them again into the face of day, and soon after seven o'clock the whole arrived at Harborough, where a sumptuous dinner was provided, consisting of abundance of turtle, venison, turbot, and every rarity in season, with a profusion of fresh water fish – liberally sent by J. Cradock, Esq of Gumley. – After dinner, the banner given by Mrs. Cradock, was presented in her name by Mr. Meredith to the two companies – in an elegant and appropriate speech Mr. M. very pertinently discoursed on the glory which had been attendant on the banners of the country during a long and destructive period of warfare – and hoped the banners which were unfurled on the present occasion would not be less successful in the commercial prosperity of the country. – An ode written on the occasion was also ably delivered by a gentleman present – great gaiety and good humour prevailed during the day, and the festive board was not departed from until a very late hour.

Such is the convenience of this New Canal to the public, that the fly-boats of Messrs. Pickfords, which arrived here loaded from London in the morning, returned reladen for the Metropolis the same evening.'

The last words regarding the opening of the Grand Union Canal are taken from *Foxton: Locks and Barge Lift* by Peter Gardner and Frank Foden:

'*Thus was opened the Grand Union, aptly named, for it forged the last link of the ambitious grand design to connect the East Midlands coalfields to London, a total distance of 168 miles. The furthest northward extent of the system was Langley Mill at the end of the Erewash Canal.*'

★ ★ ★ ★ ★

In conclusion, the construction of the three canals, as described at some length above, dramatically enhanced the commercial prospects for the Nottinghamshire and Derbyshire coalfields in the Erewash Valley. The canals jointly provided a radically improved route southwards to London. At the end of the 18th century, the best route for East Midlands coal to reach London was by means of the Erewash, the Trent & Mersey, the Coventry and the Oxford canals, and finally the River Thames. By 1814, however, with the opening of the Grand Union Canal, an alternative and more efficient route to London was available, by means of the Loughborough Navigation, the Leicester Navigation, the Leicestershire & Northamptonshire Union, the Grand Union and the Grand Junction canals (**Figure 4**).

This new route between the Trent Junction near Nottingham and the Thames at Brentford in London was nominally 80 miles shorter, although it did contain forty-eight more locks. It is not easy to be definite about travel times for horse-drawn boats at the beginning of the 19th century

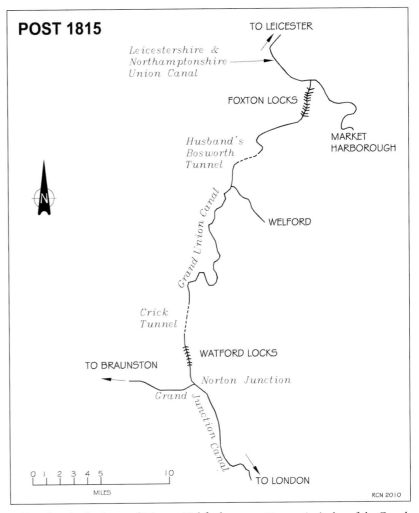

FIGURE 4: *A plan of the Grand Union Canal, after 1815.* DRAWING PREPARED BY THE AUTHOR & ROSS NORVILLE *The overall length of the Grand Union Canal, from the Grand Junction Canal at Norton Junction to the Leicestershire & Northamptonshire Union Canal at the bottom of the Foxton Locks, is 23¼ miles. The GUC included two tunnels, at Crick and Husband's Bosworth, two flights of locks, at Watford and Foxton, and a short navigable arm to Welford.*

but it is illustrative to compare the predicted travel times on both routes today. By reference to Chris Clegg's excellent *Canal Time Map*, a diesel-powered boat today would be expected to take around 94 hours to travel between Brentford and the Trent Junction via the Thames, the Oxford Canal, the Coventry Canal and a short section of the Trent & Mersey Canal, assuming that conditions on the Thames were favourable. In contrast, on the new route using the Grand Junction Canal, the Grand Union and the Leicestershire navigations, the travel time for the same journey would be around 74 hours. In commercial terms the 20 hours reduction would have been very significant. These journey times, however, take no account of:

• the greater traffic volumes of the early 19th century, leading to possible congestion at the numerous narrow locks on the old route, as opposed to the relatively few narrow locks on the new route
• the slower speed of horse-drawn vessels when compared to diesel-powered boats
• the transshipment of cargos between canal narrowboats and Thames barges at Oxford

Any of these factors could have resulted in yet longer journey times on the old route. The difference between the two routes might reasonably be compared to building a new dual carriageway road between two cities that had previously only been connected by roads that meandered through local towns and villages.

And so it was that, by 1814, just fifty-three years after the construction of the Bridgewater Canal, arguably the first inland waterway in Britain, the main arteries of the canal system between the East Midlands and London were in place.

Sources For This Chapter

The Canals of the East Midlands, Charles Hadfield, David & Charles, 1966
British Canals – An Illustrated History, Charles Hadfield, Phoenix House, 1950
The Illustrated History of Canal and River Navigations, Edward Paget-Tomlinson, Sheffield Academic Press, 1993
British Waterways Inland Cruising Booklet 8 – Cruising on the Grand Union Canal Part 1: Regent's Canal Dock and Brentford to Braunston Junction, circa 1960
British Waterways Inland Cruising Booklet 9 – Cruising on the Grand Union Canal Part 2: Braunston Junction to Birmingham, and adjoining canals, circa 1960
British Waterways Inland Cruising Booklet 10 – Cruising on the Grand Union Canal: Part 3: Norton Junction to Trent Lock, circa 1960
Foxton: Locks and Barge Lift, Peter Gardner & Frank Foden, Leicestershire County Planning Dept in association with the Leicestershire branch of the Council for the Protection of Rural England, 2nd ed. 1979
Foxton Locks and Inclined Plane – A Detailed History, compiled by members of the Foxton Inclined Plane Trust and published by Department of Planning & Transportation, Leicestershire County Council, c1986
Chris Clegg's Canal Time Map, Version 2.1, 2002
The Leicester Line, Philip A. Stevens, David & Charles, 1972
Leicester Journal, 20th October 1809
Canals, Barges and People, John O'Connor, Art & Technics Ltd, 1950
Other documents at the Foxton Inclined Plane Trust Archives
The Map That Changed The World, Simon Winchester, Viking 2001

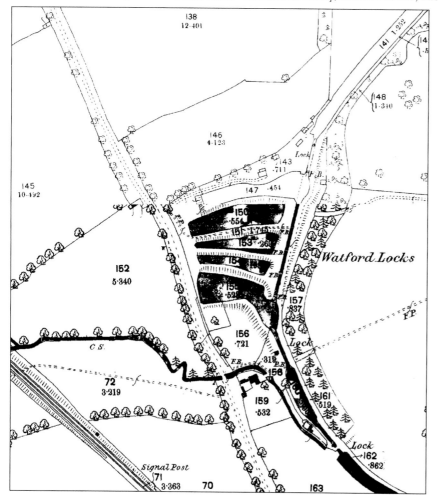

Detail from the 1885 25 inch OS, showing the Watford Locks. Courtesy, www.old-maps.co.uk The building of the locks took several years and was completed circa 1814. The locks are at the southern end of the summit section of what was originally the Grand Union Canal but which, in September 1894, had been taken over by the GJCC and was thereafter referred to as the Leicester Section of the Grand Junction Canal. At Watford, the canal descends firstly by means of a single lock, then a staircase of four locks, followed by two more single locks. The total rise provided by the seven locks is 52ft 6ins.

CHAPTER 2

1814 TO 1894
COALS TO LONDON

'When the connection to the Grand Junction opened in 1814 long distance through traffic commenced, chiefly in coal from the Nottinghamshire coalfields for London and the south; road-stone from Mountsorrel and Quorndon, also south, and general merchandise in both directions. By the 1830s trade was at its peak, then gradually falling away under the onslaught of the railways.'
From The Old Union Canals of Leicestershire and Northamptonshire *by the* Old Union Canal Society

As summarised so neatly above, with the completion of the Grand Union Canal, the last link of the new and more efficient inland waterway route, between the coalfields of the East Midlands and London, was finally open. All the physical components were then in place, once the political and economic conditions were right, to facilitate the construction of the Foxton Inclined Plane around eighty-five years later.

In this chapter, I will endeavour to present a coherent picture of the eighty years or so of canal history after the opening of the Grand Union Canal, as far as it is relevant to the Foxton Inclined Plane. This chapter will therefore cover the period from 1814 to 1894, the time that the Grand Junction Canal Company (GJCC) first begin to show interest in addressing the bottlenecks posed by the flights of narrow locks at Foxton and Watford. In transport terms, it covers the post-boom years of the canal age and the beginning of the railway age.

★ ★ ★ ★ ★

By way of a review, the new East Midlands to London waterway route, which was completed in 1814, consisted of six separate canal companies. From north to south, these were the Erewash, the Loughborough Navigation, the Leicester Navigation, the Leicestershire & Northamptonshire Union, the Grand Union and the Grand Junction. The six canals had been built at different times over different landscapes, with the consequence that, although they all had the same basic function, that of transport, they were far from being equal in status.

During the period of thirty years or so before the coming of the railways, the various river and canal concerns tended to be run on a local basis, often with competition between the companies on the same route but especially between companies on competing routes. This competition resulted in the situation in which the financial success of one canal company, on a particular route, did not necessarily mean that other companies on that same route were equally successful. The financial viability of a canal company at the start of the 19th century depended on numerous factors; these included:

• The amount of compensation monies that had been paid out by the canal promoters to achieve the withdrawal of objections to allow the passage of the Parliamentary Bill. Objections were typically raised by land-owners affected by the proposed canal route as well as overland carriers and other canal companies whose trade might be threatened by the proposed canal

• The extent of any pecuniary clauses inserted in the Act of Parliament, which could restrict the level of tolls to be charged to carriers

TABLE 2.1: APPROX. ANNUAL DIVIDENDS PAID BY CANALS & NAVIGATIONS BETWEEN 1800-14

YEAR	LOUGHBOROUGH NAVIGATION	LEICESTER NAVIGATION	LEICS & NORTHANTS UNION	GRAND JUNCTION
1800	63%	5%	-	-
1805	80%	5%	-	-
1810	94%	5%	-	6%
1814	108%	7%	2%	7%

Data taken from *The Canals of the East Midlands* (Hadfield, 1966)

• The initial construction cost of the canal. This, in turn, depended on numerous factors including the overall length of the canal; the terrain over which it ran, hence the number of locks, tunnels and aqueducts; the underlying geology; the adequacy of the natural water supply; and the social and political circumstances pertaining at the time of its construction

• The commercial imperative for the canal, whether on its own account or as part of a route with several participating canal companies and hence the amount of traffic generated, whether as local or through traffic

• The ability of the canal company to set its own toll rates. This would be at its greatest if the company was in a monopolistic situation, where the canal connected the areas of production to the market place without competition from other canals. The ability to set tolls, however, would be reduced if several canal companies made up the route and would be reduced still further if alternative routes were available to the carriers. Furthermore, a small canal company on a particular route would be likely to be less successful than a connecting larger company

Without getting too involved with the detailed historical intricacies, which are arguably not of particular relevance to the story of the Foxton Inclined Plane, it is of value to consider the profitability of the main companies on the new route between the East Midlands and London. This might best be done by consideration of the annual dividends paid out by the companies to their shareholders. Those for the fourteen years prior to the opening of the Grand Union are thus shown in **Table 2.1**.

As can be seen, the Loughborough Navigation was hugely successful during this period, paying very high returns to its shareholders, whilst in contrast the other three canals gave relatively modest rates of return. The high dividends paid out by the Loughborough Navigation can be explained by two factors. Firstly, by the low cost of its construction, which took place prior to the inflation of material costs caused by the Napoleonic Wars (1800-1815); secondly, it had the good fortune of being part of a lucrative waterway link between the coalfields of the East Midlands and the market place of Loughborough from 1778 onwards, and then Leicester from 1794 onwards.

The balance of the network between the East Midlands and London changed in 1814 with the opening of the Grand Union Canal, the last link in the alternative route that avoided the vagaries of navigation on the River Thames. By all accounts, long distance traffic on the new route built up rapidly with the main cargo being coal moving southwards towards London from the coalfields of the East Midlands but also hosiery goods in the same direction from the Leicester mills. **Table 2.2** presents the annual dividends paid out prior to the onset of competition from the railways.

TABLE 2.2: APPROX. ANNUAL DIVIDENDS PAID BY CANALS & NAVIGATIONS BETWEEN 1815-35

YEAR	LOUGHBOROUGH NAVIGATION	LEICESTER NAVIGATION	LEICS & NORTHANTS UNION	GRAND UNION	GRAND JUNCTION
1815	112%	8%	3%	0%	8%
1820	134%	9%	3%	0%	9%
1825	153%	12%	4%	0%	12%
1830	151%	11%	3%	1%	13%
1835	92%	7%	3%	1%	12%

Data mostly taken from *The Canals of the East Midlands* (Hadfield, 1966) and *British Canals – An Illustrated History* (Hadfield, 1950). Data for the Grand Union Canal from *The Leicester Line: A History of the Old Union and Grand Union Canals* (Stevens, 1972) and assuming an original share value of £100

Paddington, the first bridge on the Grand Junction Canal.
This illustration is taken from English Rivers and Canals *by F. Eyre & C. Hadfield, Britain in Pictures Series, Collins 1945. A coloured aquatint, it shows an accommodation barge going down the canal to Uxbridge and was originally published in 1801.*

During this pre-railway period, the profitably of the various canals was effectively in three tiers, with the Loughborough remaining hugely profitable but now with the Leicester Navigation and the Grand Junction Canal paying reasonable returns to their investors, whilst the Leicestershire & Northamptonshire Union and the Grand Union were noticeably less profitable. In his book *The Canal Age*, Charles Hadfield explains one reason why some of the earlier canal companies, for example the Loughborough Navigation, were so profitable:

> *'As traffic grew, the old companies benefited disproportionately, both because their original cost had been low, and because newer canals which had joined them introduced fresh business. Hence high rates of dividend upon small issued capital.'*

However, the following extract from *British Canals* (Edwin Pratt, 1906) critically addresses the behaviour of several of the early canal companies, in taking advantage of their monopolistic positions when compared to other forms of transport:

> *'It is clear from all this that, however great the benefit which canal transport had conferred, as compared with prior conditions, the canal companies had abused their monopoly in order to secure what were often enormous profits …'*

It was evident from the dividends paid, as summarised in **Table 2.2**, that the Grand Union Canal Company was the poor relation of the canals on the East Midlands to London route. This conclusion is supported by the following extract from *Canals of the East Midlands*:

> *'From the beginning it [the Grand Union Canal] suffered from one great disadvantage. It lay in a line of canal controlled by an extraordinary large number of different companies: Derbyshire coal to London probably had to pass the Cromford, Erewash, Loughborough, Leicester Union, Grand Union and Grand Junction Canals, and perhaps the Regent's also. The Grand Union was the weakest link, for as its motto Juncta Jovebunt, implied, it depended almost entirely upon its through trade, whereas the others had substantial local business. Therefore when bargaining was done, the Grand Union usually came off worst.'*

The three locks at Stoke Hammond, Buckinghamshire on the Grand Junction Canal. From English Rivers and Canals, *F. Eyre & C. Hadfield, Britain in Pictures Series, Collins 1945. This engraving was first published in J. Hassell's* Tour of the Grand Junction Canal *in 1819.*

Compared to its neighbours, the Grand Union, especially, struggled financially for four obvious reasons, as follows:

• The Grand Union Canal Company was burdened financially, possibly both at the time of passing the Act of Parliament in 1810 and throughout the life of the canal, with payments to compensate other canal companies and other parties for their potential losses
• The initial construction cost per mile of canal was high compared to the other canals, apart from the Grand Junction. This was due to the fact that the topography traversed by the Grand Union Canal was relatively difficult, with the need for ten locks at Foxton to ascend the Northampton Uplands and seven at Watford to descend to the Grand Junction Canal. Additionally, there were two long tunnels; one at Husbands Bosworth and the other at Crick. As explained previously, the choice of narrow locks at Foxton and Watford may have been partly due to an effort to reduce construction costs as well as to minimise the loss of water from the summit
• The canal was relatively short in length and ran through a mostly rural landscape without any significant urban centres on its line. As a result, unlike the other canals on the route, it was almost entirely dependent on through traffic coming from the other canals, whether from the north or the south, for an income
• The reservoirs at Naseby, Sulby and Welford were built not only to provide water to the long summit section of the Grand Union Canal but also to replace water that was inevitably transferred downhill into the adjacent canals, both to the south and the north

For these reasons, the Grand Union Canal Company was heavily dependent on financial support from the GJCC in order to remain solvent.

★ ★ ★ ★ ★

By 1840, however, all of the inland waterways were, to a greater or lesser extent, facing increasing competition from the new, faster transport system, the railways. As stated by Hadfield in *British Canals – An Illustrated History*:

'So ended the canal age, which had added to the navigable rivers some 3,600 miles of artificial waterway in the eighty years to 1840, during which it had provided the chief means of transporting goods in bulk. By its means the Industrial Revolution had taken place, and the country now stood on the threshold of the new era – the Victorian age.'

The good times for the canals were relatively short lived, just eighty years after the start of the 'Canal Mania' period. Those canals that had been built early on in the canal age, on commercially successful routes, had made eye-watering returns for their investors, to the extent that these canal companies faced severe criticism for not reducing their toll rates to their customers. Other canals, however, built only a relatively short time later but still on commercially viable routes, managed to pay more modest dividends to their investors, whilst others in less advantageous positions either struggled to pay dividends or failed completely.

Overall, it seems that those businesses that had hitherto been dependent on the canals to carry their raw materials and products, were ready to welcome the railways with open arms. The railways challenged the monopolistic position of the canals and, consequently, led to the reduction of carriage tolls, both by rail and canal.

From around 1840 onwards, the canal companies faced a common enemy – the up and coming railways. Like the canal companies before them, the railways were promoted and developed privately, on a piecemeal basis, with investors rushing to put their money into this new market hoping for high returns.

By all accounts, the Grand Junction Canal was the most actively managed of all the canals on the East Midlands to London route. The GJCC was heavily committed to making the canal more competitive against the new and rapidly increasing threat of the railways. In practice, the GJCC, and presumably also the Oxford Canal Company, began to feel the threat of the railways as early as 1824, when plans for a line between London and Birmingham were first mooted. The London & Birmingham Railway was eventually opened in 1838, by which time the GJCC had already carried out a number of improvement works to increase the competitiveness of the canal.

In 1847, with the withdrawal of Messrs Pickfords as carriers on the Grand Junction Canal, the Company decided, perhaps with little choice given the threat to their trade posed by the railways, to diversify into carrying. A sum of £93,700 was raised to support the venture by the issue of preferential shares. In 1864, the company set up a fleet of steam powered narrowboats that generally operated with 'butty' boats in tow. The fleet operated over the full length of the canal route between the coalfields of the East Midlands and London. To attract yet more traffic onto the canals and, hence, away from the railways, the company established a series of depots, several located away from the canal itself. However, despite trading for nigh on thirty years, the venture into carrying by the GJCC was a financial failure and was abandoned in 1876.

Not long after, the GJCC began consultations with neighbouring canal companies to find ways of reducing tolls charged to carriers, in an attempt to hold on to their share of the traffic between the Midlands and London. As pointed out by Hadfield in *Canals of the East Midlands*, it was a battle that the canal company was ultimately going to lose:

'The Grand Junction Canal notably failed to hold, still less to increase, the carriage of coal to London against competition from the railways, notably the L&NWR [London & North Western Railway] and the Great Northern. The following figures, [Table 2.3] taken at five-yearly intervals, of coal imports to London paying the coal duties, must be read against an import by sea that remained fairly constant at about 3 million tons annually.'

The increasing competition from the railways continued to draw trade away from the canals and force tolls downwards, to the extent that the GJCC sought closer working arrangements, which fell only just short of amalgamation, with the Leicestershire & Northamptonshire Union Canal.

TABLE 2.3: TONNAGE OF COAL TRANSPORTED TO LONDON 1845-65 BY CANAL AND RAIL		
YEAR	BY CANAL	BY RAIL
1845	60,311	8,377
1850	29,479	55,096
1855	23,251	1,137,835
1860	19,593	1,477,546
1865	8,532	2,733,057

Data taken from *The Canals of the East Midlands* (Hadfield, 1966)

In 1863, the GJCC contacted the various canal companies on the Birmingham, Coventry and Leicester lines to initiate enquiries into the feasibility of closer co-operation and possible amalgamation of the waterways, in order to increase their competitiveness. Seemingly, there was initial interest in the idea from some although, crucially, not all of the other canal companies but this soon waned and the first opportunity for concerted action against the railways was missed.

Another opportunity for more efficient working on the canals arose at the end of 1885. According to the Minute Book of the GJCC, on 4th November, the Board members:

> 'Read letter dated 28th ulto from Henry I. Marten Esq C.E. stating that at a meeting of an influential Committee composed of gentlemen largely concerned in the manufactures of the South Staffordshire District as well as of Representatives of various trading Associations in that District and formed for the purpose of considering the question of improving the carrying capacity of the Canals between Birmingham and London and held in Birmingham on Thursday the 15th inst he was requested to ascertain whether the Directors of this Company would so far aid in this important investigation, as to afford him, as the Engineer appointed to report to the Committee on the subject, the requisite facilities for making an inspection of the Canal and for retaining such information as will enable him to make a reliable report on the feasibility and cost of effecting such improved carrying capacity.'

Not wholly unsurprisingly, this letter received a guarded response but, having asked for and being in receipt of more details, the GJCC agreed that its Engineer at that time, Hubert Thomas, should meet with Mr Marten on behalf of the promoters of the scheme and the Engineers from the other canals affected; this turned out to be the Warwick & Birmingham Canal, the Warwick & Napton Canal and the Oxford Canal.

In response to another letter on the canal improvement subject, received about six months later, which advised that the 'Trent Navigation was contemplating deepening their navigation to provide more capacious and efficient carrying appliances', the GJCC responded by declining an invitation to join 'a committee for the federation of canals' until such time as the matter had been explored further by the various canal companies affected.

The proposal for the improvement of the Birmingham to London canal route rumbled on over the next three or four years. It eventually seemed to fade away when, in October 1890, the Board of the GJCC informed the promoters that the possible canal amalgamation was somewhat premature given the impending 'Classification of Tolls' by the Board of Trade.

Around the same time, in 1886, the largest and perhaps best known of the canal carrying companies, Messrs Fellows, Morton & Clayton, took over the trade of the London & Midland Counties Carrying Company and by so doing became far more influential with regard to the setting of tolls for inland transport between the East Midlands and London. Before long, they would play a key part in the expansion of the GJCC but more of this later.

The Minute Book around this time also reveals that the GJCC had regular meetings at which proposed legislation that might be relevant to the company's interests was identified and evaluated. Records indicate that, towards the end of the century at least, parliamentary business was closely monitored. Any Parliamentary Bills, which would have included canal or railway development, that might affect the business of the GJCC, was referred to Messrs Grahames & Co. Ltd for their attention and, where appropriate, to ensure that clauses to protect the GJCC's interests were inserted in any Act of Parliament.

According to the Minute Book of the GJCC, in August 1891, and with the proposal to improve the Birmingham to London canal route seemingly fading away, the Company began negotiations with the Grand Union and Leicestershire & Northamptonshire Union canal companies, with a view to entering into an arrangement for improving and increasing the traffic on the Leicester route. These negotiations would primarily have been driven by the need to increase the volume of through traffic between the East Midlands and London, thereby making the Grand Junction Canal more competitive with the railways. However, the value of the summit section of the Grand Union Canal, as a supply of water to the Grand Junction Canal, would also have been a significant factor.

Before long, however, the focus of the negotiations had moved onto a take-over by the GJCC of the other two canals, rather than mere co-operation, with an initial purchase price of £25,000 for both canals being considered. It was during the course of these negotiations that Mr J. Fellows, of Fellows, Morton & Clayton, became involved and played what appears to have been a crucial role by acting as arbiter between the three canal companies concerned. Clearly, the carrying company was greatly worried about the poor condition of the two Union canals and was keen to encourage the GJCC in its plans to purchase, so that the line to Leicester could be improved. This, in turn, would enable Fellows, Morton & Clayton to reduce their freight charges on the route between the East Midlands and London, making them more competitive with other canal carriers and the railways. For their part, the GJCC sought guarantees from Fellows, Morton & Clayton, regarding the volume of traffic that they would commit to the Leicester line in the event of the canal amalgamations going through.

According to Charles Hadfield in *Canals of the East Midlands*, in February 1893, whilst these negotiations were ongoing, the Engineer to the Grand Union Canal Company reported to his directors that the canal might do better if:

*Lock houses at Foxton – A colour engraving by John O'Connor taken from **Canals, Barges and People** by John O'Connor, Art & Technics Ltd, 1950.*
This is a view looking generally northwards from part way up the flight of locks at Foxton, with the Market Harborough Arm in the right background.

> '... more energy were thrown into the matter of Boat accommodation, expedition and canvassing for trade, particularly on the part of the principal Carriers, Messrs. Fellows, Morton & Clayton Ltd.'

Subsequently, the Grand Union Canal Company met with Mr Fellows and it was perhaps during the course of the ensuing dialogue that the proposal for removing the bottlenecks posed by the narrow Foxton and Watford flights of locks was first raised.

Mr Fellows' interventions on behalf of the GJCC, regarding the purchase of the two other canals, eventually bore fruit for, on 12th July 1893, the minutes of the Board record that:

> '... they authorised Mr J. Fellows as Agent for the Company to purchase the canals with all freehold and leasehold estates, water rights and plant in connection therewith and that he had acquired the Grand Union Canal for the sum of £10,500 and the Leicestershire &

TABLE 2.4: ANNUAL DIVIDENDS FOR THE GRAND JUNCTION CANAL IN THE RAILWAY ERA, 1840–90	
DATE	DIVIDEND
1840	8%
1845	7%
1850	4%
1855	2%
1860	3½%
1865	4%
1870	4%
1875	3%
1880	4%
1885	4%
1890	4%

Data taken from *The Grand Junction Canal* (Faulkner 1972)

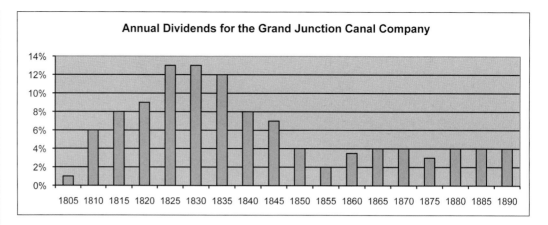

Northamptonshire Union Canal for the sum of £6,500 together with £250 to be paid to the Clerk as compensation for the loss of his office making a total of £17,250.'

It would seem that Mr Fellows had negotiated, on behalf of the GJCC, a reduction of £7,750. The Royal Assent for the transfer bill allowing the purchases was finally completed on 29th September 1894.

The GJCC clearly felt it needed to gain control of the Leicester route if there was to be any chance of reversing the decline of the traffic between the East Midlands and London in the face of railway competition. This decline is explained by Alan Faulkner in his book *The Grand Junction Canal*:

> *'In 1850 some 125,000 tons of Derbyshire coal had reached the Grand Junction, but this had declined to 73,000 tons in 1855 and to a mere 4,700 tons by 1894. This drop reflected the intense railway competition for this lucrative traffic, particularly from the Midland Railway.'*

To complete the picture, the declining profitability of the canals in the face of competition from the railways from 1840 onwards can be illustrated by reference to the annual dividends paid out by the GJCC, as shown in **Table 2.4**.

On the basis that pictures speak louder than words, also shown above is a bar chart of the annual dividends paid out by the GJCC from its opening in 1805 to 1890.

★ ★ ★ ★ ★

It is of interest to note that, whilst giving evidence twelve years later on 6th November 1906 to the Royal Commission into Canals & Inland Navigations in the United Kingdom, Gordon Thomas, the Engineer to the GJCC at that time, advised that:

> *'The object* [of purchasing the Leicestershire and Northamptonshire Union and the Grand Union canals] *was to form a through route under one control for carriage by water of coal, stone, iron and the products of those parts of Nottinghamshire and Derbyshire which are served by the Cromford and Nottingham Canals owned respectively by the Midland and Great Northern Railway Companies.'*

Gordon Thomas went on to advise the Royal Commission that through-toll agreements had been entered into by the GJCC with the above two canals, together with the Leicester Navigation, the Loughborough Navigation and the Erewash Canal. These agreements were intended to make the canal route more attractive to carriers by offering reduced tolls for through traffic. However, in order to secure these through-toll agreements, the GJCC had to give minimum toll guarantees to the five other canal companies. This meant that, on a year-by-year basis, if sufficient through traffic was not generated, then the GJCC would compensate the other canal companies up to the minimum toll guarantees.

★ ★ ★ ★ ★

Finally, there was a rather bizarre intervention in 1894, by Bertram William Cook who, at that time, was the manager of the Northern District of the Grand Junction Canal. Prior to the finalisation of the purchase of the Leicestershire & Northamptonshire Union and the Grand Union canals by the GJCC, Cook presented proposals, which he entitled 'The Future of Canals', to replace the above two canals with a railway between Leicester and Watford. His idea was surprising given that it was seemingly at odds with the GJCC's apparent determination to fight against the remorseless growth of the railways.

Cook's idea was to construct a railway along the line of the canals with steam engines pulling wagons carrying narrowboats with their cargos, each with a laden weight of around 40 tons. The changes in ground level between Leicester and the summit reach, including that at the Foxton flight of locks, were to be overcome by railway inclines with gradients of 1 in 100, whilst the change in level at the Watford flight would be overcome by a railway incline of 1 in 50 gradient. Cook proposed branch lines to connect the new railway to the Midland Railway line at Leicester and the London & North Western Railway line at Watford. A typical train using the new line would have consisted of a steam locomotive pulling four wagons. How the laden narrowboats would have been put onto the wagons, however, is not clear but, as stated by Dave Goodwin in his *Foxton Locks & the Grand Junction Canal Co.*, the scheme had all the hallmarks of not having been fully thought through. He goes on to say:

> 'Surely Cook's ideas would be seen as a sell-out in the eyes of the Canal hierarchy. They would
> have been incredulous at such a chilling proposition – the future of canals was railways – rank
> disloyalty!'

Seen in another light, however, Cook could be viewed as a pragmatist, given the very poor condition of the two canals that the GJCC were on the verge of purchasing and the inevitability of the dominance of the railways in the future.

Not surprisingly, however, given the circumstances at that time, Cook's idea did not find favour with the GJCC. Perhaps coincidentally, within two years of his controversial proposal, Cook left the employ of the canal company and was replaced by Thomas Millner.

Sources For This Chapter

The Canals of the East Midlands, Charles Hadfield, David & Charles 1966
British Canals – An Illustrated History, Charles Hadfield, Phoenix House 1950
British Canals, Edwin A. Pratt, John Murray, 1906
The Canal Age, Charles Hadfield, David & Charles 1968
The Leicester Line: A History of the Old Union and Grand Union Canals, Philip Stevens, David & Charles 1972
The Grand Junction Canal, Alan Faulkner, David & Charles 1972
Foxton Locks and the Grand Junction Canal Co., Dave Goodwin, Leicestershire County Council c1988
The Illustrated History of Canal and River Navigations, Edward Paget-Tomlinson, Sheffield Academic Press 1993
The Minute Books of the Committee of the Grand Junction Canal Company, the National Archives, Kew
'Minutes of Evidence given to the Royal Commission on the Canals & Inland Navigations of the United Kingdom', the National Archives, Kew – Evidence given by Gordon Thomas on 6th November 1906

Oil on canvas portrait by William Armfield Hobday in 1796, of William Reynolds (1758–1803), the designer of the Ketley Inclined Plane near Coalbrookdale in Shropshire.
COURTESY THE MUSEUM OF IRON, COALBROOKDALE
William Reynolds was a Quaker ironmaster, entrepreneur and manager of the Ketley branch of the Coalbrookdale Company and the Madeley Wood Company. In his left hand, he is holding a drawing of the Longdon-on-Tern Aqueduct, the first cast iron aqueduct in the world, which was designed by Thomas Telford. Over his left shoulder can be seen the Ketley Inclined Plane. William Reynolds was 38 years of age at the time of the portrait.

CHAPTER 3

1750 TO 1887
EARLIER INCLINED PLANES

'Inclined planes appeared to have been first applied to the purpose of conveying vessels from one reach of a canal to another at a greater elevation, by Mr. William Reynolds on the Ketly [sic] Canal, in Shropshire, about the year 1789; they were afterwards adopted on the Shropshire Canal, – the Duke of Bridgewater's Canal, (upon which they have since been discontinued), – and more recently, they have been, on a much larger scale, successfully employed on the Morris Canal, United States.'
Part of a statement made by Mr James Leslie, M. Inst. C.E. at a meeting on 24th January 1854 as recorded in the Proceedings of the Institution of Civil Engineers

My objective in this chapter is to provide a brief history of inclined planes that have been used to convey river and canal boats between one level and another. I will focus mainly on those inclined planes built in Britain prior to 1900, as these are the ones that would most likely have been referred to during the development and design of the Foxton Inclined Plane. The time period of relevance to this book is between the start of the Industrial Revolution, circa 1750, and the end of the 19th century.

My main sources of information for this chapter are two books, the first by David Tew entitled *Canal Inclines & Lifts*, dated 1984, and the other by Hans-Joachim Uhlemann entitled *Canal Lifts and Inclines of the World*, dated 2002. It seems quite likely, however, that Uhlemann would have made use of David Tew's book with respect to the British inclines that I concentrate on below. I have also made reference to papers written circa 1854 by James Leslie, the designer of the Blackhill Inclined Plane of the Monkland Canal in Scotland, and to recent booklets prepared by the Chard History Group. Unfortunately, these documents are not always mutually consistent.

Please note that I have been very deliberate with my use of terms in this chapter. Although some authors refer to inclined planes under the general heading of boat lifts, I have chosen to restrict my use of the words 'boat lift' to a structure that raises and lowers boats vertically between two levels, as is the case for the Anderton Boat Lift, as opposed to 'inclined plane' that raises and lowers boats between two levels by means of a relatively shallow angled slope.

The Anderton Boat Lift in 2011, following its restoration to working order by British Waterways in 2001. AUTHOR

★ ★ ★ ★ ★

The extract at the top of the chapter demonstrates that there is rarely anything new under the sun. For example, Edwin Clark, the designer of the Anderton Boat Lift, drew upon the examples of earlier boat lifts built in Britain. Similarly, Gordon Thomas, the Engineer to the Grand Junction Canal Company, who was generally credited with the design of the inclined plane at Foxton, would presumably have learnt from the construction and operation of earlier inclined planes. Whilst I have found no written evidence to support this, in my opinion it is inconceivable that the Foxton Inclined Plane was designed without any reference to earlier structures. However, whilst there are many similarities between that at Foxton and

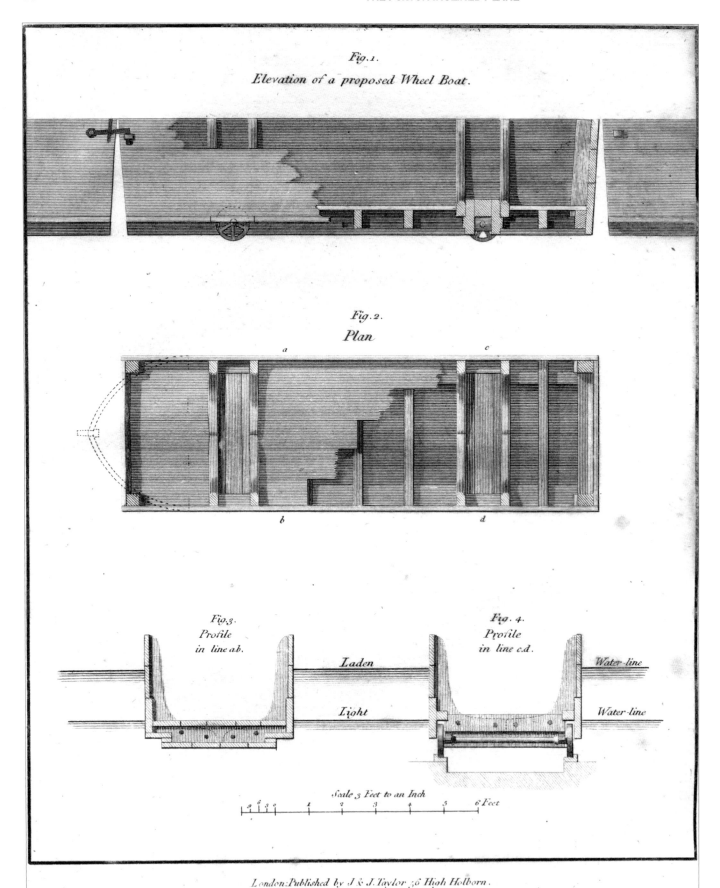

Plate 2 from **A General History of Inland Navigation** *by* **J. Phillips, 1795.** NEIL PARKHOUSE COLLECTION
Proposed wooden 'Wheel Boats' for conveying coal and other bulk goods on canals in mines and onto the inland navigations. The boats would be capable of being towed by a horse whilst afloat in a canal and also being taken out of the water onto rails and drawn up or down an inclined plane between canals at different levels. The boats are rectangular so that they can more easily accommodate the square boxes or crates that contained the coal.

earlier inclined planes, the Foxton incline contained a number of unique aspects, as will be expanded upon later.

★ ★ ★ ★ ★

The first recorded use of an inclined plane to convey boats between two levels was circa 1700 BC in Egypt, at Mirgissa near Wadi Halfa on the River Nile. It comprised a 3 to 4km long slipway, that made use of fixed wooden slats lubricated with wet river silt to slide boats around rapids that, at certain times of year, were impassable. It is likely that boats were pulled along the inclined plane with their hulls in contact with the slats; that is to say without the use of separate support frames. The plane was seemingly built to enable quarried stone to be transported downstream and provisions transported upstream. The site of this inclined plane is now under water due to the construction in the 1960s of the Aswan High Dam.

Many centuries later, circa 600 BC, an inclined plane referred to as the Diolkos (slipway) was built to carry ships over the Isthmus of Corinth, in modern-day Greece, between the Gulf of Corinth and the Saronic Gulf. The inclined plane was paved with stone and was 6½km long and, in places, 10m wide. Archaeologists believe from the existence of grooves in the stonework that the boats were hauled along the incline on wheeled cradles or carriages. In order to reduce weight, the cargos from the boats were unloaded and conveyed over the isthmus by more conventional road transport. The Diolkos enabled boats to avoid the arduous and potentially hazardous voyage around the isthmus. It is possible that the Diolkos was in use over a period of 300 years or more.

The next recorded use of inclined planes was circa 300AD, with the Chinese using a series of seven relatively short inclines on the Ssu River section of the Grand Canal. The planes made use of capstans that were either operated by oxen or teams of men. By all accounts, these inclined planes, or at least others of similar design, continued in use until modern times.

Perhaps not surprisingly, the first recorded use of inclined planes on navigable waterways in Europe was in the Low Countries, that is to say Holland and Belgium, in the 12th century AD. Whilst there were various different configurations and hauling methods for these inclines or 'overtooms', they were generally relatively short and were used for conveying small boats of between 6 and 8 tons over earth embankments or dykes between waterways. Several continued in use up to the beginning of the 19th century. Other inclined planes were built around the same time in Russia, Italy and Germany.

In Britain, the construction of inclined planes on waterways began as part of the 'Canal Mania' period that started in the middle of 18th century. The inland navigation system that resulted provided a reliable and economic means of transporting bulk goods, particularly coal, essential for the fuelling of the Industrial Revolution. Although rivers had been used for navigation for many centuries previously, it is the Bridgewater Canal, built in 1761 to carry coal from the Duke of Bridgewater's mines at Worsley to the market place of Salford and Manchester, which is generally recognised as being the first commercial canal to have been constructed in Britain. Somewhat fittingly, for reasons that will be revealed in the next chapter, it was on this canal that one of the earliest inclined planes in Britain was built.

In *A General History of Inland Navigation*, written by J. Phillips and published in 1795, the author discusses the methods of moving coal at the Worsley mines and, for specific situations, suggests the use of inclined planes to convey wheeled boats between the canals at different levels within the mines:

'The higher Canal where it crosses the main tunnel, has a pit communicating with the side of it, down which the coals are sent from the upper to the lower boats, and by their descent raise a proportionate quantity of limestone up another pit to the surface of the ground. The charge of the operation is not great; but the frequent delay attendant upon this method, is such, as may render it eligible in some instances to convey the boats themselves from the upper to lower Canal; and in all situations where the dip or fall of the [coal] seam is sufficiently great, for the weight of the

TABLE 3.1: SUMMARY DETAILS OF MOST OF THE INCLINED PLANES BUILT IN BRITAIN 1750-1900

LOCATION OF INCLINED PLANE	IN OPERATION	DESIGNER	SUMMARY DETAILS
St Columb Canal, Cornwall			
Morgan Porth and St Colomb Porth	1773-1881	John Edyvean	Gravity and horse powered winding gear, with boxes filled from boats and then lowered down incline
Ducart's Canal & Lagan Navigation, Northern Ireland			
Brackaville	1777-1787	Davis Ducart	Double-tracked and counterbalanced with assistance from horses
Drumreagh			
Fernlough			
Ketley Canal, Shropshire			
Ketley	1788-c1816	William Reynolds	Double-tracked with counterbalanced cradles with a chamber at the top of each track
Donnington Wood Canal, Shropshire			
Hugh's Bridge	1790-1873/79	Poss. John Gilbert	Originally a hoist but in 1790 converted to an incline for boxes, which may later have been converted for boats
Shropshire Canal, Shropshire			
Wrockwardine Wood or Donnington Wood	1792-c1858	William Reynolds	Double-tracked and counterbalanced with reverse slopes at the top. Initially operated by horses but soon after completion converted to steam engine operation
Windmill Farm	1792-c1858		
Hay Incline at Coalport	1792-c1894		
Brierley Hill, Coalbrookdale	1794-c1800	Unknown but William Reynolds	Replaced a counter-balanced vertical shaft which had operated since 1792. The incline was double-tracked and counterbalanced
Shrewsbury Canal, Shropshire			
Trench Incline	1793-1921	William Reynolds	Double-tracked and counterbalanced. Its operation was steam engine assisted. This was the last working inclined plane in Britain
Bridgewater Canal, Lancashire			
Ashton's Field at Worsley	1797-1822	John Gilbert	Double-tracked, counterbalanced and self-operating with initial assistance by manual winches
Redding Canal, South Wales			
Cadoxton	1818	Unknown	No details
Tavistock Canal, Devon			
Mill Hill	1819-1831/44	John Taylor	Single-tracked and operated by horses
Morwellham Quay	1817 to 1883		Operation was waterwheel assisted
Bude Canal, Cornwall			
Marhamchurch	1819 to 1891	James Green	Waterwheel assisted
Hobbacott Down			Small steam engine provided
Vealand (Venn)			Waterwheel driven for wheeled boats
Merrifield			
Tamerton			
Werrington or Bridgetown			
Torrington or Rolle Canal, Devon			
Weare Giffard	1827-1871	James Green	Waterwheel driven, probably for wheeled boats
Grand Western Canal, Devon			
Wellisford	1836-1837	James Green	For tub boats floating in caissons
Chard Canal, Somerset			
Thornfalcon	1837-1868	Sir William Cubitt	Double-tracked with water-filled counterbalanced caissons operated by water being added to descending caisson
Wrantage			
Ilminster	1841-1868		Either double-tracked with water-filled counterbalanced caissons or single-tracked 'dry' incline, operated by a water turbine
Chard Common	1841-1868		Single-tracked 'dry' incline operated by a water turbine
Kidwelly & Llanelly Canal, South Wales			
Pont Henry	1838-1867	James Green	Probably counterbalanced with hydraulic pump operation
Capel Ifan			
Hirwaun-isaf			As above but never completed
Monkland Canal, Scotland			
Blackhill Inclined Plane	1850-1887	James Leslie	Double-tracked and counterbalanced. Operated by steam engines

A Demonstration of the Theory of Canals, from a coloured engraving by J. Pass, 1800. From English Rivers and Canals, F. Eyre & C. Hadfield, Britain in Pictures Series, Collins 1945. This illustration shows three different forms of early canal inclined planes. The top picture appears to show a counterbalanced dry inclined plane, with the weight of the descending boat helping to raise another boat up the incline. It is not clear whether the boats going down are laden and hence heavier than the boat going up but, if this is the case, then no additional power input is likely to be needed. The middle picture shows the top of an inclined plane for a single boat on a dry slope, with the lifting power seemingly being provided by lowering a water-filled container down a vertical shaft. The weight of a boat going down the slope would presumably be sufficient to lift the container back up to the top of the shaft. The lower picture shows an inclined plane for a single boat on a dry slope, this time with the motive power being provided by water-wheel driven by water drawn from the upper section of the canal. The horse that would be used to tow the boat along the canal is being led down to the bottom of the incline

laden boats to overcome friction and other impediments to drawing the light ones up, I conceive the system of inclined planes and wheels under the boats might be adopted with advantage.

It would appear that this document pre-dated the use of the inclined planes in the Duke of Bridgewater's Worsley mines and may well have been the catalyst to their construction.

Table 3.1 lists, in chronological order, the inclined planes that records indicate were built in Britain prior to 1900. The information was generally taken from Hans-Joachim Uhleman's book.

Focussing on these relatively recent inclined planes in Britain, several facts which are relevant to the Foxton Inclined Plane can be drawn from the table:

• There were broadly two types of inclined planes – the 'dry' type in which boats were conveyed up and down slopes out of the water, and the 'wet' type in which boats were conveyed whilst floating in a water-filled tank or caisson. The earlier inclined planes tended to be of the 'dry' type for the conveyance of small tub-boats

• An obvious advantage of the 'wet' type was that, barring accidents, the structural integrity of the boats being conveyed was not put at risk; conversely, boats on 'dry' inclined planes were supported on frames that imposed point loads on their hulls, for which they had not been designed

• Another advantage of the 'wet' type is that, due to the displacement of water by the boat, the weight of the water-filled caisson remained constant whether containing a boat or not. Consequently the energy required to haul a caisson up a slope was predictable and, if two counterbalanced caissons were used, relatively minor

• The inclined plane at Foxton was just one in a long line of inclined planes in Britain, some commercially successful and many not, built and operated over the preceding 150 or so years

Of the many inclined planes built in this country, those that I particularly wish to highlight are: the **Ketley Inclined Plane** (1788), because it was one of the first, if not the first, to be built in Britain; the **Ilminster Inclined Plane** on the Chard Canal (1837), which was one of the first to convey boats floating in water-filled caissons, albeit relatively short tub-boats; and finally, the **Blackhill Inclined Plane** (1850) for being the last incline to be built in Britain prior to the development of the Foxton Inclined Plane, this time for full-sized barges floating in water-filled caissons.

As stated previously, it is inconceivable that Gordon Thomas and his co-designers had not researched earlier inclined planes in Britain, and perhaps in Europe, prior to setting about designing the Foxton Inclined Plane. It is quite likely that they studied the advantages and disadvantages of the inclines that I have singled out for closer attention below.

The Ketley Inclined Plane, near Hadley in Shropshire

It is interesting to note that, according to Hans-Joachim Uhlemann, the first use of an inclined plane on navigable waterways on the British mainland was by John Edyvean, on the St. Colomb Canal in Cornwall in 1773. This, however, seems to be contradicted by James Leslie, the designer of the Blackhill Inclined Plane (see the quotation at the head of this chapter), who suggests that the Ketley Incline was the first. Leslie's view is supported by David Tew. The discrepancy might, however, be explained by David Tew's suggestion that the planning stages of the incline on the St. Colomb's Canal may have preceded the construction of the incline on the Ketley Canal.

The Ketley Incline, whether or not the first on the British mainland, was brought into service in 1788 and was the first of six very similar inclined planes to be built in the Coalbrookdale area of Shropshire. It was designed by William Reynolds (1758-1803), who was a local ironmaster, entrepreneur and manager of the Ketley branch of the Coalbrookdale Company and the Madeley Wood Company.

This incline was particularly notable because it used two counterbalanced wheeled carriages, or cradles, to reduce the energy input required for its operation. It was a 'dry' type of inclined plane, for transferring relatively small tub-boats, nominally 20 feet long by 6 feet 4 inches wide by 3 feet 10 inches deep, laden with 8 tons or so of iron ore or coal, down to the iron foundry at Ketley. At the top and bottom of the plane were lock chambers that enabled the tub-boats to be floated over the cradles. The water in the chambers was then drained away to leave the tub-boats fully supported on the cradles, thereby allowing the cradles and boats to be raised and lowered on rails. The cradles had large wheels at the front end, with smaller wheels at the back, so as to go some way, at least, to keep the tub-boats horizontal whilst on the incline.

The cradles were linked together by means of a rope wound round a large wooden drum, located at the summit of the plane. The motive power was provided by the greater weight of the top cradle, which contained a fully laden tub-boat, whilst the lower cradle would have contained an empty or only partly laden tub-boat. The movement of the cradles was effected by a brakeman controlling the descent of the heavier cradle.

The Ketley Incline was approximately 225 yards long and overcame a vertical height of some 73 feet, which represented a slope of nominally 1 in 9 gradient. It linked the upper and lower sections of the Ketley to Oakengates Canal.

By all accounts, the Ketley Inclined Plane was much admired, coming to the attention of such notable engineers of the time as Thomas Telford and James Watt. Thomas Telford wrote about William Reynolds' achievements and these were included in a book entitled Plymley's Shropshire – General View of the Agriculture of Shropshire, published in 1803:

'There seemed insuperable difficulties, and most probably might have proved so for ages to come, had not Mr. WILLIAM REYNOLDS, of Ketley, (whose character is too well known to need any eulogium), discovered the means of effecting this desirable object: for he, about this time, having occasion to improve the mode of conveying iron-stone and coal, from the neighbourhood of Oaken Gates to the iron-works at Ketley, these materials lying generally at the distance of about a mile and a half from the iron-works, and at 73 feet above their level; he made a navigable canal, and instead of descending in the usual way, by locks, continued to bring the canal forward to an abrupt part of a bank, the skirts of which terminated on a level with the iron-works. At the top of the bank he built a small lock, and from the bottom of the lock, and down the face of the bank, he constructed an inclined plane with a double iron railway.'

Furthermore, as stated in a Wrekin Local Studies Forum Leaflet of 2004:

'When it first opened, the inclined plane at Ketley was one of the industrial marvels of the world. Many ironmasters and engineers came to view the plane, and many Frenchmen were refused access because the ironmasters wanted to protect trade secrets during wartime.'

According to David Tew, William Reynolds wrote to James Watt on 16th May 1789 to advise that:

'… our inclined plane answers my most sanguine expectations. We have already let down more than forty boats a day each carrying eight tons – on an average thirty boats a day and have not yet had an accident.'

The Ketley Inclined Plane remained in operation until about 1816, a working life of some twenty-eight years. Today, there is no evidence of it remaining on the ground, apart from a road named 'The Incline'.

As a result of his success with the Ketley Incline, William Reynolds and his colleagues went on to design and construct a further five inclined planes in the Coalbrookdale area. One of these, the Trench Incline on the Shrewsbury Canal, remained in operation for over 120 years and only finally closed in 1921, by which time it was the last working canal incline in Britain. As such, it was in service throughout the development, design, construction and operation stages of the Foxton Inclined Plane. Another, the Hay Incline, has been partly restored and can be visited today as part of the Blists Hill Victorian Town Museum at Coalport.

The two plates reproduced overleaf are taken from Plymley's Shropshire. They show details of apparently two different, but similar, inclines on the Shropshire Canal, although the headings on the plates simply refer to No. 1 and No. 2 without giving any specific location for them. Again,

The Trench Inclined Plane on the Shrewsbury Canal, circa 1890. COURTESY THE IRONBRIDGE GORGE MUSEUM TRUST
The tub-boats on the two carriages are just visible on the plane in the middle background, whilst the haulage ropes from the wheeled cradles run up the middle of the tracks on rollers. In the background are the numerous chimneys of the Shropshire Ironworks.

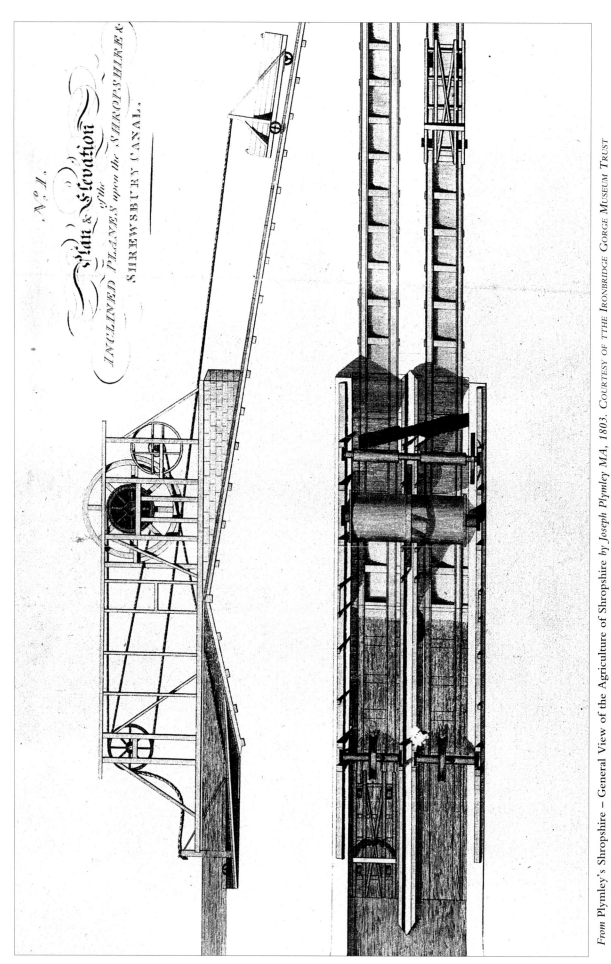

From Plymley's Shropshire – General View of the Agriculture of Shropshire by Joseph Plymley MA, 1803. COURTESY OF TTHE IRONBRIDGE GORGE MUSEUM TRUST

Plate No. 1 – Sectional side elevation and plan of the headworks of one of the inclined planes on the Shrewsbury Canal.

Note the reverse incline at the top of the plane. This was a significant improvement on the arrangement at the top of the earlier Ketley Inclined Plane which included a chamber and guillotine gate, with the consequence that a chamber of water was lost from the top pound each time a tub-boat descended.

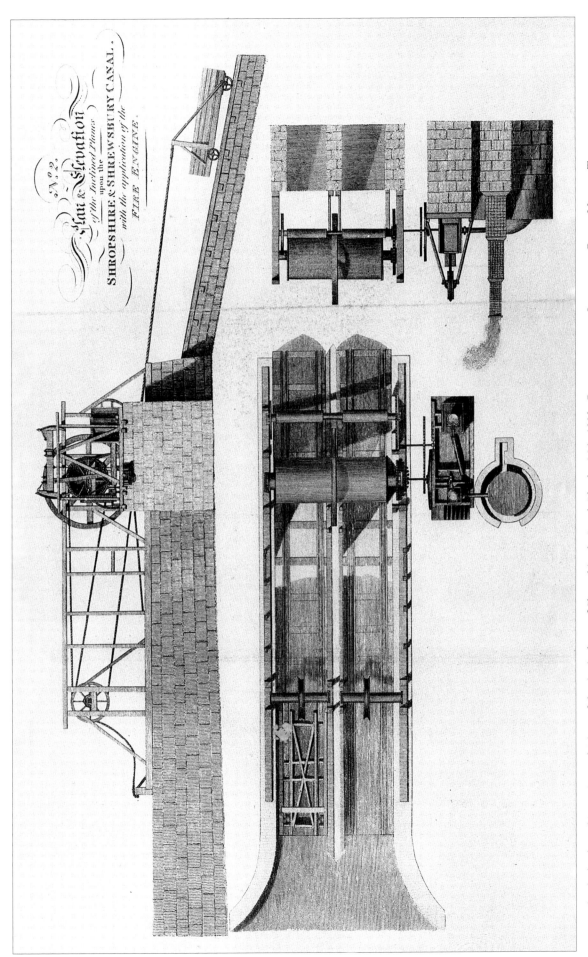

From Plymley's Shropshire – General View of the Agriculture of Shropshire by Joseph Plymley MA, 1803. Courtesy of the Ironbridge Gorge Museum Trust
Plate No. 2 – Side and end elevations and plan of the headworks, together with the steam engine, of the another of the inclined planes on the Shrewsbury Canal.
Note the location of the steam engine on the plan and the end elevation. The impression gained is that this inclined plane also has a reverse slope, rather than a chamber, at the top of the incline.

ABOVE: The hauling mechanism and engine house at the top of the Trench Inclined Plane on the Shrewsbury Canal, circa 1890. COURTESY THE WATERWAYS TRUST Notice the laden tub-boat moored at the wharf and an empty one in the left-hand chamber just having completed an ascent. The engineer in charge of the steam engine, William Jones, is standing in the doorway, whilst the brakesman, Frank Owen, is standing on the central pier at the top of the incline.

RIGHT: The Trench Inclined Plane circa 1910. COURTESY THE IRONBRIDGE GORGE MUSEUM TRUST A view up the incline, which was 223 yards long and climbed 75 feet in height.

Telford's observations were used to refer to them:

'The inclined planes which were adopted on the Shropshire canal, were upon the same principle with that which Mr. REYNOLDS had erected on the Ketley canal; and the only variations from it were, that in place of the upper canal ending in a lock, it was terminated by a small inclined plane, which commenced at the bottom level of the canal, and was brought up above top water level of the canal, and a steam engine was so placed as to work the axis of the wooden barrel of the upright frame formerly described. By means of this engine, not only the loaded boats

ABOVE: **The Hay Inclined Plane, Shopshire Canal, circa 1905.** NEIL PARKHOUSE COLLECTION
The Coalbrookdale Branch of the Shropshire Canal was in two parts, with the Hay Inclined Plane leading down to a short section which ran alongside the River Severn before terminating at Coalport. Here, tub-boats laden with coal were tipped into waiting up-river trows for onwards transportation It was last used around 1894, so this circa 1905 picture postcard shows it after about a decade out of use. It was 350 yards in length and had a drop of 208 feet.

LEFT: **The Hay Inclined Plane, Shopshire Canal, August 1972.** COURTESY THE WATERWAYS TRUST
A view of the trackbed of the inclined plane, showing the brick arch bridge glimpsed in the previous picture, which spanned the incline bottom.

are raised out of the upper canal, up the small inclined plane, without loss of water, but there is brought from the lower level, up the inclined plane, a boat with a load equal to that which passes down at the same time. The form of this machine, and the manner in which the steam-engine is connected with it, will be readily comprehended by referring to the annexed engravings marked No. 1 and 2, which have been carefully copied from those made out by Mr. HENRY WILLIAMS, the resident engineer, under whose directions the machines were erected, and on whose accuracy and veracity the public may with confidence rely: the distances, rise and fall of the canal having likewise been furnished by him, may be considered as equally correct.'

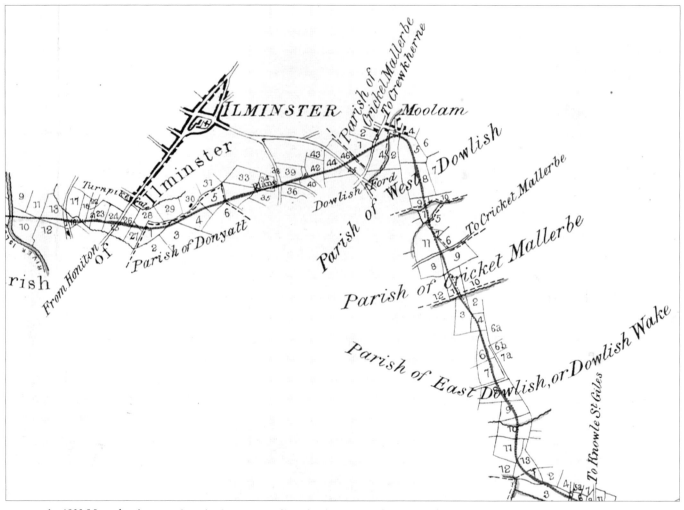

The Ilminster Inclined Plane on the Chard Canal in Somerset

According to an article in the *The Engineer* of 22nd January 1897, which addressed trials of a model inclined plane for possible use at Foxton, the first time that 'wet' inclines were used in England was in the middle of the 19th century with the construction of inclined planes for tub-boats on the short-lived Chard Canal, near Taunton in Somerset.

The design of the Chard inclines is generally credited to Sir William Cubitt, which is confirmed by the proceedings of the Institution of Civil Engineers on 24th January 1854:

'Since writing the account of the Blackhill Incline, which had appeared in the 'Transactions of the Royal Scottish Society of Arts', Mr. Leslie had learned that three inclined planes for boats were constructed, about ten years ago, by Sir William Cubitt, on the Chard Canal, Somersetshire, and they had acted very satisfactorily.'

In fact there were four inclines, not three, these being at Chard Common, Ilminster, Wrantage and Thornfalcon (for whatever reason, James Leslie makes no reference to the incline at Thornfalcon). The tub-boats used on the canal and inclines measured 26 feet long by 6 feet 6 inches wide and mostly carried coal and stone.

The inclines at Thornfalcon and Wrantage were of similar construction, overcoming vertical heights of just 28 feet and 27 feet 6 inches respectively. Both inclines made use of two water-filled and counterbalanced caissons, each with six wheels, presumably of different sizes to keep the caissons horizontal. They were connected together by a chain that passed around a drum at the top of the incline. The movement of the caissons was achieved by increasing the water level in the upper caisson so as to overcome the frictional resistance of the system. Brakes were fitted to the caissons in order to control their speed.

James Leslie, the Chard History Group and Joachim Uhlemann all suggest that the

Ilminster Incline was of similar design to that at Wrantage and Thornfalcon, with two water-filled caissons. This, however, is contradicted by David Tew who, by reference to a recently discovered drawing of the Ilminster Incline, concluded that it was *'worked by an overshot waterwheel located at the foot of the incline operating what appears to be an endless chain through gearing.'*

The vertical height overcome by the Ilminster Incline was nominally 82 feet. Unfortunately, David Tew is unable to provide any other details of it.

All references agree that the fourth structure, that at Chard Common, which overcame a vertical height of 86 feet, was a single-tracked 'dry' incline. According to the Chard History Group, it was the only such incline to have been built in Britain. As with the arrangement at the Ketley Inclined Plane, a tub-boat going up the incline would have been floated over and then lowered onto a wheeled cradle on rails, before being pulled up the slope. The motive power was by means of a rope driven by a water turbine located at the foot of the incline; that is to say, a similar mechanism to that suggested by David Tew for Ilminster.

The cradles on the inclines had two pairs of wheels, with one pair larger than the other in order to keep the tub-boats horizontal on the incline. At the top of the inclines, the cradles ran down a short reverse slope into the upper section of the canal but this time seemingly using a different pair of wheels (or rails), to keep the tub-boats reasonably horizontal.

David Tew, Joachim Uhlemann and the Chard History Group agree that the gradient of all four of the inclines was nominally 1 in 9 – although in another document the Chard History Group states that the slopes for the Chard Common incline was 1 in 12, whilst the slope for the other three was 1 in 6.

A Pen and Ink Sketch of the Operating Machinery at the bottom of the Ilminster Inclined Plane, circa 1852. COURTESY LUTON CULTURE
The bottom of the plane, with its descent into the lower canal, can be seen on the right with the pulleys for the hauling chain, whilst in the background is the overshot waterwheel which was used to power the movement of the water-filled caissons.

The Blackhill Inclined Plane on the Monkland Canal near Glasgow

This structure is significant as it was the last incline to be built in Britain prior to the construction of the Foxton Inclined Plane. It was designed by James Leslie and provided an alternative route for full-sized but empty barges travelling up the Monkland Canal. The bulk of the laden traffic on this canal, which carried ironstone, limestone and manure, was downwards.

By the middle of the 19th century, the existing flight of four double locks was becoming heavily trafficked and was wasteful in both time and water. It was therefore decided to construct an inclined plane to convey the empty barges up the slope, whilst the laden barges continued to use the locks to descend, although the incline plane occasionally took empty barges down. The depth of water in the caissons was just 2 feet, which was sufficient draft for an empty barge and minimised the weight of each caisson. The overall weight of the water-filled caissons, with or without a barge, was between 60 and 70 tons.

The following is another extract from the proceedings of the Institution of Civil Engineers on 24th January 1854, that describes the operation of the Blackhill Incline:

'On that incline each boat, of about 60 tons burden, is taken up afloat, in a water-tight caisson, set level on a carriage, running on twenty wheels, and fitted with portcullis gates, at each end. The caisson, after being hauled up to the top of the incline, and being pressed hard against the gates of the upper reach of the canal, so as to form a water-tight joint, acts as a portable lock, out

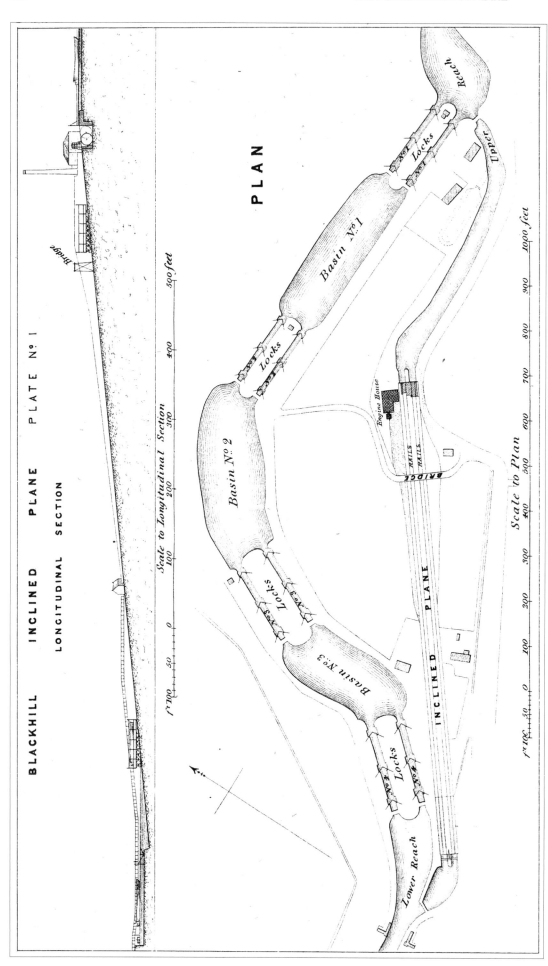

A General Plan and Sectional Side Elevation of the Blackhill Inclined Plane, on the Monkland Canal in Scotland. COURTESY THE TRUSTEES OF THE NATIONAL LIBRARY OF SCOTLAND

The following three plates of the Blackhill Inclined Plane accompanied a paper by its designer, James Leslie: 'Description of an Inclined Plane, for conveying Boats from one level to another, on the Monkland Canal, at Blackhill, near Glasgow, constructed in 1850; from Designs by JAMES LESLIE, Civil Engineer, Edinburgh.' Take note of the four original double locks that were bypassed by the inclined plane to relieve traffic congestion. The inclined plane was designed and operated primarily to convey empty barges up the incline.

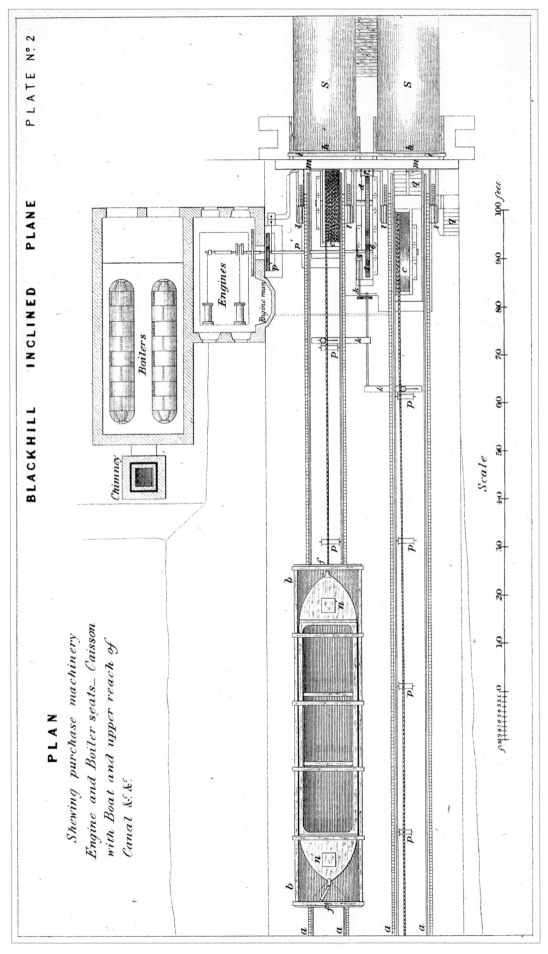

BLACKHILL INCLINED PLANE PLATE Nº 2

PLAN

Shewing purchase machinery
Engine and Boiler seats_ Caisson
with Boat and upper reach of
Canal &ᶜ &ᶜ.

Scale

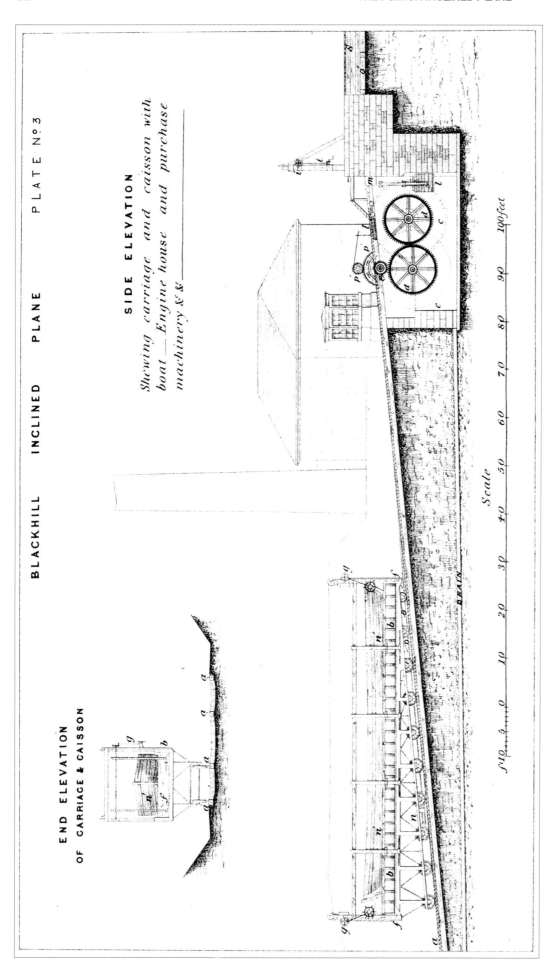

BLACKHILL   INCLINED   PLANE   PLATE · N°· 3

SIDE ELEVATION

Shewing carriage and caisson with boat — Engine house and purchase machinery &c &c

END ELEVATION

OF CARRIAGE & CAISSON

Scale

A Sectional Side Elevation of the Top of the Blackhill Inclined Plane, on the Monkland Canal in Scotland. Courtesy the Trustees of the National Library of Scotland

of which the boat is floated into the upper reach, and vice versa, in the case of vessels descending. There are two lines of rails, so that the ascending and descending carriages balance each other.'

This extract is particularly pertinent as it not only describes the working of the Blackhill Inclined Plane but could equally well be used to describe the working of the Foxton Inclined Plane, built some fifty years later. Another similarity between the inclines at Blackhill and at Foxton was that both used steam engines to provide the motive power; the Blackhill Incline used two 25 horsepower engines to drive vertical drums with steel ropes attached to the caissons, whilst at Foxton there was a single 25 horsepower engine driving a horizontal drum, again with steel ropes attached to the caissons. The Blackhill Incline needed two engines, in order to provide enough power to overcome the effect of the hydraulic upthrust on the descending caisson as it entered the water of the lower canal. Only one engine was needed at Foxton, due to a unique arrangement of the curvature of the rails at the top of the slope for the ascending caisson.

The Blackhill Incline was generally used to convey barges, 66 ft long by 13 ft wide, whilst floating in caissons mounted on rails. The caissons were 70 feet in length, 13 feet 4 inches wide and 2 feet 9 inches deep. Interestingly, the profile of the caissons was designed to best match that of the boats, with a hollow space for the keel, in order to minimise the volume of water and hence the overall weight of the caissons. The gauge of the tracks was 7 feet.

The vertical height to be overcome by the incline was 96 feet, with a gradient of 1 in 10. Consequently, the overall length of the incline was 1,040 feet. The time taken for the transfer of a boat from one level to the other by the incline was reported not to exceed 10 minutes, which included 2 minutes each for loading and unloading a boat from the caisson and hence just 6 minutes for the journey time. In comparison, the time taken for boats to pass through the eight adjacent locks was 30 to 40 minutes.

The description of the safety system on the Blackhill Incline, as included in the proceedings of the Institution of Civil Engineers on 24th January 1854, is worthy of repetition:

'For the sake of safety, there was a line of ratchets alongside each rail, and the ascending carriage [or caisson] had four palls [sic] constantly working into the teeth of the ratchets, so as, in the case of accident, to prevent the carriage from running down. The descending carriage could never have the palls constantly working, but should anything go wrong with the rope, a large draught-spring under the carriage, to which it was attached, would, by its opening out when the tension was removed, allow the palls to fall down.'

The Blackhill Incline differed from the Foxton Inclined Plane in one important aspect; at Blackhill the caissons travelled 'longitudinally', or 'line astern', up and down the plane, or as stated in the previously quoted article from *The Engineer* for 22nd January 1897:

'… in a direction corresponding with the length of the barges, and not at right angles to it, as in Mr. Thomas's arrangement.'

The caissons at Blackhill were kept horizontal by the downslope end of them being set much higher above the rails than the upslope end, hence the need for the relatively gentle gradient to provide them with more stability. On the Foxton Incline, however, the caissons travelled 'laterally', or line abreast', up and down the plane, with the result that they were significantly more stable. By such means, the Foxton Incline was able to adopt a steeper gradient of 1 in 4, resulting in a much shorter incline and, hence, significantly less use of land (see diagram below). This was one of the main aspects of the Foxton design that made it so innovative.

★ ★ ★ ★ ★

Finally, it is of interest to note the views of several prominent Victorian engineers regarding the use of inclined planes on canals, as revealed in the discussions that followed the

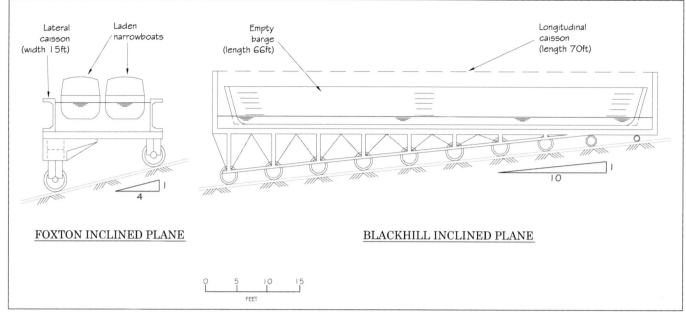

Lateral caisson (width 15ft)   Laden narrowboats   Empty barge (length 66ft)   Longitudinal caisson (length 70ft)

FOXTON INCLINED PLANE   BLACKHILL INCLINED PLANE

0   5   10   15
FEET

An illustration of the differing alignments of the caissons on the Foxton and Blackhill inclined planes. DRAWING PREPARED BY THE AUTHOR & ROSS NORVILLE
The gradient of the Foxton Inclined Plane could be relatively steep due to the lateral alignment of the caissons, whereas the gradient of the Blackhill Inclined Plane had to be shallower, to safely accommodate the longitudinal alignment of the caisson. The caissons on both of the inclined planes were capable of carrying full length narrowboats.

presentation of the paper by James Leslie in 1854, referred to at the top of the chapter:

'MR. HAWKSHAW *said, that whether the traffic was carried on by lifting water, or by lifting the boats and cargo, the result was the same: the nature of the locality must decide which plan was most advantageous. The system of lockage was, however, an easier and more economical mode; the lockage capacity could be multiplied, by pumping up again the water already used, and it precluded the necessity for the cumbrous machinery of inclines. On the Grand Junction Canal, the pumping system was beginning to be adopted.*

MR. GIBBS *admitted, that as a general rule, the system of lockage and pumping was preferable to that of inclines, which ought only to be used in exceptional cases. He thought, however, that many continuous lines of rivers in England might be made available for traffic, by means of these inclines.*

Mr. HOMERSHAM *mentioned the case of the Peak Forest Railway, in Derbyshire, where the summit level was 400 feet above the summit level of the adjoining Peak Forest Canal, and was reached by means of four inclines.*

MR. RENDEL, – *President* [of the Institution of Civil Engineers in 1854] *– remarked, that the perpendicular lifts on the Great Western Canal, described by Mr. Green, were now almost useless. The system of pumping, the cost of which was remarkably small on the Birmingham Canal, was superior to that of inclines, which should only be adopted under exceptional circumstances.'*

Given these comments, it is, perhaps, quite surprising that about forty-five years later, the Grand Junction Canal Company was embarking on a major engineering project of replacing the flights of locks at Foxton with an inclined plane and considering another to replace the locks at Watford.

Sources For This Chapter
Canal Inclines and Lifts, David tew, Alan Sutton, 1984
Canal Lifts and Inclines of the World, Hans-Joachim Uhlemann (translated & edited by Mike Clarke), Internat, 2002
'Description of an Inclined Plane, for conveying Boats from one level to another, on the Monkland Canal, at Blackhill, near Glasgow, constructed in 1850'; from 'Designs by JAMES LESLIE, Civil Engineer, Edinburgh' – a paper given by James Leslie to the Royal Scottish Society of Art on 28th April 1851
'Description of an Inclined Plane, for conveying Boats over a Summit, to and from different Levels of a Canal', a paper given by James Leslie to the Institution of Civil Engineers on 24th January 1854
Article on the Bulbourne model from *The Engineer*, 22nd January 1897
The Roads, Canal and Railways of Chard, Chard History Group, 2001
Plymley's Shropshire – General View of the Agriculture of Shropshire, first published c1812

CHAPTER 4
1894 TO 1897
THE DEVELOPMENT OF THE FOXTON INCLINED PLANE

'Since 1894, when the Grand Union Canal and the Old Union Canal were purchased by the Grand Junction Canal, the Grand Junction Company has had under consideration the idea of providing accommodation for barges at these locks [Watford and Foxton], *either by rebuilding the locks to the wide gauge, or by substituting for the inclined plane lifts, which latter plan would have the advantage of greatly economising water.'*
Extract from an article in The Engineer *of 22nd January 1897*

With the acquisition, in September 1894, of the Grand Union Canal and the Leicestershire & Northamptonshire Union Canal (jointly referred to as the Old Union Canal), which gave greater influence over the tolls being charged by the Leicester, Loughborough and Erewash canals, the Grand Junction Canal Company (GJCC) was finally able to begin making the route between the East Midlands and London more competitive. Almost immediately, the GJCC carried out a detailed survey of these new assets and then embarked on an extensive dredging campaign on the canals, under the direction of their Assistant Engineer, Gordon Thomas. The dredging works were started at Norton Junction at the southern end of the Grand Union Canal and proceeded northwards. The Grand Union and Leicestershire & Northamptonshire Union canals had clearly been poorly maintained for many years previously, presumably due to shortage of revenue, as the dredging works took about four years to complete, with a total of 319,545 tons of silt being removed.

Foxton Locks in winter, circa 1901. COURTESY THE WATERWAYS TRUST
This photograph is one of six which accompany a paper entitled The 'Thomas' Lift constructed at Foxton Leicestershire by the Grand Junction Canal Company, *written by Gordon Thomas circa 1904, the Engineer to the canal company and the lead designer of the Foxton Inclined Plane. Note the two cottages (the left hand cottage is now demolished) in the background at the top of the flight and the edge of the major earthworks for the inclined plane on the far left. The lock gates appear to be in relatively poor condition. The six photographs were commissioned from professional photographers Wakefield of Brentford.*

In this chapter, I will attempt to shed some light onto the likely development of the Foxton Inclined Plane; a process that seemingly started with a memorandum dated June 1894 and culminated in a finished design for an inclined plane that was intended to replace the flight of locks at Foxton.

It should be noted that, at this time, and for the next six years or so, Gordon Thomas was officially the Assistant Engineer to the GJCC but it is clear that he was gradually taking on more and more of the responsibilities of Engineer from his father, Hubert Thomas. This is evidenced by the fact that, six years later, in April 1900, Gordon Thomas was formally appointed as Engineer, with the appointment being back-dated to 13th June 1894. Notwithstanding this, where appropriate in this chapter, I will continue to refer to Hubert Thomas as the Engineer and to his son, Gordon Thomas, as Assistant Engineer.

★ ★ ★ ★ ★

Within a few months of the acquisition of the Grand Union and Leicestershire & Northamptonshire Union canals, and with the background of continued promptings by Fellows, Morton & Clayton for improvement of the Leicester Line, Gordon Thomas was in receipt of a hand-written memorandum dated 4th December 1894, (hitherto referred to as the 1894 Memorandum). The 1894 Memorandum was from Messrs Thomas & Taylor, a consulting engineering practice based in Victoria Street, London, and dealt with the possible construction of inclined planes to replace the narrow locks at Foxton and Watford.

Apart from the clause in the original 1810 Act of Parliament for the Grand Union Canal, it would appear that the 1894 Memorandum was the first documented reference to the possibility of inclined planes on the Grand Union Canal. Rather oddly, however, there is no reference to the 1894 Memorandum in the Minutes of the Board of the GJCC, whilst the inclined planes were surprisingly only first referred to in the Minutes almost two years later, in October 1896. Without further evidence, therefore, it is only possible to speculate as to the circumstances leading to the receipt of the 1894 Memorandum. Although possible, it seems very unlikely that it arrived on Gordon Thomas' desk without any forewarning. Most probably, it was the outcome of collusion between Gordon Thomas and Thomas & Taylor. This line of thinking is supported by the family connection that is confirmed by Edward Paget-Tomlinson in *The Illustrated History of Canal & River Navigations*:

> '*G.C. Thomas was involved with plans to widen the Leicester line and he planned the Foxton inclined plane, with his cousin B.J. Thomas of Thomas & Taylor, civil engineering consultants of Westminster.*'

Although any collusion may have been unofficial, the most likely explanation is that Gordon Thomas was acting as Engineer to the GJCC, whilst also being formally involved with Thomas & Taylor, a practice that would not have been particularly unusual at that time.

The 1894 Memorandum contained eighteen numbered paragraphs that described in some detail the workings of the proposed inclined plane. Unfortunately, the accompanying drawings seem not to have survived, so that it is difficult to be certain just how far the design had been developed at that stage and, therefore, how much additional work would have been required before it could be constructed. However, the following extracts from the Memorandum show that the proposals had obvious similarities with the structure that was eventually to be built at Foxton around six years later:

> '*1. The principle of this Lift is shewn in the General Plan, Section and Details prepared in Jan. 1886 and now completed and submitted to you.*
> *2. The essential principle of the Lift (which is to be used in lieu of a Flight of Locks) is floating of the barge or vessel into a tank and the conveying of that tank with its floating load broadside up or down a slope or inclined plane to a higher or lower pond of the Canal respectively into which*

it is floated from the tank, which is left ready for another Barge going in the opposite direction. The system does not <u>necessarily</u> include a balance lift – that is to say – duplicate tanks working up & down duplicate inclines in reverse direction. It is equally applicable to a single tank and a single incline.

3. Obviously the balance lift will do twice the work, in the same time, and, beyond this, the power required to operate the lift, although of the same intensity, would be only usable during a small portion of the rise instead of during the whole.

4. The Lift will practically prevent all loss of water by Lockage under the present system. Instead of a "Lock" (or 9,000 c.ft. of water) being lost by the passage of a barge (or boats) through the ordinary wide lock, only about 90 c.ft. or one – 100th part of a Lock, would be passed down the Canal by the passage of one barge down the Canal and another barge up.'

Further on, the Memorandum provides an estimate of cost and other significant details for the construction of the inclined plane, with a direct reference to Watford and Foxton:

'11. A preliminary and approximate estimate of the cost of such a Balance Lift, as is shewn on the Drawing, constructed under ordinary circumstances, on a suitable site, with Engine and appliances complete, but excluding land and approaches, is about £14,000.

12. The Watford Locks on the Grand Union Canal are we believe 7 in number with a total rise of 56 feet and the Foxton Locks 10 in number with a total rise of 75 feet."

The final paragraphs, intriguingly, make reference to the design of the inclined plane having been carried out some eight years earlier:

17. There is no doubt that this system of Lifts is perfectly practicable. Whether a single Lift costing little more than half the Balance Lift is advisable or not can only be determined on working out the details of the site where it is required to be constructed, & the conditions under which it would have to be worked.

It would not be an expensive or difficult matter to make a working model of the Proposed Lift to a scale of say ¼ inch to a foot and upon this model the whole arrangement and system of working could be shewn with model barges and proportionate tackle.

18. All the principal details of the scheme are laid down in the foregoing or in the Drawings. The matter has received our closest & most careful consideration and although the details were worked on in 1886 for another Canal in the Manchester District (but not used) they are all to all intents and purposes equally applicable to the Grand Union Canal, when that Canal is improved, to be of the same working capacity as the Grand Junction Canal and to carry the same vessels.'

(The full text of the 1894 Memorandum is contained in Appendix A of *Foxton: Locks and Barge Lift* by Peter Gardner & Frank Foden)

It is likely that the other canal referred to in the last paragraph of the Memorandum was the Bridgewater Canal, at Worsley. Also, it is interesting to note the phrase in the same paragraph referring to the Grand Union Canal – '*when that canal is improved.*' This clearly reveals that the author of the Memorandum knew about the GJCC's intention to address the traffic congestion issues caused by the narrow staircases of locks at Watford and Foxton, and further reinforces the conjecture of familial collusion.

Rather intriguingly, Gardner & Foden's book reveals that there is a hand-written note on the front cover of the original Memorandum that says '*nothing will be done until an Act is obtained for the acquisition of the Leicester Canals.*' It does not seem to be unreasonable to assume that this note was written by Gordon Thomas and probably indicates the attitude of the Board of the GJCC at that time. In practice, as will be dealt with later on in this chapter, the GJCC did eventually open negotiations for the purchase of the so-called Leicester Canals

– presumably the Leicester Navigation and the Loughborough Navigation. For various reasons, however, an Act of Parliament was never obtained; a fact that could go some way to explain why it took three years, from the receipt of the 1894 Memorandum, for the decision to be made by the GJCC to proceed with the construction of an inclined plane at Foxton.

★ ★ ★ ★ ★

As explained in the Memorandum, the proposed inclined plane would have many advantages over the existing flight of locks, including passage for barges, as opposed to just narrowboats. However, according to Gordon Thomas, from his two papers on the Thomas Lift dated 1902 and 1906, the most significant benefit was:

> '... THE GREAT SAVING OF WATER, APPROXIMATING TO 90 PER CENT OF THE QUANTITY USED BY THE LOCKAGE SYSTEM, AND THE SAVING OF TIME.'

From this, it is clear that the loss of water from the long summit section of the old Grand Union Canal was of major concern to the GJCC.

★ ★ ★ ★ ★

The three year period covered by this chapter, from September 1894 to November 1897, was a busy time in the development of the Foxton Inclined Plane. It seems reasonable to assume that, relatively early on, Thomas & Taylor were appointed by the GJCC, under the supervision of Gordon Thomas, to develop the design of the inclined plane and to make it more directly applicable to the conditions at Foxton and Watford.

By all accounts, during this period Fellows, Morton & Clayton continued to apply pressure on the GJCC to carry out improvements to the Grand Union Canal. According to the Minutes of the Board of the Company, the carriers were in contact on a number of occasions expressing their disappointment with the delays in developing major improvement works at both Foxton and Watford Locks. In particular, the carriers' letter of February 1896 asked the canal company:

> 'to consider the desirability of enlarging the locks on the Leicester Section at Watford and Foxton to enable them to work wide boats which they anticipated would lessen the cost of haulage and enable them to increase the traffic from the Leicester and Nottingham Districts to London.'

On 22nd April 1896, just over a year after the 1894 Memorandum, an application for patenting of the design for the inclined plane was made jointly by:

> 'We, BARNABAS JAMES THOMAS and JOSEPH JEX TAYLOR both of 1, Victoria Street, Westminster, Civil Engineers, and GORDON CALE THOMAS of Marsworth, in the County of Bucks, Civil Engineer.'

The application makes no mention of either Thomas & Taylor or the GJCC, presumably details that were not required by the patenting process. It is interesting to note that, today, Gordon Thomas is generally identified as being the designer of the Foxton Inclined Plane but perhaps, given the wording of the patent, it should also be attributed to Barnabas Thomas and Joseph Taylor. At the very least, however, the inclusion of Gordon Thomas in the patent application adds weight to the suggestion of collusion between him and Thomas & Taylor. The patent application goes on to say:

> 'This invention relates to lifts for transferring barges and other vessels from one level to another on canals and other waterways in lieu of an ordinary lock or flight of locks, the object of

the invention being to obviate the loss of water from the higher to the lower level by lockage inseparable from the ordinary system and to provide the passage of vessels simultaneously in both directions and at a single lift and between levels of widely different altitude whereby the loss of time incidental to the passage through a flight of locks is in great measure avoided.'

What seems to have made the design worthy of patenting, and distinguished it from earlier inclined planes, was the previously untried arrangement of raising and lowering boats within caissons that were aligned laterally (or '*broadside*' as described in the 1894 Memorandum) across the plane. Earlier inclines had conveyed boats in a longitudinal alignment on the slope. One particularly interesting issue that was addressed by the patent was the adopton of a curvature at the top of the plane, in order to offset the effects on the operation of the inclined plane of the descending caisson entering the water in the lower canal basin:

'The disturbance of the balance which would occur by the immersion of the lift in the water at the foot of the inclined way may be automatically compensated by varying the effective diameters of the winding drums of the balance ropes, or by bringing auxiliary power into operation at the required moment.'

Other aspects of the design described in the patent application had obvious parallels with previous inclined planes, especially the Blackhill Incline on the Monkton Canal in Scotland and the inclines on the Chard Canal in Somerset. The patent application was accepted on 3rd April 1897.

★ ★ ★ ★ ★

In parallel with these technical developments, in March 1896, Hubert Thomas, acting as Clerk to the GJCC, was authorised to begin negotiations with the Leicester Navigation, Loughborough Navigation and Erewash Canal companies, initially to seek agreement on more advantageous through-toll arrangements but, subsequently, for the outright purchase of the three waterways. Not surprisingly, the GJCC clearly wanted to build on the recent acquisitions of the Leicestershire & Northamptonshire and Grand Union canals in order to gain greater influence over the whole of the inland route between London and the East Midlands.

By December 1896, Hubert Thomas' negotiations had progressed to the stage that initial sale prices of £38,075, £25,000 and £20,000 for the Leicester, Loughborough and Erewash canals respectively, had been agreed. The prices for the latter two canals, however, allowed for certain properties being retained by the current owners. These valuations were significantly higher than those paid by the GJCC for the Leicestershire & Northamptonshire and the Grand Union, and presumably reflected the greater profitability of these three canals. However, the GJCC was clearly unhappy about the proposal to exclude various properties from the sale. Hubert Thomas was consequently instructed to return to the negotiating table with the underlying threat that the possible canal improvements at Foxton and Watford might be postponed until such time as satisfactory agreements had been reached. Within a month, Hubert Thomas had acquired revised options on the purchase of the Loughborough Navigation for £26,500, albeit with one wharf in Loughborough still being excluded from the sale, and the Erewash Canal for £21,000 with all properties now included.

Before proceeding with the canal purchases, the GJCC opted to take legal advice on the prospects of getting the necessary Bill through Parliament. Perhaps it was at this stage that the purchase of the canals by the GJCC began to founder, possibly on the basis that there were likely to be too many objections to the Bill. It is of interest that the GJCC had previously investigated some form of amalgamation with the Warwick & Birmingham and Warwick & Napton canals but, due to objections, this too had foundered at the Parliamentary stage in June 1895.

So, the matter of purchasing the Leicester Navigation, the Loughborough Navigation and the Erewash Canal was held in abeyance, with only sporadic references to the subject in the Minute Book of the GJCC thereafter. For example, in November 1900, it is recorded that:

> 'the Sub-committee were of the opinion that an amalgamation of the three Companies Leicester, Loughborough and Erewash, inter se, was desirable and that the Grand Junction Company should endeavour to obtain a controlling interest therein.'

The Board concluded that its Chairman and Hubert Thomas should, therefore, keep in touch with the representatives of the three canals. Just over a year later, in January 1902, the Leicester, Loughborough and the Erewash canals were offered to the GJCC for the combined sum of £50,000, a significant reduction compared to the earlier valuations. Again, any decision to proceed was initially deferred but about a month later, the offer was declined by the GJCC.

A letter from the GJCC to Fellows, Morton & Clayton neatly summarises the failed attempt to gain direct control of the whole route between London and the East Midlands:

> 'The Company have expended, as pointed out to your Directors by my Chairman, a large sum of money in improving and reinstating the Old and Grand Union Canals, with the view of developing traffic, which has not had the effect anticipated and the Capital expenditure from this point of view is at present unremunerative, and the Committee feel they are not justified in advising their Proprietors to acquire the remaining Canals necessary to complete the through route to Langley Mill, on such terms.
>
> I may however say they are disappointed, after all their labours, to have to abandon a much cherished scheme of canal amalgamation and the hope of developing the Coal traffic from the Nottingham District to parts of their Canal to London, but taking into consideration the cost of reinstating the Canals to meet the requirements of traders, together with the high purchase price, there would be little chance of my Company receiving an adequate return on such outlay.'

★ ★ ★ ★ ★

The GJCC, presumably assisted by Thomas & Taylor, continued with investigations into the viability of an inclined plane to replace the Foxton Locks. It seems, however, that there was some doubt about the technical viability of the design of the proposed inclined plane, which necessitated the construction of two working models. The first was a 1:48 scale model (¼ inch to the foot), similar to that which was originally proposed in the 1894 Memorandum by Thomas & Taylor. It seems likely that it was either built by the consultants, or that they assisted Gordon Thomas in having it built. This small model was inspected by the Chairman of the Board in May 1896, at the company's depot at Bulbourne, near Tring in Hertfordshire. It would appear, however, that doubts still existed about aspects of the inclined plane, for the GJCC then instructed Gordon Thomas to arrange for the construction of a larger model.

Within five months, the larger model had been built at the Bulbourne depot. There must have been considerable interest in the proposed inclined plane in the engineering profession, indicated by an article in *The Engineer* for 22nd January 1897, relating to the trials associated with the second model. The purpose of it was described thus:

> 'With a view to determining the suitability of an inclined plane lift for this purpose [presumably to replace the narrow locks at Watford and Foxton] a large size model has been constructed and worked by Mr. Thomas, the engineer of the Grand Junction Canal Company, at the company's works Bulbourne near Tring.'

The model was, in some aspects, full size, presumably to increase the relevance of the trials. The caissons were large enough to accommodate 13 foot wide barges but were significantly shorter than the 80 foot length that was eventually adopted at Foxton.

The Bulbourne Model as photographed for The Engineer of 22nd January 1897. *Courtesy the Foxton Inclined Plane Trust*
The photograph shows a demonstration of the working model at the GJCC's depot at Bulbourne, near Tring, Hertfordshire, on 13th November 1896. The construction of the model and the trials were organised by Gordon Thomas, Engineer to the GJCC and lead designer of the Foxton Inclined Plane. Standing on the bank between the two caissons are directors of the GJCC along with invited guests, including representatives of the carriers Fellows, Morton & Clayton and the engineering company Hunter & English. The trials resulted in some important improvements to the design of the Foxton Inclined Plane. Interestingly, a typed caption to the original photograph refers to the model as the 'proposed slide in lieu of locks'.

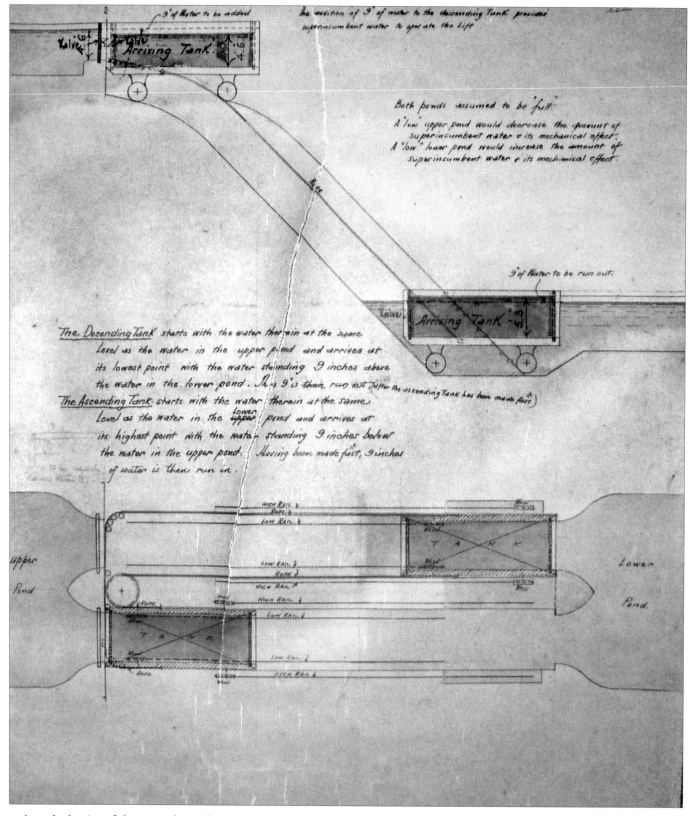

The addition of 9" of water to the descending Tank provides
superincumbent water to operate the lift

Both ponds assumed to be 'full'.

A 'low' upper pond would decrease the amount of
superincumbent water & its mechanical effect.
A 'low' lower pond would increase the amount of
superincumbent water & its mechanical effect.

9" of Water to be added

9" of Water to be run out.

Arriving Tank

Arriving Tank

The Descending Tank starts with the water therein at the same
Level as the water in the upper pond and arrives at
its lowest point with the water standing 9 inches above
the water in the lower pond. This 9" is then run out (after the ascending Tank has been made fast)

The Ascending Tank starts with the water therein at the same
Level as the water in the lower pond and arrives at
its highest point with the water standing 9 inches below
the water in the upper pond. Having been made fast, 9 inches
of water is then run in.

An early drawing of the proposed curved arrangement at the top of the inclined plane, possibly based on the Bulbourne Model, circa 1896.
COURTESY THE WATERWAYS TRUST

The curvature was designed to offset the effect of the partial immersion of the descending caisson into the lower canal basin. Note that the movement of the caissons on this sketch is achieved by having 9 inches greater depth of water in the upper caisson than the lower caisson. This method is similar to that adopted in earlier inclined planes and the hydraulically operated version of the Anderton Boat Lift. The motive power on the Foxton Inclined Plane was eventually provided by a steam engine.

The model had two identical caissons, or water-filled tanks, each with a set of wheels at each end, to allow the caissons to run on the rails in a broadside manner up and down a relatively short slope of 1 in 4 gradient. The caissons on the model, unlike those on the inclined plane itself, were principally constructed from timber and were connected to each other by a single wire rope, the ends of which were attached to the uphill facing side of both of them. The cable passed round guide pulleys at the top of the slope. By this means, with both the caissons filled with water they counterbalanced each other, with the result that the effort to raise and lower them was significantly less than would be the case if only one caisson was involved. The caissons were raised and lowered in the trial by means of a portable steam engine.

According to the article in *The Engineer*:

'On 13th November last [1896] *a large party of the leading canal managers and engineers visited Bulbourne, and inspected the working of the model.'*

The Minutes of the Board of the GJCC, for 11th November, record that the firm of Sir W.G. Armstrong & Co. Ltd was originally invited by the Board to make an inspection in order to advise upon its suitability and, subsequently, to provide an estimate for the cost of constructing the machinery, presumably full size, associated with the inclined plane. However, this company subsequently declined the invitation by saying that:

'… *it was out of their province to advise on the Model Lift and being full of work they were unable to tender for the construction.'*

It seems likely that the large party of leading canal managers and engineers that inspected the model on 13th November 1896 included, at the invitation of Gordon Thomas, representatives from Messrs Hunter & English and also Fellows, Morton & Clayton. By all accounts, the trials were successful and Hunter & English came back with a ringing endorsement of the model:

'*It appeared to be admirably adapted for its purpose and will work satisfactorily with a small expenditure of power.'*

Fellows, Morton & Clayton were similarly impressed because, soon after, they wrote to the GJCC advising of their satisfaction with the model and the efforts being made to address the obvious bottlenecks at Foxton and Watford locks on the Grand Union Canal.

Subsequently, in March 1897, it would appear that Hunter & English were asked to prepare an estimate of costs for the provision of the mechanical components of a proposed inclined plane at Watford. They were eventually paid £105 for their work and Gordon Thomas was instructed to provide comparative estimates of operating costs for the inclined plane and the existing locks.

★ ★ ★ ★ ★

Valuable lessons were learnt from the Bulbourne trials, with the design of the inclined plane being modified in key areas. This particularly applied to changes needed to address the adverse effect on the balanced movement of the caissons, when the descending caisson makes contact with the water in the lower canal basin. Rather than modifying the winding drum or bringing in auxiliary power as envisaged earlier, a curve was introduced to the rails at the top of the slope, so that, instead of continuing at the gradient of 1 in 4, they gradually rounded off to a shallower slope. The reducing gradient at the top of the slope counteracted the hydraulic uplift force, or buoyancy effect, as the descending caisson entered the water in the lower canal basin. The curvature of the rails on its own, however, would have led to the caissons tilting over as they approached the top of the plane but this was remedied by

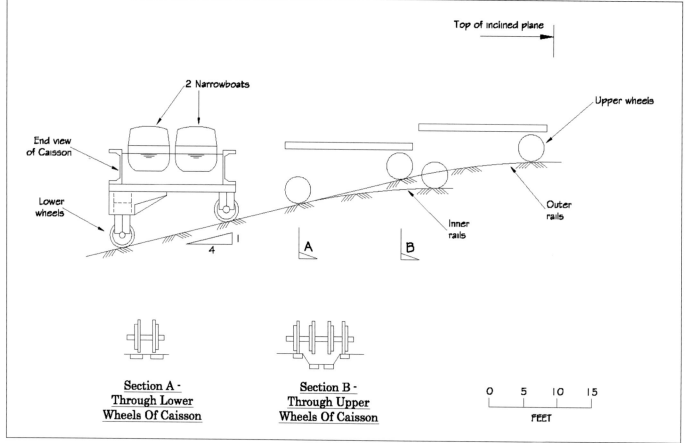

Section A -
Through Lower
Wheels Of Caisson

Section B -
Through Upper
Wheels Of Caisson

0   5   10   15
FEET

Diagram of the top of the Foxton Inclined Plane. Drawing Prepared by the Author & Ross Norville; Based on a Diagram in Foxton: Locks and Barge Lift

The diagram shows the curved section of rails that was introduced into the design to compensate for the effect of the descending caisson entering the water in the lower canal arm. It also shows the additional outer rails that were added in order to keep the caisson upright as it moves over the curved section to and from the remainder of the plane.

the introduction of a second set of outer rails and wheels on the caissons. This was a very neat and relatively simple solution to a complex problem. It is possible that the design of the curved and double-tracked rails at Foxton owed something to the earlier arrangement at the top of the Chard Common Inclined Plane on the Chard Canal in Somerset.

On 14th November 1896, the day after the Bulbourne trials, a second, smaller patent was applied for by Barnabas James Thomas, Joseph Jex Taylor and Gordon Thomas. This was needed in order to secure the revised detail regarding the curvature of the rails at the top of the slope, and the inclusion of a second set of wheels and rails on the uphill side of the caissons, so that they would remain vertical as they passed over this curved section. This patent was accepted on 13th November 1897.

★ ★ ★ ★ ★

Fellows, Morton & Clayton wrote again to the GJCC, on 8th July 1897, stating that their commercial interests were being jeopardised by the delay in progressing with the improvement works, which prevented the use of barges along the full route between the East Midlands and London. Whether this latest letter from the carriers was the final catalyst, or whether the arrival of the letter just happened to be coincidental, the GJCC made the decision, a week later, to back the recommendations of Gordon Thomas. The Minutes of the Board of the GJCC on 14th July 1897 record the decision that:

> 'Land to be purchased and plans and estimates prepared for Mechanical Boat Lift at Watford and Foxton Locks and tenders obtained for the work and Fellows Morton & Clayton be requested to state the amount of capital they will expend on suitable craft for use on this section of the Canal.'

It is of interest to note that, at this stage, the GJCC had every intention to proceed with the construction of inclined planes at both Foxton and Watford.

Soon after, Fellows, Morton & Clayton wrote to the GJCC to advise that, on the basis of the Company improving the Grand Union Canal to pass 50-ton barges, they would be prepared to work additional narrowboats on it while the improvement works were ongoing.

★ ★ ★ ★ ★

During the course of this correspondence, Gordon Thomas had obtained competitive tenders from three firms for the machinery and steelwork. He then prepared a hand-written report to the Board, dated 12th October 1897, as follows:

'Gentlemen -

In accordance with your instructions of the 11th August, plans have been prepared and are herewith submitted for your consideration of a Lift or Slide to take the place of the 10 Locks that now serve as the means for passing the traffic at Foxton Locks

The total Lift or rise from the Lower to the Upper Pond is 75 feet 2 inches.

Three firms of Mechanical Engineers have been asked to tender for the machinery and steelwork under conditions embodied in a Specification of Terms a copy of which is hereto appended.

The Specifications and tenders of the three firms viz:-

Messrs. Hunter & English of Bow   *£12,930*
Messrs. Glover & Sons of Warwick   *£9,942*
Messrs. J. & H. Gwynne of Hammersmith   *£14,130*

Allow for expenses   *£500*
            £14,630

Are hereto attached

There is no individual Specification which appears to embrace the whole of the mechanical conditions to be dealt with: but there are many good points contained in the Specifications of Messrs. Glover & Messrs. Gwynne: and it would appear that a combination of certain parts of these two schemes would produce a highly satisfactory machine.

For instance the Hauling Drums proposed by Messrs Glover are without doubt the best system and these can be applied to the original idea which has been adopted by Messrs Gwynne viz:- 1 Free Balance Rope and two Hauling Ropes to each tank. Then Messrs Gwynne's proposal for equalising the strain on each individual rope by means of connected Hydraulic Rams is most satisfactory as also is their suggestion for actuating the lift up gates by means of Hydraulic Pressure utilizing the Engine for pumping up the Accumulator.

The three firms appear to be consonant with respect to the small Steam Power required to actuate the Lift viz: about 25 H.P. noml. Likewise they unanimously advocate the adoption of the tail rope to insure uniformity of motion. This does not appear to be altogether necessary having regard to the grade of the inclines, but possibly the Condition of the Bond has induced them to add this so as to prevent the semblance of a hang to the descending tank.

Hereto is appended an Estimate of the Cost of the Works suggested to be constructed Departmently by the Canal Company the total of which may roundly be put at £12,000.

A general Plan showing the proposed position of the Lift and contingent works accompanies this Report together with the Drawings which have been submitted by the three firms of Mechanical Engineers who have tendered for the Machinery and Steel Work.

I am, Gentlemen

Your obedient servant.

Signed. Gordon Thomas

An advertisement for John & Henry Gwynne, circa 1900. COURTESY THE FOXTON INCLINED PLANE TRUST *J. & H. Gwynne supplied and fabricated the steelwork for the Foxton Inclined Plane.*

As can be seen, Gordon Thomas favoured Glover's proposal for the system of hauling drums and Gwynne's proposals for two hauling ropes for each caisson, the use of hydraulic rams between the hauling ropes and the caissons to reduce the strain on the ropes, and the use of the rams or 'jiggers' connected to the hydraulic accumulator, to operate the guillotine gates on the ends of the caissons and those on the ends of the aqueducts from the upper canal arm. The final arrangement as installed by J.&H. Gwynne seemingly incorporated all of these innovations.

On 3rd November 1897, the GJCC, no doubt on the recommendation of Gordon Thomas, accepted the most expensive of the three tenders, that submitted by J.&H. Gwynne, on the basis that:

> *'it included hydraulic machinery for operating the whole of the gates and connections with the tanks and conduits instead of hand power provided for by the other tenders.'*

The extracts above strongly suggest that the three firms had been asked to submit tenders against a set of general or conceptual designs that lacked many of the finished details needed for fabrication and installation. The companies were either required to put forward their own proposals for the more complex issues of the structural and mechanical aspects of the inclined plane or, at least, provide alternative suggestions to aspects of the original design.

★ ★ ★ ★ ★

And so, after all the activity over the preceding four years, everything was at last in place to allow the construction of the first of the inclined planes, that at Foxton, to be commenced. The estimated cost of the combined works, civil, structural and mechanical, amounted to £26,630, which is effectively a doubling of the £14,000 estimate that was given by Thomas & Taylor in their 1894 Memorandum.

There remains, however, the question as to what extent Gordon Thomas can be credited with the design of the Foxton Inclined Plane. There seems little doubt that he had been involved with Thomas & Taylor at the very outset of the concept of it in around 1886 and that he was the driving force behind the subsequent trials at Bulbourne depot and the ensuing development of the design. Somewhat confusingly, however, J.&H. Gwynne refer to Gordon and his cousin Barnabas Thomas in a publicity brochure as the inventors of the inclined plane, and to themselves as the designers and manufacturers of the tanks and machinery. My interpretation of the situation is that Gordon Thomas, Barnabas Thomas and Joseph Taylor can best be described as the designers of the Foxton Inclined Plane, with Gordon accredited as lead designer, whilst J.&H. Gwynne carried out the design and detailing of the steelwork elements to general arrangement drawings prepared by the designers.

Sources For This Chapter

The minutes of the Board and various committees of the Grand Junction Canal Company held at the National Archive, Kew

The Canals of the East Midlands, Charles Hadfield, David & Charles, 1966

The Illustrated History of Canal and River Navigations, Edward Paget-Tomlinson, Sheffield Academic Press, 1993

Foxton: Locks and Barge Lift, Peter Gardner & Frank Foden, Leicestershire County Planning Dept in association with the Leicestershire branch of the Council for the Protection of Rural England, 2nd ed. 1979

Foxton Locks and Inclined Plane – A Detailed History, compiled by members of the Foxton Inclined Plane Trust and published by Department of Planning & Transportation, Leicestershire County Council, c1986

Article on the Bulbourne model from *The Engineer*, 22nd January 1897

The archives of the Foxton Inclined Plane Trust at Foxton

CHAPTER 5
1897 TO 1898
THE DESIGN OF THE FOXTON INCLINED PLANE

'THE 'THOMAS' LIFT, which is of very simple design, is an apparatus constructed for the purpose of transferring barges and other vessels from one level to another on canals and other waterways, in lieu of an ordinary lock or flight of locks, its object being to minimise the loss of water from the higher to the lower level, which is inseparable from the ordinary system of lockage, and to provide for the passage of vessels simultaneously in both directions at a single operation between levels of widely different altitude, whereby the loss of time incidental to the passage through a flight of locks is in a great measure reduced.'

From a paper entitled Surmounting of Great Ascents, the 'Thomas' Canal Barge Lift, *written by Gordon Cale Thomas for the 9th International Navigation Congress at Dusseldorf in Germany in 1902*

This description of the design and operation of the Foxton Inclined Plane was written by its lead designer and protagonist, Gordon Thomas, the Engineer to the Grand Junction Canal Company (GJCC). The extract also appears word for word in a paper entitled 'The 'Thomas' Lift constructed at Foxton, Leicestershire by the Grand Junction Canal Company', which was also written by Gordon Thomas approximately four years later. These two papers and the plans contained therein, will be

The upper section of the Foxton Inclined Plane, circa 1901. COURTESY THE WATERWAYS TRUST
Note the curved section in the foreground, a unique aspect of the Foxton Inclined Plane, that offset the uplift effect as the descending caisson entered the water in the lower canal basin and hence allowed the continued movement of the caissons without the need for extra power input from the steam engine. The winding house and one of the control cabins are on the right, whilst a narrowboat is waiting in the right hand aqueduct. One of the caissons has just started its descent down the incline from the left hand aqueduct, also with a narrowboat. Two of the large horizontally-mounted cast iron pulleys with the hauling ropes for the caissons are clearly visible in the right foreground.

"PhotoWakefield.Brehtford."

my primary source of information for this chapter. Unfortunately, both papers are relatively brief and, hence, somewhat lacking in detail. I have, therefore, also made extensive use of two other publications; namely *Foxton Locks and Inclined Plane – A Detailed History* compiled by members of the Foxton Inclined Plane Trust, and *Foxton: Locks and Barge Lift* by Peter Gardner & Frank Foden.

In this chapter, I will describe the overall layout of the Foxton Inclined Plane, together with each of its main components. For reasons of clarity, I have attempted to keep the descriptions simple and have deliberately avoided too much detail. The reader may need to make regular reference to the various diagrams provided.

★ ★ ★ ★ ★

In his 1902 paper entitled 'Surmounting of Great Ascents, the 'Thomas' Canal Barge Lift', Gordon Thomas gave a very simple explanation of the working of the Foxton Inclined Plane:

> *'The essential principle of this Lift is that of two weights suspended over pulleys, viz: two weights acting in opposite directions upon planes of equal declivity whereby the sum of the gravity of one weight is consonant with the gravity of the other weight.*
> *Hence to produce movement in both of the weights all that is necessary is to provide power sufficient to overcome the friction of the working parts of both weights.'*

So to expand on this, the weights referred to by Gordon Thomas are the two identical caissons, or tanks, that were connected together by wire ropes. The caissons sat laterally across the plane, on wheels that ran on steel rails, similar to those used on the railways, aligned longitudinally down the full length of the plane. Due to the weights of the water-filled caissons, the rails were heavier section than those used on standard railways. The caissons contained water at a constant depth, sufficient to allow canal boats to float, with any excess water being displaced. By this means, both caissons, with or without canal boats, always weighed the same. As a consequence, the caissons balanced each other and were consequently in static equilibrium in any position on the inclined plane.

The interconnecting wire ropes passed over a system of pulley wheels to the top of the plane, where they were separately attached to a large drum. A steam engine provided the power necessary to turn the drum to overcome the static friction in the whole system, thereby moving the caissons up and down the plane. Hence, the essential simplicity of the design expressed by Gordon Thomas; but now for the more complex details, starting with the various fixtures and fittings of the inclined plane.

★ ★ ★ ★ ★

The civil or fixed elements of the Foxton Inclined Plane can best be considered in three main parts: the inclined plane itself, the lower canal basin and the upper canal arm. These three are described separately below:

Inclined Plane – Put simply, this is a sloping surface with a gradient of 1 in 4 over the greater part of its length. It is made up of two distinct parts, each wide enough to accommodate one of the 80-foot long caissons. When looked at from above, the two parts of the plane are staggered horizontally by approximately 28 feet to facilitate loading and unloading of the caissons, whether at the top or at the bottom of the plane. Gordon Thomas uses the word 'echeloned' to describe this horizontal stagger. The plane was built into the natural escarpment that forms the northern edge of the Northampton Uplands. The selected gradient and alignment of the plane necessitated extensive excavation at the bottom of the escarpment and extensive filling at the top.

The overall height to be overcome by the plane, from the Leicestershire & Northamptonshire Union Canal up to the summit section of the Grand Union Canal, was 75 feet and 2 inches.

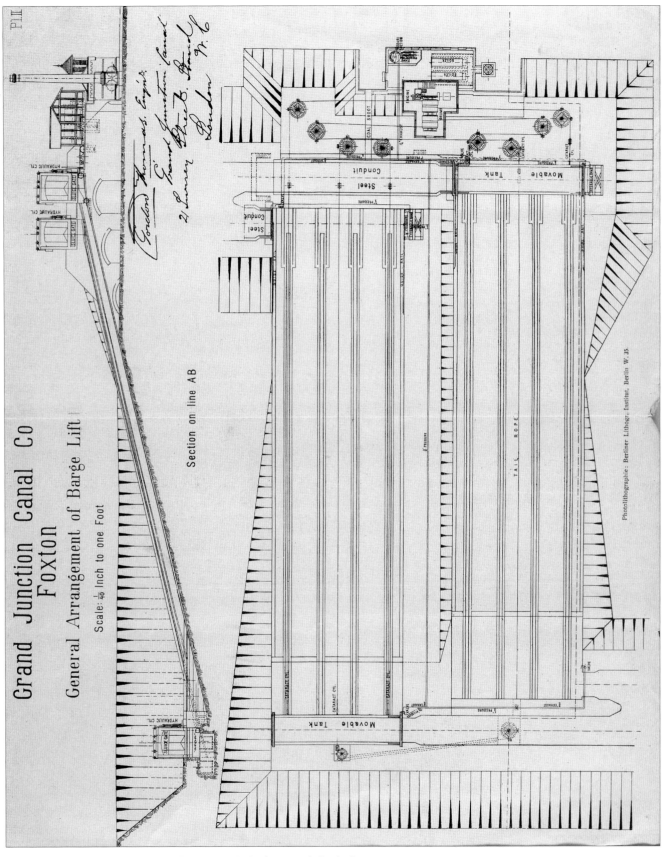

PLII

Grand Junction Canal Co
Foxton
General Arrangement of Barge Lift

Scale: 1/40 Inch to one Foot

Section on line AB

A general arrangement drawing of the Foxton Inclined Plane with a full sectional elevation and plan, as taken from the report by Gordon Thomas entitled 'Surmounting Great Ascents – The 'Thomas' Canal barge lift', 1902. COURTESY THE WATERWAYS TRUST

The plan is signed by Gordon Thomas in the top right hand corner, in his role as Engineer to the GJCC.

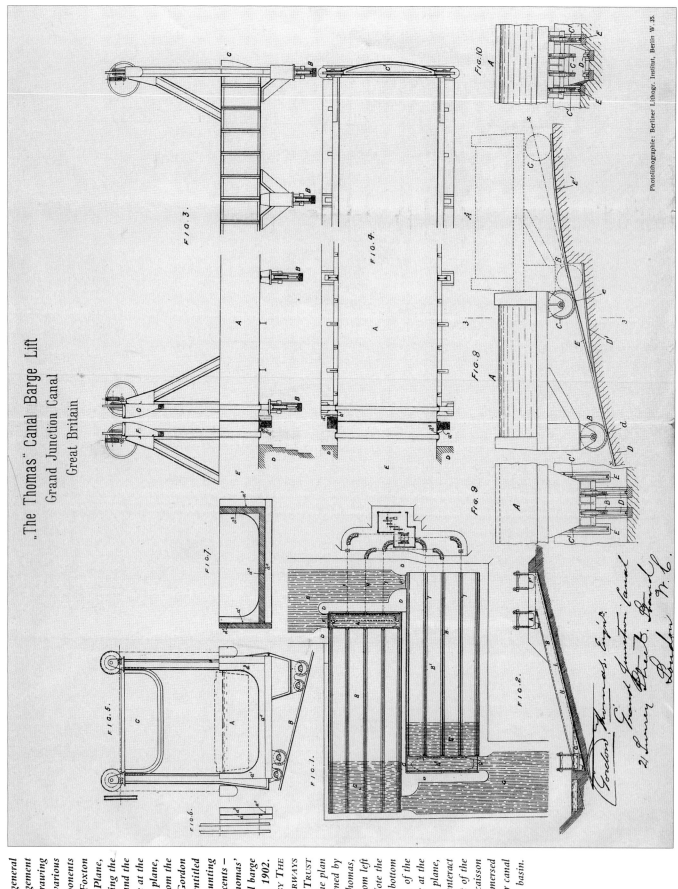

"The Thomas" Canal Barge Lift
Grand Junction Canal
Great Britain

A general arrangement drawing of various components of the Foxton Inclined Plane, including the caissons and the curvature at the top of the plane, as taken from the report by Gordon Thomas entitled 'Surmounting Great Ascents – The 'Thomas' Canal barge lift', 1902.
COURTESY THE WATERWAYS TRUST

Again the plan is signed by Gordon Thomas, in the bottom left corner. Note the detail, bottom right, of the curvature at the top of the plane, to counteract the effect of the descending caisson when it immersed in the lower canal basin.

At the lower end, the plane descended below the normal retained water level in the lower canal basin, so as to permit boats to float in and out of the caissons. The overall length of the plane measured down the slope was over 300 feet.

In order to counteract the upthrust caused by the gradual submersion of the descending caisson in the Lower Canal Basin, the upper end of the plane was curved so that the gradient diminished. This meant that the upthrust on the descending caisson was balanced by the reduced gravitational pull, down the slope, of the upper caisson as it passed over the curved section of the plane. This curved arrangement, which was introduced to the design following the Bulbourne model trials, allowed the caissons to continue moving up and down the plane without the need for an increased power input.

There were eight pairs of steel rails set longitudinally down the full length of the plane, four for each of the caissons, and eight further pairs of rails just on the upper curved section of the plane, which ingeniously ensured that the caissons remained upright despite the change in gradient of that part of the plane. It is possible that the design of this was a modification of a similar feature at the top of the plane for the Chard Common Incline on the Chard Canal in Somerset, which was built in 1841. The Chard Common arrangement was designed to keep tub-boats on cradles horizontal, whether on the main part of the plane or on the reverse slope at the top of the incline to lower the tub-boats into the upper canal.

The rails were fastened down by coach screws into 14 foot long timber sleepers laid in the same alignment as the rails, which in turn were set into the below-ground concrete foundations. Between the rails, the plane was covered with a layer of granite chippings.

Lower Canal Basin – This was excavated at the bottom of the plane, with a connection to the old Leicestershire & Northamptonshire Union Canal (now the Market Harborough Arm), a short distance to the east of the bottom of the locks. The basin was approximately 400 feet long and 40 feet wide, allowing two barges (or wide boats) to pass without difficulty.

Upper Canal Arm – This was built to take boats from the summit section of the canal to the top of the inclined plane. It was approximately ¼ mile in length and, like the lower canal basin, about 40 feet wide. The construction of the upper canal arm required extensive earthworks, both excavation and filling, particularly as it approached the top of the inclined plane.

★ ★ ★ ★ ★

The various structural and mechanical components of the inclined plane, whether static or mobile, were simply described by Gordon Thomas in his 1902 paper entitled 'Surmounting of Great Ascents, the 'Thomas' Canal Barge Lift', as follows:

> 'The plant consists of two fixed conduits [aqueducts] and two moveable docks [caissons], together with the necessary hydraulic gates and rams, steam engine and boilers, hydraulic pumps, accumulator, steel wire ropes, hauling drums, guide and deflecting pulleys, &c.'

Before describing each of these components, however, it might be helpful to identify the various buildings associated with the inclined plane:

Boiler House and Winding House – These were located together centrally at the top the plane.

The boiler house was set below the top of the inclined plane. It was a brick built structure, with three arched windows in the side overlooking the locks, with two more in the end wall facing up the locks, and a round window and entrance door in the end wall facing down the locks. The boiler house had a flat roof and ornate castellations built into the brickwork along the top of the walls' edge.

The winding house was at a higher level than the boiler house. It was of planked timber construction, with a sloping slate roof and windows on all four sides that provided good

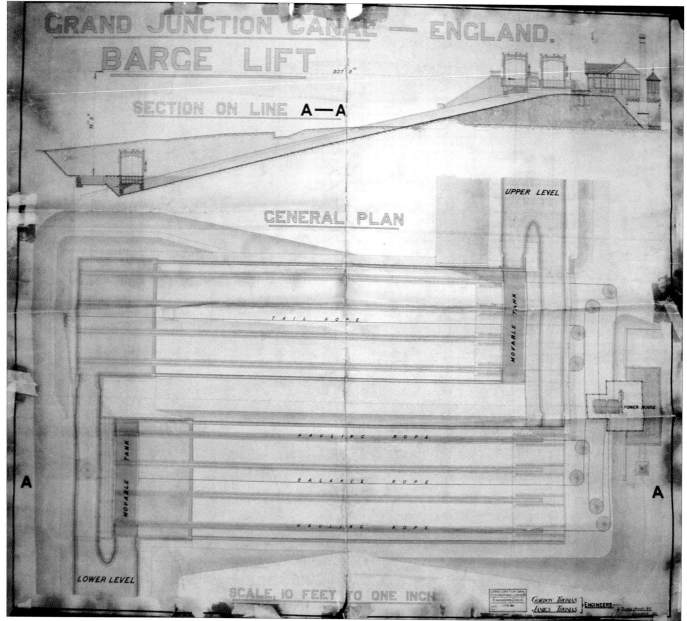

An original GJCC plan of the proposed inclined plane at Foxton, circa 1898. COURTESY THE WATERWAYS TRUST A sectional elevation of the inclined plane is at the top with the plan given below. It is interesting to note that, in the bottom right corner, the Engineers are named as Gordon Thomas and James Thomas. The latter's name does not appear in other records, so perhaps in reality it was Barnabas James Thomas, cousin to Gordon, co-designer of the inclined plane. He was appointed by the GJCC in 1898, as its Resident Engineer for the construction works on site.

views of the inclined plane, the locks and the Leicestershire countryside. It had the external appearance of a railway signal box.

Today, the winding house no longer exists, whilst the reconstructed boiler house accommodates the Museum of the Foxton Inclined Plane Trust.

Accumulator House – This was an ornate tower that was located on top of the boiler house and adjacent to the winding house. It accommodated the upper section of the accumulator, which was based in the boiler house below. Similar to the winding house, it was of timber construction with sloping slate roof. The accumulator house no longer exists.

Control Cabins – There were four, relatively small, timber control cabins on site, one for each caisson at the top and bottom of the inclined plane. The lower cabins contained the controls for operating the guillotine gates on the caissons in the lower canal basin, whilst the upper cabins contained the controls for the gates on the caissons and the aqueducts, together with the controls for jacking the caissons laterally in order to achieve a watertight seal with the aqueducts.

★ ★ ★ ★ ★

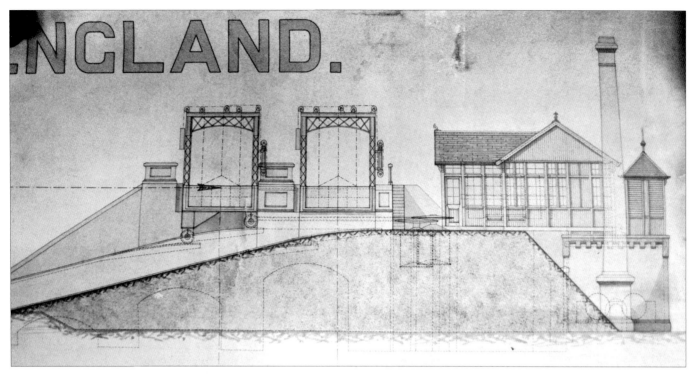

The main structural and mechanical components are now described, in turn:

Aqueducts – These comprised two steel, water-filled troughs located at the top of the plane linking the upper canal arm with the caissons. Although no specific dimensions are available for the aqueducts, reference to the drawings reveal that they were approximately 28 feet apart, centre to centre, which matched the horizontal stagger of the two parts of the inclined plane. One of the aqueducts was around 130 feet long, whilst the other was around 18 feet long. Both were approximately 18 feet wide and presumably 5 feet deep, as for the caissons. The aqueducts were supported above the top of the plane on brick piers with concrete foundations.

A detail close-up of the top right corner of the GJCC plan of the proposed inclined plane at Foxton. COURTESY THE WATERWAYS TRUST
This shows a side elevation of the aqueducts, the boiler house, the winding house, the accumulator housing and the chimney.

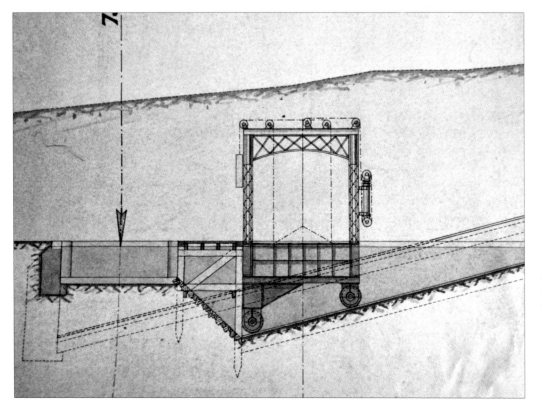

A detail close-up of the top left corner of the GJCC plan of the proposed inclined plane at Foxton. COURTESY THE WATERWAYS TRUST
This shows a sectional elevation through the lower canal basin, with a caisson immersed in water up against the timber staging.

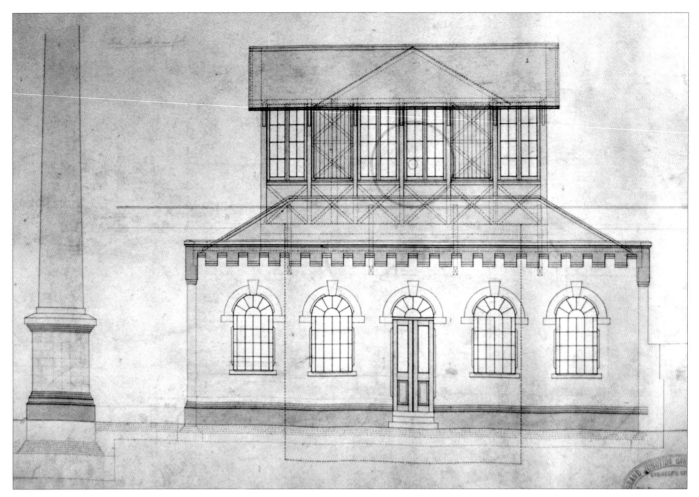

At the end of each aqueduct was a guillotine gate which was operated by 'jiggers', or hydraulic rams, and chains wrapped around two pulleys. When the rams extended, the pulleys were pushed apart, effectively making the free length of chain shorter and hence lifting the gate. The power for these rams came from the hydraulic accumulator in the boiler house.

The ends of the aqueducts that interfaced with the caissons had flat sealing faces finished with timber sections, 7 inches wide. The aqueducts and gates were fabricated from riveted structural steel sections and plates.

Caissons – The two caissons were rectangular in shape and measured 80 feet long by 15 feet wide by 5 feet deep. Each was capable of accommodating two laden 33-ton narrowboats, or one laden 70-ton barge, or wide boat. The caissons had a guillotine gate at each end, similar to those on the aqueducts, to facilitate the loading and unloading of the canal boats. These gates were also operated by 'jiggers', as previously described for the aqueduct gates.

Each caisson was mounted on four separate wheel assemblies, each of which ran on double rails on the incline. Each assembly had six wheels, four of which were on the upper axle and the other two on the lower axle. The two lower wheels and the middle wheels on the upper axle made contact with the rails on the linear (1 in 4 gradient) section of the plane, and the outer two wheels on the upper axles only came into play when they made contact with the short sections of rails on the upper curved section of the plane, thereby keeping the caissons upright.

The ends of the caissons that interfaced with the aqueducts had flat steel sealing faces, also with a width of 7 inches.

The caissons were generally fabricated from riveted structural steel sections and $^3/_8$ inch thick plates. When operational, that is to say full of water, with or without boats, each caisson weighed nominally 230 tons.

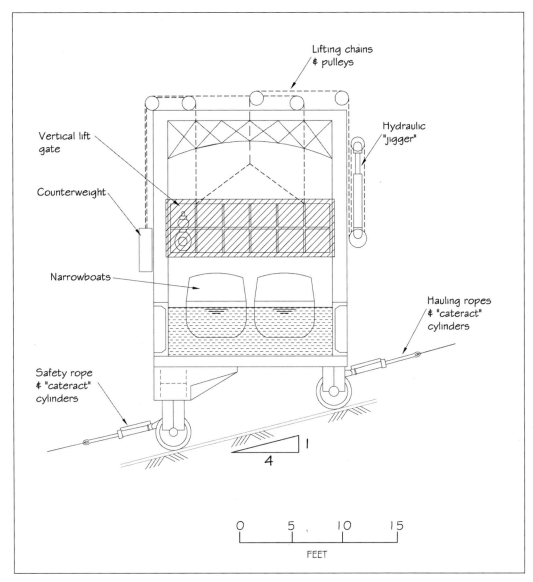

A sectional end elevation of the caisson at the Foxton Inclined Plane, with two narrowboats. DRAWING PREPARED BY THE AUTHOR & ROSS NORVILLE; BASED ON A DIAGRAM IN FOXTON: LOCKS AND BARGE LIFT
This diagram shows the key components of the caisson and gate mechanisms.

Wire Ropes – The caissons were held in position on the plane by means of two systems of 2½ inch diameter multi-stranded wire ropes; one that controlled the movement of the caissons by the steam engine via the winding drum, whilst the other was primarily for safety reasons.

Two wire hauling ropes were attached to the upper side of each caisson, close to the ends. The connection was made by means of hydraulic cylinders (or cataract cylinders) that equalised the forces applied by each rope. The ropes passed up the plane supported on small vertically-mounted pulleys and then through 90 degrees at the top of the plane by means of large horizontally-mounted pulleys. The upper ends of the hauling ropes were attached to the winding drum at the centre top of the plane. As the winding drum was turned, one pair of ropes from a caisson was wound onto the drum causing it to ascend the plane, whilst the other pair of ropes from the other caisson was unwound at the same rate, allowing it to descend the plane by means of gravity.

The safety system consisted of a continuous loop of a single wire rope that ran all the way round the plane between the two caissons, again making use of vertical and horizontal pulleys. The rope was connected to the mid-point on the upper and lower sides of each caisson, attached, as for the hauling ropes, through hydraulic cylinders. This system had two functions; firstly to ensure that the caissons were not solely reliant on the hauling ropes for holding them on the plane, and secondly to ensure that the caisson about to be descend from the top of the plane was actually pulled away from its starting position, rather than just relying on gravity to overcome any static friction and inertia in the system.

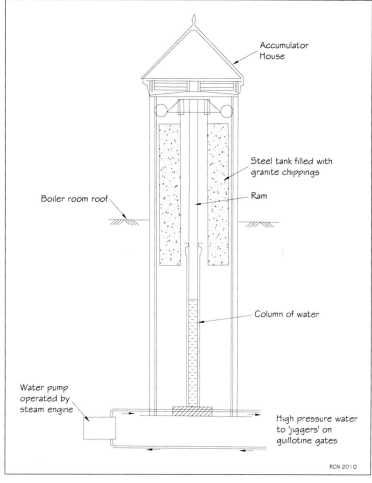

Sectional diagram of the accumulator. DRAWING PREPARED BY THE AUTHOR & ROSS NORVILLE; BASED ON A DIAGRAM IN FOXTON: LOCKS AND BARGE LIFT

This diagram shows the key components of the accumulator, which provided a constant supply of water at high pressure, needed to raise and lower the guillotine gates of the caissons and aqueduct, and to push the upper caisson against the sealing face of the aqueduct end.

Guide Pulleys – Large horizontally-mounted cast iron guide pulleys for the various hauling and safety ropes were located at the top and bottom of the inclined plane. These were over 10 feet in diameter with 24 spokes. Elsewhere, the wire ropes were supported vertically by smaller guide pulleys.

Winding Drum – A large cylindrical drum was located within the winding house with its axis horizontal. It was made from cast iron and was nominally 10 feet in diameter and 14 feet in length. It was driven directly by the steam engine through worm gearing, both of which were also contained within the winding house. The four wire hauling ropes from the caissons were each attached to the drum in such a way that, whichever way it was turned, two ropes would be wound onto the drum, thereby raising a caisson, whilst the other two would be unwound from the drum allowing the second caisson to descend.

Boilers – Two Lancashire-type steam boilers were installed in the boiler house; one duty and one standby (a Lancashire boiler has two flues that contain the furnaces and extend through the boiler from end to end). According to Dave Goodwin, in *Foxton Locks & the Grand Junction Canal Co.*, the boilers may not have been manufactured by J.&H. Gwynne but were more likely to have been procured by them from Marshall's, a specialist firm based in Gainsborough. The boilers were simple and robust in design, about 20 feet long by 6 feet diameter and had the capacity to meet rapidly changing demands for steam.

Steam Engine – The power to the hauling drum was provided by a double-cylinder, high-pressure, jet-condensing type steam engine, that delivered nominally 25 horse power. This was a relatively small rating, which reflected the fact that the caissons were in equilibrium on the plane, so the engine only had to overcome the friction and inertia in the system. The engine was thought to have operated at a pressure of between 100 and 120 pounds per square inch, at around 50 revolutions per minute. Reversing of the engine, needed during the raising and lowering of the caissons, was achieved by the use of Stephenson reverse link motion gearing.

Hydraulic Operating System – The hydraulic operating system made use of water with added anti-freeze, rather than the specialist oils that are available for similar uses today.

Water Pumps – Two small water pumps were housed in the boiler house, both being driven by the steam engine. They are thought to have been horizontal duplex pumps with outside plungers. One of the pumps was used to deliver water to the boilers, whilst the second delivered water to the hydraulic accumulator. The capacity of the latter pump was 20 gallons per minute.

The Hydraulic Accumulator – The lower part of this was located in the boiler house, whilst its upper section projected through the roof of and was contained within its own housing, alongside the winding house. The accumulator provided a large volume of water at a constantly high pressure, needed to operate the 'jiggers' that lowered and raised the guillotine gates on the aqueducts and the caissons. It also provided water to operate the hydraulic rams that jacked the caissons horizontally against the aqueduct end faces, in order to achieve watertight seals. The accumulator was capable of providing a volume of 9,000 cubic inches, or approximately 32 gallons of water, at a pressure of 700 pounds per square inch.

The accumulator was effectively a column of water in a vertical cylinder that supported, and hence was pressurised by, a heavily weighted ram. The diameter of the cylinder and ram was 9 inches, whilst the stroke, or maximum lift, of the ram was 12 feet. The weight was provided by a steel tank filled with granite chippings.

It seems likely that the accumulator would have had a device fitted so that when the ballast had reached the bottom of its travel, the water pump started up automatically to recharge the accumulator, or raise the ballast. A similar device would have switched off the pump when the accumulator was fully charged.

★ ★ ★ ★ ★

As with all new great inventions, for example the Anderton Boat Lift, the design of the Foxton Inclined Plane was ingenious for its simplicity, whilst the scale of the structure was breathtaking even by Victorian standards. By the end of the 19th century, inclined planes to convey canal boats from one level to another were by no means a new idea but the arrangement settled upon by Gordon Thomas and his co-designers for the Foxton Inclined Plane generally took what was good from the earlier designs and then developed the concept still further. Quite rightly, the Foxton Inclined Plane was recognised by Victorian engineers as a civil engineering masterpiece and its lead designer, Gordon Thomas, was justly heralded by his peers. One of the many accolades for him occurred in 1904, when the design was awarded a gold medal and diploma at an exhibition in St. Louis in the United States of America.

Sources For This Chapter

'Surmounting of Great Ascents – The 'Thomas' Canal barge lift' – a professional paper written by Gordon Cale Thomas for the 9th International Navigation Congress in Dusseldorf, circa 1902

'The 'Thomas' Lift constructed at Foxton, Leicestershire by the Grand Junction Canal Company', a professional paper written by Gordon Cale Thomas, circa 1904

Foxton: Locks and Barge Lift, by Peter Gardner & Frank Foden, Leicestershire County Planning Dept in association with the Leicestershire branch of the Council for the Protection of Rural England, 2nd ed. 1979

Foxton Locks and Inclined Plane – A Detailed History, compiled by members of the Foxton Inclined Plane Trust and published by Department of Planning & Transportation, Leicestershire County Council, circa 1986

Foxton Locks and the Inclined Plane – Three Years of Restoration, 200 Years of History, by members of the Foxton Inclined Plane Trust, 2009

Foxton Locks and the Grand Junction Canal Co., Dave Goodwin, Leicestershire County Council

The archives of the Foxton Inclined Plane Trust at Foxton

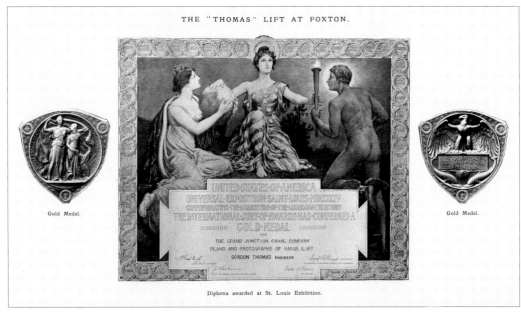

The Gold Medal and Diploma awarded to the Grand Junction Canal Company for the design of the Foxton Inclined Plane at an exhibition in St. Louis in the United States of America in 1904. COURTESY THE WATERWAYS TRUST The image accompanies a paper entitled 'The 'Thomas' Lift constructed at Foxton Leicestershire by the Grand Junction Canal Company', written by Gordon Thomas circa 1904.

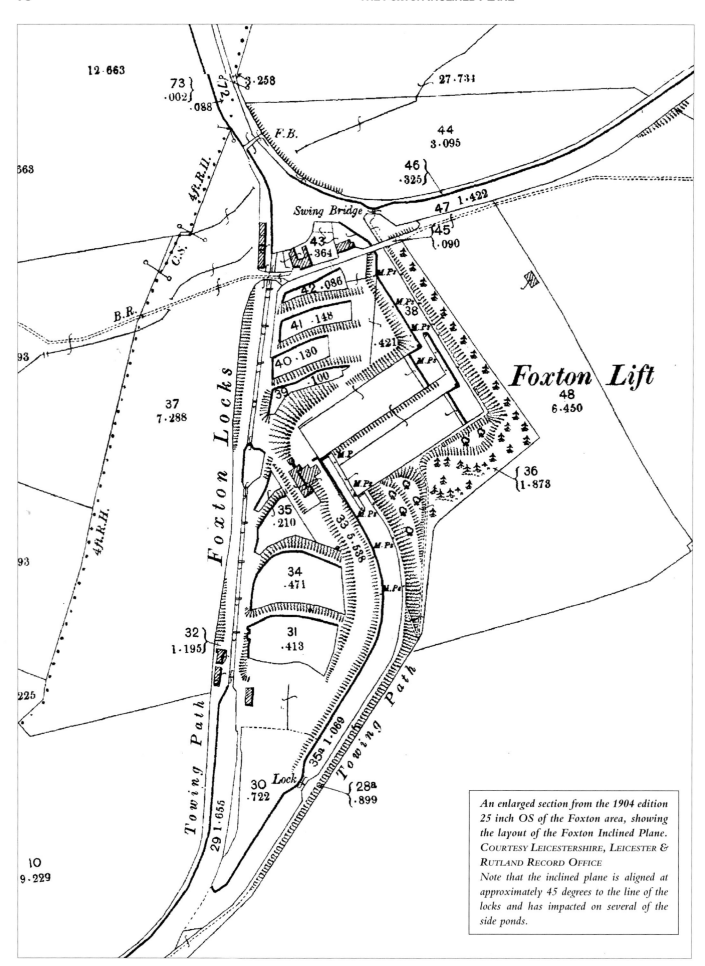

An enlarged section from the 1904 edition 25 inch OS of the Foxton area, showing the layout of the Foxton Inclined Plane.
COURTESY LEICESTERSHIRE, LEICESTER &
RUTLAND RECORD OFFICE
Note that the inclined plane is aligned at approximately 45 degrees to the line of the locks and has impacted on several of the side ponds.

CHAPTER 6
1898 TO 1900
THE CONSTRUCTION OF THE FOXTON INCLINED PLANE

'It is apparent that the whole of the work below ground level was completed in 18 months by the summer of 1899, which left 9 months for the erection of the machinery and other work, to be ready for trials in April 1900. Obviously there would have been some overlap, but this is essentially the time scale of the construction.'
Extract from Foxton: Locks and Barge Lift *by Peter Gardner & Frank Foden*

I n this chapter, I will attempt to describe the significant events during the two and a half or so years of construction of the Foxton Inclined Plane. This period effectively began in November 1897, with the acceptance by the Grand Junction Canal Company (GJCC) of a tender for the fabrication of the structural and mechanical components of the inclined plane and ended with its formal opening in July 1900.

Before embarking on the main subject of this chapter, however, it is worthy of note that Thomas Millner, the Manager of the Northern District of the Grand Junction Canal between 1896 and 1929, was a very keen and competent amateur photographer and was known to take his camera to the canal company's work sites. It is quite likely, therefore, that many of the photographs of the construction of the Foxton Inclined Plane in this chapter, along with many of the photographs in subsequent chapters, were taken by Millner.

Also worthy of note is the fact that Millner was not thought to have become involved in the day-to-day progress of the construction of the inclined plane, even though the Leicester Section was part of the Northern District. This was most likely due to the fact that his superior, Gordon Thomas, who was the Engineer to the GJCC and the lead designer of the inclined plane, took a personal interest in the construction and worked very closely with Barnabas James Thomas, the Resident Engineer for the works on behalf of the Company. Barnabas Thomas was also Gordon Thomas' cousin and co-designer of the inclined plane.

★ ★ ★ ★ ★

On 3rd November 1897, the Minute Book of the Board of the GJCC records, in rather prosaic terms, the decision to proceed with the construction of an inclined plane at Foxton, by appointing J.&H. Gwynne to design and fabricate the structural and mechanical elements:

'Resolved: That the recommendation of the Sub-Committee be adopted subject to Messrs Gwynne entering into a proper contract and giving security for the due performance of the work and in addition to the amount of the tender a further sum not exceeding five hundred pounds be allowed for experiments that may be found necessary provided the same are sanctioned by the Company's Engineer.'

The £500 referred to in the extract above *'for experiments'*, is presumably the same £500 referred to in the report by Gordon Thomas dated 12th October 1897 as being *'expenses'*.

Soon after, suitable land for the inclined plane to the east of the flight of locks was purchased by the GJCC from a Mr J. Crisp. The purchase of two parcels of land is recorded in the Company's minute book on 8th December 1897. The first parcel was slightly over 10 acres in size and was bought at a cost of £125 per acre, whilst the second, smaller parcel of

A photographic portrait of Barnabas Thomas circa 1905, cousin of Gordon Thomas and Resident Engineer in charge of supervising the construction of the Foxton Inclined Plane.
COURTESY THE FOXTON INCLINED PLANE TRUST
Thomas is here seen apparently dressed in the uniform of a lift attendant for the inclined plane.

just over one acre was priced at £200 per acre.

Whilst J.&H. Gwynne were awarded the contract for the mechanical and steelwork elements of the inclined plane at a contract price of £14,630 (the tender price of £14,130 plus £500), the civil engineering works were to be carried out by the direct labour force of the GJCC at an estimated cost of £12,000, under the day-to-day supervision of Resident Engineer Barnabas Thomas.

It should, however, be recognised that although cheaper, the civil engineering works were not insignificant, as they included:

• Major earthworks to the land immediately to the east of the locks, in order to create a stable slope for the plane
• Extensive foundations for the rails on the inclined plane and the various mechanical components
• Major channel and basin works at both the top and bottom of the proposed inclined plane

By the beginning of 1898, Gordon Thomas had been authorised to purchase appropriate materials and equipment needed for the construction of the inclined plane, which included amongst other things, a portable engine and a concrete mixer. A month or so later, the Engineer also gained approval to purchase three portable hoisting engines for the site works.

By all accounts, work on site began sometime during the spring of 1898 as, on 21st May, the Board of the GJCC made what was presumably the first of several visits to Foxton to inspect the works. The Minute Book records that general satisfaction was expressed with the progress being made.

The work on site and that at the premises of J.&H. Gwynne at Hammersmith in London can be assumed to have been carried out in parallel over the following months. Gordon Thomas would presumably have made frequent inspections of both the civil works at Foxton and the mechanical fabrication works in London to monitor progress and to address any issues that may have arisen.

★ ★ ★ ★ ★

The landscape in the Foxton area contained a north facing escarpment with a natural gradient of 1 in 12 or so, which marks the northern edge of the Northampton Uplands. The flight of ten narrow locks had been built circa 1810, down the escarpment generally at right angles to the contours.

The underlying geology that forms the Northampton Uplands in the Foxton area is Lower Lias deposits, which contain strata that vary in consistency from relatively soft clay to hard shale. The Lower Lias, when undisturbed, is said to be resistant to erosive forces but when the clays are exposed to the water they can become unstable and difficult to work with. As a consequence, excavated slopes exposed to adverse weather can be liable to slips and filled areas can be prone to settlement.

The position and gradient selected for the inclined plane presents a bit of a conundrum to today's observer, in that the plane tends to be aligned diagonally down the escarpment with a footprint that overlays four of the nine side ponds of the locks. Filling over the side ponds for the locks would almost certainly have created problems given the need to displace water and silt, whilst the chosen alignment and slope led to very large volumes of excavation and filling. Gordon Thomas is on record as having stated that the chosen arrangement necessitated the moving of around 60,000 cubic yards of excavated material.

A more sensible arrangement might have been to construct the plane further to the east of and parallel to the locks, with a gradient shallower than 1 in 4, thereby avoiding any interference with the side ponds and also reducing the volumes of cut and fill.

It is interesting to note that the 1894 Memorandum, as written by the consulting engineers Thomas & Taylor on the subject of a possible inclined plane at Foxton and Watford, (see Chapter 4), reveals that the 1 in 4 gradient was not an essential part of the design:

> '7. The incline or slope in the example is taken as 1 in 4 as being that which offers the greatest convenience; but it is not necessarily 1 in 4; and it may be varied without detriment, according to the peculiarities of pits or other pertinent circumstances.'

The reference in the extract to 'pits' clearly indicates that the 1 in 4 slope was chosen to suit a different location, most probably the Worsley mines in relation to the Bridgewater Canal. If there ever was a case for reducing the gradient, the site at Foxton appears to be it. A gentler slope would have significantly reduced the volume of cut and fill required, resulting in shallower foundations and an inherently more stable arrangement.

The actual location and configuration of the plane chosen are difficult to explain. Perhaps the increased area of land that would have been needed for the alternative configuration of the inclined plane was not available for purchase or perhaps there was an underlying geological problem. One cannot help wondering, however, whether the 1 in 4 gradient shown in the 1894 Memorandum was adopted by Gordon Thomas without being adequately challenged.

★ ★ ★ ★ ★

Gordon Thomas (centre), Barnabas Thomas (left), with surveying rod in his left hand, and possibly Joseph Jex Taylor (right) standing outside the GJCC office at the bottom of Foxton Locks, circa 1900.
COURTESY THE WATERWAYS TRUST
If the man on the right is Joseph Jex Taylor, then all three were partners in the consulting engineering practice of Thomas & Taylor, which was closely involved with the design of the Foxton Inclined Plane and for the 1894 Memorandum.

As stated earlier, the earthworks needed to construct the plane were an enormous undertaking. To stabilise the filling works, the escarpment slope was terraced in order to expose relatively strong geological strata. Then, in order to achieve a better material for filling and compaction, some of the excavated clay material was baked in a 'clamp' on site, prior to mixing and re-use.

As a consequence of the terraced construction procedure and the 1 in 4 slope, the depth of excavation required in places was as much as 30 feet. The filling and concrete foundations had to be of similar depths. Arches were incorporated into the track foundations, so that they were supported by undisturbed material and, therefore, would not be subject to settlement. Apparently, the arched foundations were stabilised by being tied together by means of steel ducts that ran laterally across the plane.

The foundations for the winding house and the large horizontal pulleys were evidently constructed on the filled ground at the top of the plane. By all accounts, other heavy items, such as the winding drum and the steam engine, would have had solid foundations, possibly through the fill material to undisturbed ground, in order to reduce the risk of settlement.

The earthworks, whether cut or fill, would have been carried out almost entirely by hand tools, with up to 140 men being employed on site at the busiest times. Excavated material was moved around site either by means of wooden wheelbarrows or by steel trucks running on temporary rails. The trucks would either have been pushed by hand or horse-drawn. On steep slopes, however, the movement of the trucks may have been facilitated by the use of portable steam engines and cables.

As stated in the extract at the beginning of this chapter, the civil engineering works on site lasted for around a year and a half, with the result that adverse weather conditions would almost certainly have been encountered. It is therefore surprising, given the sensitive ground

A group photograph, possibly taken from inside the partially built winding house, during the construction of the Foxton Inclined Plane. COURTESY THE FOXTON INCLINED PLANE TRUST
This might be an inspection by the directors of the Grand Junction Canal Company. Gordon Thomas, the Engineer, is on the far left of the group, holding his shooting stick, and alongside him is his cousin, Barnabas Thomas. The formidable figure of Thomas Holt, the Area Engineer of the Leicester Section of the Grand Junction Canal, is in the middle of the front row holding an umbrella in his right hand. Behind the group is a lifting frame, below which are two of the large horizontal pulleys for the hauling ropes.

conditions and lack of modern safety measures, that just two accidents to workmen are recorded in the Minute Book of the GJCC, on14th December 1898:

'Accident at Foxton Works in which Mr G. Sharman injured his finger whilst engaged in tipping wagons on 8th November. £5-5-0 gratuity offered by the Company, but they do not admit liability. Offer eventually accepted.'

The second and far more serious accident was recorded as follows:

'George Robinson, one of the navvies employed at Foxton killed by a fall of earth. Inquest returned verdict of accidental death.'

The fatality occurred on 5th December 1898, when a fall of earth trapped the unfortunate workman against a tipping wagon, thereby breaking his back. It would appear that George Robinson had no relatives and so his fellow workmen contributed towards his funeral expenses. It is not recorded whether the GJCC made any contribution.

At least one other serious accident occurred, as there is reportedly a gravestone in St. Andrew's Church in Foxton village for John Joseph Allen, who died in December 1899, as a result of an accident during the construction of the incline plane at Foxton. No details are known of the accident that befell Mr Allen, although given the date, it may have been related to the fabrication of the mechanical components by Messrs Gwynne.

★ ★ ★ ★ ★

Whilst the civil engineering aspects of the works were ongoing on site, fabrication of the structural and mechanical elements would have been progressing at the premises of J.&H. Gwynne. It is reasonable to assume that the various components would have been delivered to Foxton, most likely along the Grand Junction Canal, to coincide with the completion of the civil works in the summer of 1899. Fabrication and installation on site would have taken place over the following nine months or so.

The caissons, which were fabricated from steel plates and structural steel sections, were assembled piece-by-piece in position half way down the plane, at the point where they would pass when in operation. Once completed, they would not need to be relocated prior to attaching the two hauling cables. It is of interest to note that the caissons were subsequently parked up in this position at night and during other periods of non-operation.

Apart from the above references to accidents, the Minute Books reveal very little information about the works on site. This might lead one to assume, perhaps wrongly, that the works on the inclined plane at Foxton were progressing well. However, nominally two years after the start of construction, the Minute Book of the GJCC, on 11th April 1900, records that the company had received a letter from J.&H. Gwynne, dated 29th March 1900, expressing regret about the delay in the completion of the machinery in connection with the Foxton Lift. The Minute Book also recorded on the same day that:

'Mr De Salis reported that he and Mr Praed [both Board members] were present unofficially with the Company's Engineer and viewed a trial of the Lift on the 5th inst and the Engineer stated that there were certain alterations required before he could certify for a further payment.'

It may be partly, if not wholly, as a consequence of this delay that the GJCC subsequently decided to stop, until further notice, the widening works that had just been started to the Watford flight of locks.

It is worthy of note that, also on 11th April 1900, after all the good work carried out on the GJCC's behalf by Gordon Thomas in progressing the improvements to the Leicestershire & Northamptonshire Union Canal and the Grand Union Canal, the Board decided to formally promote him to the post of Engineer to the Company. This decision was back-dated to 13th June 1894, when his father, Hubert Thomas, took on the role of Clerk to the Company. It is not stated whether the backdating of Gordon Thomas' appointment had any monetary implications but, whether or not, it reveals the esteem that he was held in by the GJCC.

Just over a month later, on 18th May 1900, J.&H. Gwynne wrote to Gordon Thomas stating that, in their opinion, the next payment for the structural and mechanical works should be made on the basis that the machinery at Foxton had recently successfully completed an official trial. The Minute Book on 13th June 1900 confirmed the success of the trial and recorded the Engineer's request to the GJCC for payment of 25% of the contract value to J.&H. Gwynne, and also:

'recommending that the ordinary cost now incurred in working the lift before it is finally taken over be allowed out of the £500 which has been specifically reserved in the Contract.'

The Board agreed that a payment of £3,593 16s 6d should be made to J.&H. Gwynne but deferred a decision with respect to the running costs. Soon after, at the next meeting, the Board agreed that the cost of working the inclined plane should be met by the company.

★ ★ ★ ★ ★

The Foxton Inclined Plane was formally declared open to traffic on 10th July 1900. Although no contemporary account of the opening is available today, it can be assumed that the opening of the inclined plane was, as is usual for such events, accompanied by appropriate ceremony and celebrations.

Finally, on 11th February 1901, after the designated maintenance period of twelve months,

The lower canal basin of the Foxton Inclined Plane circa 1901, looking northwards. COURTESY THE WATERWAYS TRUST
The caisson, containing a narrowboat, is about to enter the lower canal basin. Note the two control cabins in the centre of the picture and the inspection pit on the right bank of the basin, which was for access to one of the horizontal pulleys for the tail rope to the caissons. Temporary stoplogs in a shelter with a pitched roof are visible between the caisson and the control cabins. It is not known who the two well-dressed gentlemen are on the right bank, although the one standing on the left, with an umbrella in his hand, shows some resemblance to Gordon Thomas, the Engineer to the Grand Junction Canal Company and the lead designer of the Foxton Inclined Plane. It is interesting to note that, for some unknown reason, the lower sections of the lattice uprights of the gantries at the outer ends of the caisson appear to have been painted in a different colour than the rest of it.

during which time, one assumes, the new structure had worked satisfactorily, the contract for the structural and mechanical elements of the Foxton Inclined Plane was effectively completed. A final payment was made to J.&H. Gwynne in the amount of £1,413, subject to:

> '*Mess'rs Gwynne providing and fixing new axles to the wheels of the tanks as and when necessary.*'

This inclusion in the Minute Book suggests that there may have been some problems with this aspect of the inclined plane but this is put in perspective by the fact that a spare axle and set of wheels were eventually purchased from J.&H. Gwynne almost exactly four years later, on 8th February 1905, for the sum of £60.

★ ★ ★ ★ ★

To close this chapter, I include below two extracts that neatly summarise the development and construction of the Foxton Inclined Plane. The first is from *The Canals of the East Midlands*:

> 'The plane was designed by the canal's engineer, G.C. Thomas, and his brother, to raise two narrowboats or one barge a vertical distance of 75ft 2ins. Tenders were received in November 1897, and that of J. & H. Gwynne & Co. of Hammersmith for £14,130 was accepted. Construction began early in 1898 and the plane was opened for traffic on 10 July 1900, at a cost of £39,224 including the land'

The only doubt in this extract is that Charles Hadfield refers to the co-designer of the plane, presumably Barnabas James Thomas, as being the brother of Gordon Thomas, whereas other authors, including Edward Paget-Tomlinson and David Tew, refer to him as a cousin.

The second extract is taken from a paper entitled 'Surmounting of Great Ascents – The 'Thomas' Canal Barge Lift', which was written by Gordon Thomas for presentation at the 9th International Navigation Congress in Dusseldorf in 1902:

> 'The total cost of the works, (inclusive of plant, machinery and land) together with expenditure due to forming the upper and lower connecting Canals, which extend for a distance of about a half-mile and comprise on the upper level a high embankment and on the lower level a cutting of considerable depth, together with bridges, protecting walls and works has amounted to a sum of nearly £40,000.'

All in all, therefore, for a project of this magnitude, the construction of the Foxton Inclined Plane seems to have been carried out with the minimum of fuss and generally without incident. By all accounts, the work to install the structural and mechanical elements overran by a few months, whilst by reference to the above extract, the cost of the project was significantly higher than the original estimate, *i.e.* £12,000 for the civil works and £14,630 for the structural & mechanical works. It should be noted, however, that the total cost of £37,500, as quoted elsewhere by Gordon Thomas, includes bridge building, protecting walls and other incidental works that were presumably not covered by the original estimates. Even allowing for this, there does seem to have been a sizeable cost overrun, most of which is likely to have been associated with the civil works, possibly as a result of the difficult ground conditions on site.

And so, after a period of nominally six years of planning, development and construction, the extraordinary Foxton Inclined Plane was finally in service.

Sources For This Chapter

The Minute Books of the Committee of the Grand Junction Canal Company held at the National Archives, Kew
The Canals of the East Midlands, Charles Hadfield, David & Charles, 1966
Canals, Inclines and Lifts, David Tew, Alan Sutton Publishing Ltd, 1984
The Illustrated History of Canal and River Navigations, Edward Paget-Tomlinson, Sheffield Academic Press, 1993
Foxton: Locks and Barge Lift, by Peter Gardner & Frank Foden, Leicestershire County Planning Dept in association with the Leicestershire branch of the Council for the Protection of Rural England, 2nd ed. 1979
Foxton Locks and Inclined Plane – A Detailed History, compiled by members of the Foxton Inclined Plane Trust and published by Department of Planning & Transportation, Leicestershire County Council, circa 1986
'Surmounting of Great Ascents – The 'Thomas' Canal barge lift' – a professional paper written by Gordon Cale Thomas for the 9th International Navigation Congress in Dusseldorf, circa 1902
Article on the Bulbourne model from *The Engineer*, 22nd January 1897
The Grand Junction Canal, Alan Faulkner, David & Charles, 1972
The archives of the Foxton Inclined Plane Trust at Foxton

RIGHT: The part built boiler house and chimney. COURTESY THE FOXTON INCLINED PLANE TRUST *Note the elaborate timber scaffolding to the chimney and the staging for the workmen on the boiler house.*

BELOW: The major filling works for the upper section of the inclined plane at an advanced stage. COURTESY THE FOXTON INCLINED PLANE TRUST *The partly completed winding house, aqueduct and chimney can be seen in the middle background, as can the masonry foundations for the rails down the slope. In the foreground, running diagonally across the inclined plane, is one of the temporary track-ways for wagons moving excavated material around site.*

CHAPTER 6A
1898 TO 1900
BUILDING THE
FOXTON INCLINED PLANE
A PHOTOGRAPHIC RECORD

LEFT: A view of the construction works looking up the incline. COURTESY THE WATERWAYS TRUST
The rails for the caissons are already in place on their timber sleepers, set into the concrete foundations. The work to fabricate the caisson mid-way up the incline is just starting, with an axle and pair of wheels fixed in place on one set of rails, while a group of workmen are fabricating the wheel assembly on the rails in front of the chimney. The large frame that was to act as a buffer forcing the caisson against the aqueduct end face, to create a watertight seal, is clearly visible on the horizon.

BELOW LEFT: The steam engine about to be lifted into place within the partially completed winding house.
Gordon and Barnabas Thomas are to the left of the picture, whilst three men are at work on the engine.

BELOW RIGHT: The winding drum lifted into place in the winding house. BOTH COURTESY THE FOXTON INCLINED PLANE TRUST
Gordon (left) and Barnabas Thomas (right) again pose for the photograph.

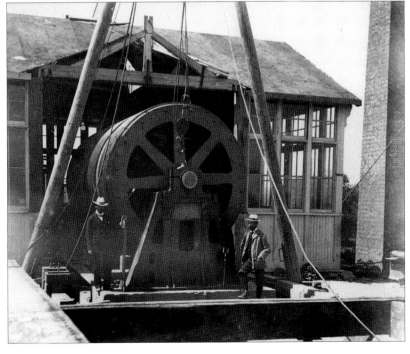

Two more views of the nearly completed winding house, with the winding drum newly lifted into place. BOTH COURTESY THE FOXTON INCLINED PLANE TRUST

In the top view, Gordon and Barnabas Thomas can be seen standing to the right of the drum, along with a shirt-sleeved workman. The foundation and axle of one of the horizontal pulleys for the hauling ropes is in the right foreground. It is believed that many of these pictures may have been taken by Thomas Millner, the Manager of the Northern District of the Grand Junction Canal, who was a very keen and competent amateur photographer.

The boiler house, winding room and chimney close to completion, looking from the west across the flight of locks. COURTESY THE FOXTON
INCLINED PLANE TRUST.
There is still staging around the housing for the accumulator and one of the aqueducts is clearly visible against the skyline on the right.

*The major excavation works
for the lower section of the
inclined plane and the lower
canal basin.* COURTESY THE
FOXTON INCLINED PLANE
TRUST
*This photograph vividly shows
the extent of the excavation,
all of which had to be done by
hand. There appears to have
been a serious landslip in the
right background, which is
being cleared away by a gang
of four workmen, making use
of tipping wagons running
on temporary rails. Pulling
these up the incline was
achieved with the assistance
of a small steam winch.
Gordon Thomas, in a light
coloured suit and panama
hat, is observing the works in
the background from a lower
terrace, perched on a shooting-
stick, whilst his wife, Mabel,
in a white dress, is standing
under a parasol part way up
the slip. She appears in a
number of these photographs.*

RIGHT: *Work progressing on the gantry to the guillotine gate of the right hand aqueduct.* COURTESY THE FOXTON INCLINED PLANE TRUST *Resident Engineer Barnabas Thomas is inspecting the work from ground level.*

BELOW: **Work in progress on the two aqueducts.** COURTESY THE FOXTON INCLINED PLANE TRUST *The aqueduct gates, the lattice steel framework and the 'jiggers' for operating the gates are clearly visible in the right foreground and middle background, whilst the winding house is just visible in the left background. Gordon Thomas and Mabel, his wife, are again posing for the photographer; the frequency with which they appear in the pictures suggests he took great pride in his design and the work being carried out to bring it to fruition.*

ABOVE: Construction of the left hand aqueduct. COURTESY THE WATERWAYS TRUST Note the temporary staging inside the aqueduct and the vertical-lift or guillotine gate, fabricated and supplied by J.&H. Gwynne. The winding house and the chimney, in the background, are effectively complete.

LEFT: The wheel assemblies for the caissons set out on the rails mid-way up the inclined plane, in readiness for the fabrication of the caissons. COURTESY THE WATERWAYS TRUST Gordon and Mabel Thomas pose behind the wheel assemblies, while a group of workmen in the right background are just beginning the next stage of erecting the caissons.

RIGHT: *A completed wheel assembly for one of the caissons.* COURTESY THE FOXTON INCLINED PLANE TRUST
Gordon Thomas here assumes a rather jokey pose for the camera, looking out from one of the wheel assemblies, his shooting stick leaning on the wheel below. In the background, work is in progress on another upturned assembly.

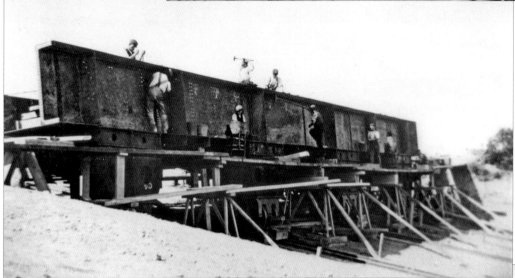

LEFT: **Early days in the fabrication of one of the caissons.** COURTESY THE FOXTON INCLINED PLANE TRUST
The metalwork elements, as fabricated and supplied by J.&H. Gwynne, are being put together mid-way up the slope on top of the wheel assemblies, with extensive use of timber scaffolding. The various elements were hot riveted together.

RIGHT: *Fabrication of one of the caissons.* COURTESY THE FOXTON INCLINED PLANE TRUST
In what appears to be fine weather conditions, many men are seen at work on fabricatiing one of the caissons. They are being observed by Gordon Thomas, in a light coloured suit and holding his shooting-stick, in the right foreground, and probably his cousin also, Barnabas Thomas, the Resident Engineer, in the left foreground.

LEFT: The left hand caisson nearing completion. COURTESY THE FOXTON INCLINED PLANE TRUST Note the staging is erected around the top of the gantry for the guillotine gate, allowing access to the pulleys so they can be worked on. The workmen's temporary accommodation huts can be seen in the background.

BELOW: The fabrication of the caissons in progress, mid-way up the inclined plane. COURTESY THE WATERWAYS TRUST Note the timber scaffolding providing access to the (higher) nearside of the caisson. It was easier to fabricate the caissons on their wheel assemblies on the incline, which thus enabled the work to be carried out on the level.

RIGHT: *Another view showing the process of building the caissons.* COURTESY THE FOXTON INCLINED PLANE TRUST

A group of workmen are seen assembling the top of the gantry for one of the guillotine gates. This is not as precarious as it looks, the timber staging protecting against any falls.

RIGHT: *A close up of one of the caissons during fabrication.* COURTESY THE WATERWAYS TRUST

The 'cataract' cylinder and hauling rope can be seen in the foreground, whilst the metalwork to the caisson is yet to be painted, with the consequence that the fabricator's reference numbers are still visible on the independent elements.

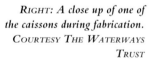

*LEFT: **One of the sets of controls that were installed in the upper control cabins.** There are three hand levers on top of the machinery, which were mechanically linked so that they could only be operated in a pre-set sequence. The labels underneath the levers, from left to right, read 'RAMS', 'CONDUIT' and 'TANK'. It is not entirely clear what actions these levers controlled but it evidently related to the procedure of creating a watertight seal between the upper caisson and the aqueduct, prior to opening the guillotine gates to allow boats to move on and off the caisson.*

*BELOW: **The completed caissons in their fabrication positions mid-way up the plane.** BOTH COURTESY THE FOXTON INCLINED PLANE TRUST*

Note that the two aqueducts in the background appear to be close to completion as well. The impression given is that the chocks have been removed, which suggests that the caissons may be interconnected by the hauling ropes, although they are not evident. Due to the lack of water, it seems likely that work was progressing at this time on the lower canal basin.

RIGHT: *Gordon Thomas sitting in the lower canal basin towards the end of its construction.* COURTESY THE FOXTON INCLINED PLANE TRUST
Thomas is sitting on the edge wall of a chamber for one of the large pulleys for the tail ropes from the caissons. The other pulley is set in a chamber in the basin wall, the arched entrance to which is just visible in the background to the left of his head. The tail rope interconnected the two pulleys by means of the pipe ducting, the end of which can be seen in the far left corner of the chamber in the foreground. Note the two planks behind, in use as wheelbarrow runs, and also the massive scale of excavation needed to create the lower part of the inclined plane and the basin.

LEFT: *The timber staging in the lower canal basin.* COURTESY THE FOXTON INCLINED PLANE TRUST
Thomas posing once again, on the timber staging erected between the base of the incline and the lower canal basin, prior to it being filled with water.

RIGHT: *Lower canal basin.* COURTESY THE FOXTON INCLINED PLANE TRUST
Another photograph which illustrates the extent of the major excavation work that had to carried out to carve the lower part of the incline and all of the lower canal basin out of the landscape. This was carried out manually using picks and shovels, the material being carted away in wooden wheelbarrows and narrow gauge wagons. Two wagons fully laden with excavated material can be seen in the middle foreground. Some of the temporary rails which were used for these to run on can be seen leant against the basin wall on the far left. In the right foreground is the arched entrance to a chamber for housing one of the large horizontal pulleys for the tail ropes from the caissons. Above the chamber entrance is the inspection pit, which is still in good condition today.

RIGHT: One of the caissons in the lower canal basin, with the guillotine gates still being worked on. COURTESY THE FOXTON INCLINED PLANE TRUST
The basin itself has been completed. In the background are the sheds that were used to accommodate the workmen, as well as for storage of materials and equipment.

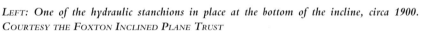

LEFT: One of the hydraulic stanchions in place at the bottom of the incline, circa 1900. COURTESY THE FOXTON INCLINED PLANE TRUST
Note that the control cabin is yet to be built around it. These would have been used by the lift attendant to enable the guillotine gates on the caissons to be opened and closed from within the control cabins. Behind it is the bare face of the excavation works for the lower canal basin.

BELOW: The lower canal basin, looking northwards, close to completion. COURTESY THE FOXTON INCLINED PLANE TRUST
Note the planks spanning the basin to enable workmen to gain access to the right bank.

RIGHT: *A view up the inclined plane when very close to completion.* COURTESY THE WATERWAYS TRUST
This photograph reveals the sheer scale of the project in all its grandeur.

BELOW: *One of the caissons in the lower canal basin.* COURTESY THE FOXTON INCLINED PLANE TRUST
The large number of rather distinguished spectators and the lack of any boat give the impression that the caisson has been lowered into the water as part of a trial run. Gordon Thomas appears to be the second spectator from the left in the foreground, with his hands clasped together behind his back. It is possible that the spectators are the Board of the Grand Junction Canal Company.

ABOVE: The winding drum and steam engine in their final positions inside the winding house, circa 1901. COURTESY THE FOXTON INCLINED PLANE TRUST
This is the last of the six photographs which accompanied Gordon Thomas' circa 1904 paper entitled 'The 'Thomas' Lift constructed at Foxton Leicestershire by the Grand Junction Canal Company'. Note the pristine condition of the room and mechanical equipment, indicating that the photograph was taken before or soon after the opening of the inclined plane in July 1900.

LEFT: A second aspect of the winding drum and steam engine inside the winding house. COURTESY THE WATERWAYS TRUST

The top of the Foxton Inclined Plane, as photographed from Foxton Locks apparently not long after completion of construction in 1900. COURTESY THE FOXTON INCLINED PLANE TRUST
In the foreground is one of the side ponds to the locks, which appears to have been drained down, whilst on the left are the newly painted winding house, the boiler house and chimney. The gate gantries for the two aqueducts and one of the caissons are also clearly visible. Lined up for the photograph in the centre is a group of twenty-five or so dignitaries, two of which appear to be female – it seems likely that this is the Board of the Grand Junction Canal Company, possibly with guests, during one of its visits. Also note what appears to be a coal chute in front of the group, leading from the aqueduct down to the boiler room, and the structure housing the stoplogs in the far right of the picture.

The staircase of four locks at Watford, showing it before refurbishment and after. BOTH COURTESY THE FOXTON INCLINED PLANE TRUST
By the circa 1900 date of the first photograph, the locks at Watford were in a very poor state of repair and hence leaking badly. The refurbishment works were carried out during the winter of 1901-2. The GJCC initially intended to replace the locks here by another inclined plane of the same design as at Foxton but the company then had doubts and, after looking at a number of options, chose to proceed with the widening of the existing locks in order to allow barges to navigate the Leicester Section. Finally, only a few weeks into the widening work, the decision was taken to simply refurbish the existing narrow locks. Notice that the whole of the balance arms have been painted white, probably to make the locks safer to use at night time.

CHAPTER 7
1894 TO 1902
IMPROVEMENTS TO
WATFORD LOCKS

'The Company's aim was to speed traffic, save water, and to use wide boats over the route. If the latter aim was to be realised, a tandem project had to be undertaken to upgrade the narrow locks at the Watford end of the summit too. Although a duplicate lift was under consideration, it is not generally known that several other options were pursued. While Gordon Thomas, as Company Engineer, was personally responsible for the Lift [at Foxton], it was Millner who was delegated to survey the Watford Locks with several alternative schemes in mind.'
Extract from Foxton Locks and the Grand Junction Canal Co. *by Dave Goodwin*

I t is in the December 1894 Memorandum from Thomas & Taylor that the first written suggestion to address the bottlenecks caused by the narrow locks on the former Grand Union Canal at Watford and Foxton can be found. By that time, the Grand Junction Canal Company (GJCC) had embarked on a strategy to gain greater control over the most direct canal route between the coalfields of the East Midlands and London. Indeed, only a few months before the receipt of the 1894 Memorandum, the GJCC had completed the purchase of the Leicestershire & Northamptonshire Union Canal and the Grand Union Canal, jointly referred to as the Leicester Section of the Grand Junction Canal. Furthermore, the company was just about to begin a programme of major capital works with respect to the newly acquired canals, which included extensive dredging and channel improvement works.

It is now my intention to discuss the GJCC's actions with respect to the Watford flight of locks, as opposed to those at Foxton dealt with in the previous chapters. For reasons of clarity, I have decided to dedicate a separate chapter to this subject.

★ ★ ★ ★ ★

Refurbishment of the locks at Watford in 1901-2. COURTESY THE FOXTON INCLINED PLANE TRUST
Work in progress within the lock chamber of one of the locks in the staircase of four. The original lock chamber walls have been carefully dismantled, with what is assumed to be the re-usable bricks stacked on the left and presumably broken bricks discarded on the right. Up to eight men are at work in the chamber, whilst the vertical earth surfaces exposed by the removal of the bricks are unsupported. A plank provides rather precarious access across the lock and a portable steam engine, presumably to operate pumping equipment to manage water levels in the canal, can be seen on the far right. The upper lock-keeper's cottage is just visible in the far left background.

Presumably due to the urgings of their Engineer, Gordon Thomas, the GJCC initially focussed its attention on dealing with the bottleneck at Foxton. It was only after the development of the inclined plane at Foxton was well under way, that the company's attention turned to the Watford Locks.

By the end of 1894, the seven narrow locks at Watford were, by all accounts, in a very poor state of repair. An un-named contemporary writer described the condition of the locks as follows:

> *'Such a tumble-up set-out I never did see in all my born days. To take 20 tons … through eleven creaky old lock gates and rotten paddles was a work not to be laughed at.'*
> *Extract from* Foxton Locks and the Grand Junction Canal Co. *by Dave Goodwin*

Goodwin goes on to say that *'some of the lock walls had bulged so badly that boats had to use block and tackle to get through.'*

In December 1895, Thomas Millner, the Manager of the Northern District of the Grand Junction Canal, had prepared a plan for the replacement of the seven narrow locks at Watford by a flight of three wide locks, each with a rise of 18 feet. Three months later, he submitted another plan, this time for a flight of four locks, each with a rise of about 14 feet. It would seem, however, that the GJCC had its hands full enough already, with the extensive canal improvement works and the preparations for the inclined plane at Foxton, with the consequence that further consideration of improvement works at Watford was deferred.

As stated in an earlier chapter on the development of the inclined plane at Foxton, Hunter & English, a firm of steelwork fabricators, were invited to witness the Bulbourne model trials on 13th November 1896. The Minute Book reveals that, soon after the trials, Hunter & English were invited to submit a competitive tender for the supply of the mechanical and structural components for the Foxton Inclined Plane and to prepare an estimate of cost for a similar inclined plane at Watford. Their estimate was considered by the GJCC on 10th March 1897. In July of the same year, the GJCC took the decision to purchase the necessary land for inclined planes both at Foxton and Watford Locks, and Gordon Thomas was instructed to prepare comparative estimates of the total cost of building and operating an inclined plane at Watford, presumably as opposed to rebuilding the locks.

The Minute Book of the GJCC records, on 13th October 1897, that:

> *'The Chairman reported that Mess'rs Hunter & English had agreed to accept a fee of £105 for their report and professional services in connection with the proposed Canal Lift at Watford.'*

There appears to have been little or no further development regarding the Watford Locks until 11th October 1899, when the Minute Book records that consideration was being given to a letter from Fellows, Morton & Clayton. The letter reminded the canal company of the desirability of

Refurbishment of the locks at Watford, 1901-2.
COURTESY THE FOXTON INCLINED PLANE TRUST
The refurbishment work to the staircase of four locks nearing completion, with the brickwork chamber walls successfully reconstructed and the new lock gates installed; the balance arms are temporarily supported by cross beams across the lock chambers.

also increasing the capacity of the locks at Watford to cater for wide barges. As a consequence, the GJCC instructed their Engineer, Gordon Thomas, to prepare two sets of plans and estimates of costs; the first, for the replacement of the existing locks by a flight of wide locks, possibly based on one of Millner's proposals; the second, for the construction of a mechanical lift, presumably an inclined plane similar to that at Foxton, most likely making use of the earlier estimate from Hunter & English.

However, within four months and several reports later from its Engineer, the GJCC had moved away from what might appear to have been the obvious option, that of another inclined plane, and had opted for widening the existing locks. As recorded in the following extract from the Minutes for 14th February 1900:

Refurbishment of the locks at Watford, 1901-2.
COURTESY THE FOXTON INCLINED PLANE TRUST
Ongoing work to one of the locks, with the partial dismantling of the chamber walls and horizontal strutting to stabilise the exposed earth faces. A temporary barrow bridge is in the foreground and heavy lifting frames can be seen in the background. Once fully dismantled, the chamber walls were rebuilt and then faced with brindle bricks, whilst granite stone was used for the coping.

> *'In accordance with the Minute of the Board of the 11th October last the Engineer has prepared plans and estimates for six schemes for the improvement of the lockage system at Watford.*
>
> *We have given the matter very careful consideration at three meetings and are unanimously of the opinion that the scheme for the widening of the existing locks should be adopted and instructions given to the Engineer to proceed with this work forthwith.*
>
> *This improvement can be effected without the purchase of land but periodical stoppages of two or three weeks will be necessary for the purposes of constructing the several works. It is not anticipated, however, that any great inconvenience will be caused to traders and proper notices will be given of such stoppages.*
>
> *The cost of the work is estimated to be £17,000 being £7,206 less than the lower estimate of the other schemes and the working expenses £50 per annum as against much higher figures in other cases.*
>
> *Should any large increases in the traffic arise by reason of completion of the widening it may become necessary to make provisions for pumping back a portion of the lockage waters but this would not entail a heavy expenditure, or any alteration in the projected works.*
>
> *It was proposed by Mr Bouverie, seconded by Mr Burnett and resolved unanimously that the scheme for the widening of the existing locks be adopted and that the Engineer be instructed to proceed at once with the work and order the necessary materials.'*

I have chosen to include such a large extract from the Minute Book in order to help shed more light on the reason why the GJCC chose to proceed with the widening of the Watford Locks, as opposed to five other options. It should be noted that, at the time of the Board meeting, the construction of the inclined plane at Foxton was well advanced. Several interesting points can be made with reference to the Board's decision to widen the existing locks at Watford, as follows:

• It is self-evident that, as for the decision to construct the Foxton Inclined Plane taken in November 1897, the GJCC's motivation for carrying out improvement works at Watford Locks was to provide a continuous route between the East Midlands and London suitable for wide barges. The Grand Junction Canal, to the south of Watford to London, had broad locks only, as had the Leicestershire & Northamptonshire Union Canal, the Leicester Navigation, the Loughborough Navigation and the Erewash Canal to the north of Foxton. So with the imminent completion of the inclined plane at Foxton, the only remaining narrow locks on the route would be at Watford

This is a view looking downstream from the bottom lock (Lock 1). A newly built brick wing wall can be seen in the left foreground, whilst workmen with wheelbarrows cross the drained down canal beyond by means of what appears to be a rather makeshift bridge constructed from wooden scaffolding poles and planks.

A similar viewpoint to that on page 103, showing major activity on the staircase of four locks and a very untidy work site. The GJCC work boat Industrious *is in the lock chamber and temporary strutting between the chamber sides is visible over its hull. The portable steam engine can again be seen on the right of the lock, with the upper lock-keeper's cottage just visible in the far left background.*

• The decision to proceed with the option of widening of the existing locks was obviously taken as it was the least expensive. Perhaps by that time, the GJCC was beginning to have doubts about the wisdom of building the inclined plane at Foxton

• The relatively lengthy entry in the Minute Book, when compared to the more usual, blander style, gives the impression that the decision to proceed with the widening works at Watford Locks was hard fought over, perhaps with some members of the Board still supporting the original idea of another inclined plane, with others possibly having doubts about any redevelopments

Refurbishment of the locks at Watford, 1901–2. COURTESY THE FOXTON INCLINED PLANE TRUST
A close up of the work in one of the lock chambers. The original brickwork has been largely dismantled and workmen are moving surplus excavated material in stages from the bottom of the lock to ground level and then into wagons for removal. Note the temporary strutting to support the sides of the excavation and what appears to be a gas lamp in the top left of the picture.

The validity of the last point may be borne out by the fact that, within just one month of the decision to proceed, the Board was expressing doubts about the advisability of continuing with the widening works at Watford Locks. Although any decision to stop the works was not taken at the time, it was decided that the costs should be more carefully monitored with reports being given to the Board on a fortnightly basis. (According to Charles Hadfield in *The Canals of the East Midlands*, Gordon Thomas may have recommended against the building of a second inclined plane at Watford even before the inclined plane at Foxton was working, although given his commitment to the project this seem unlikely).

Only four weeks after that, on 11th April 1900, the GJCC decided to delay the improvement works at Watford until such time as the inclined plane at Foxton was working satisfactorily. At that stage, seemingly costs of only £680 or so had been incurred at Watford.

By October 1900, doubts were being expressed by the Board about proceeding further with the lock widening at Watford. It was suggested that any materials left over if the works were to be aborted could be used on general canal work elsewhere on the system. Although not minuted, it would appear that soon after the GJCC finally abandoned the proposed widening works at Watford, effectively bringing to a close the many years of optimistic expansion by the company. All that remained to be done was to refurbish the dilapidated narrow locks.

The works on the narrow locks were carried out between November 1901 and January 1902, necessitating the closure of the canal to through traffic. It was also necessary to close the canal for a few days in early February, probably for finishing off works. The improvements were carried out by the GJCC workforce from the Northern District, presumably under the direction of Thomas Millner, with up to 160 men working on the locks at the busiest period. Often, the work continued on into night-time, with the need to use acetylene lamps. Rather surprisingly, given the working conditions evident in some of the photographs, only one serious accident occurred, with one of the workmen falling into Lock No. 2 and subsequently having to take fourteen weeks off work to recover.

A typewritten note, thought to have been copied from an original GJCC document and available from the Foxton Inclined Plane Trust, summarises the principal elements of the works in the following way:

'Drove two cross stanks at Locks 2 and 7. Laying temporary tramway barrow roads stagings

Refurbishment of the locks at Watford, 1901-2. COURTESY THE FOXTON INCLINED PLANE TRUST
A view of the bridge and bottom lock (Lock 1) at Watford, with the lockkeeper's cottage on the left. It seems likely that this photograph was taken close to the completion of the refurbishment works, although the canal is still drained down. The brick wing walls appear to have been rebuilt and what could be the lifting frames are stacked on the ground to the left of the bridge. Note the planks leaning against the abutments of the bridge, possibly the stoplogs, and the new building being constructed in front of the lower lock-keeper's cottage.

and water supply and fixing mortar mill and Portable Engine.

Cutting down and recasing seven locks and facing same in brindle bricks and coping in granite.

Putting in four pair lower gates and sills etc. complete also three top gates etc. complete. Twenty two new paddle frames and paddles. Repairing the paddle holes and culverts. Rebuilding the Reservoir head walls and building dry brick walls in Reservoirs. Fixed six side paddles to Reservoirs. Refitting and repairing one top, three pair lower gates and fixing new balances and gear to old gates. Rebuilding four lock tails, heads and wings at Locks 2, 3 and 7. Building five new waste weirs to Reservoirs. New 5ft 0in gauge in Watford feeder. Rebuilding two culvert fronts Watford feeder at Lock No. 1. Building bridle Road Bridge at Lock No. 1. Making and fixing six timber footbridges for Locks 2, 3, 4, 5, 6 and 7. New waste weir and waterway wall offside Locks 1 and 2. Excavating mud from five Reservoirs and three pounds and trimming and repairing the banks when mud had settled. Raising the towing path from 1ft 0in to 4ft 0in.'

The overall cost of the refurbishment works was nominally £5,545, with the cost of labour being £2,846 and materials £2,699, which excluded the costs of the new lock gates and paddles from the Bulbourne Depot.

★ ★ ★ ★ ★

The GJCC's assertive policy against the increasing threat of the railways had all started so optimistically back in 1894, with the acquisition of the Leicestershire & Northamptonshire Union and the Grand Union canals. The years that followed saw these two canals being the subject of major and costly improvement works, which included extensive dredging and reviewing the options to deal with the restrictions to wide traffic posed by the narrow locks at Watford and Foxton. The major improvement works reached their apogee in 1898, with the commencement of the construction of the Foxton Inclined Plane. In parallel with all this, the GJCC was in detailed negotiations over several years with the owners of the Leicester Navigation, the Loughborough Navigation and the Erewash Canal, initially to achieve enhanced joint working for through traffic and eventually with the objective of purchasing the three canals, which would then have given the Company complete control of the most direct canal route between the East Midlands and London.

So what had changed by 1901? What had caused the GJCC to abandon its long held plans to achieve a fast and effective through route for 50-ton barges between the East Midlands and London? The answer to this question was to some extent provided, some five years later, by Gordon Thomas, whilst giving evidence to the Royal Commission into Canals & Inland Navigations in the United Kingdom on 6th November 1906. He advised the Commission that, after purchasing the Leicestershire & Northamptonshire Union and the Grand Union canals in 1894, the traffic on the Leicester Line had not picked up as had been hoped, a fact that he put down to the very poor condition of the Cromford, Erewash and Nutbrook canals that link the coalfields to the rest of the canal system. He claimed that the Cromford Canal was almost derelict, to the extent that fully laden narrowboats were unable to travel along it. He went on to advise that this canal was in the ownership of the Midland Railway Company; a fact from which it can be assumed that railway companies in general had little motivation to spend money on improving their newly purchased waterways.

So, in summary, it seems that in choosing not to proceed with the widening of the narrow locks at Watford, the GJCC had finally accepted the inevitable fact that the railways, whether by fair means or foul, were destined to take over from the canals as the dominant form of transport in Britain. This is borne out by the responses given by Gordon Thomas to a series of questions from the Royal Commission:

'19267. What, in your opinion, has been the effect of legislation in allowing railway companies to purchase and control so many canals? – [Gordon Thomas replied] We think that it has effectively prevented any possibility of developing canals by private enterprise.
19268. Especially as regards through traffic? – [GT] Especially as regards through traffic.
19269. Has the through traffic gradually declined since certain links forming portions of through routes fell into the hands of the railway companies? – [GT] Yes.'

Sources For This Chapter

The minutes of the Committee of the Grand Junction Canal Company, available at the National Archives, Kew
The Canals of the East Midlands, Charles Hadfield, David & Charles, 1966
Foxton: Locks and Barge Lift, by Peter Gardner & Frank Foden, Leicestershire County Planning Dept in association with the Leicestershire branch of the Council for the Protection of Rural England, 2nd ed. 1979
Foxton Locks and Inclined Plane – A Detailed History, compiled by members of the Foxton Inclined Plane Trust and published by Department of Planning & Transportation, Leicestershire County Council, circa 1986
'Minutes of Evidence given to the Royal Commission on the Canals & Inland Navigations of the United Kingdom', available at the National Archives, Kew; evidence given by Gordon Thomas on 6th November 1906

ABOVE: Refurbishment of the locks at Watford, 1901-2. COURTESY THE FOXTON INCLINED PLANE TRUST The nearly completed works on Lock 2, showing rebuilt brickwork walls and steps. Note the surplus timber planking on the left which is yet to be cleared away and the lock gate balance arms that are painted entirely white, presumably in anticipation of night-time usage of the locks.

BELOW: The pound between Lock 1 and Lock 2, circa 1908. NEIL PARKHOUSE COLLECTION The lower lock-keeper's cottage alongside the bottom lock is just visible on the extreme left and the towpath is on the right.

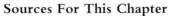

A view of Foxton circa 1910, showing both the flight of locks and the inclined plane. NEIL PARKHOUSE COLLECTION
Despite the 'old and new' caption, it is likely that this postcard view shows the locks near the completion of their refurbishment in 1910, whilst the inclined plane was just months away from the end of its working life. There is a caisson at the top of the plane and note the three shovels lying at the bottom of the bank on the left.

CHAPTER 8
1900 TO 1910
THE OPERATION OF THE FOXTON INCLINED PLANE

'In 1900 a lift was opened at Foxton with the object of superseding the staircase of locks at that place which has already been described. The general principle of the Foxton Lift was the same as the Anderton, but in this case each caisson moved sideways on sixteen wheels and eight rails down an inclined plane 307ft long representing a vertical rise of 75 ft, steam providing the motive power. Trouble was experienced with the rails which subsided owing to the great weight of the caissons, while the volume of traffic did not justify keeping a boiler constantly in steam and an engine man in attendance. Consequently the lift was abandoned after only a few years' of working.'
Extract from The Inland Waterways of England *by L.T.C. Rolt*

The Foxton Inclined Plane looking up the incline from the lower canal basin, circa 1901. COURTESY THE WATERWAYS TRUST *The nearest caisson appears to be descending and is about to enter the water in the lower canal basin. It seems to contain a single working narrowboat with a crew of two, both of whom are looking towards the camera. Note the lift attendant's control cabin in the middle foreground and the emergency stop-logs to the right of it, housed under a canopy with weather-board roof.*

This extract by the famous author and 20th century canal pioneer neatly summarises the short working life of the Foxton Inclined Plane, which was formally opened to traffic on 10th July 1900 and was closed just ten years or so later. Rolt's reference to subsidence seems to refer to the reported failure of the rail fixings under the weight of the caissons.

In this chapter, I will attempt to describe the operation of the Foxton Inclined Plane and any significant events that occurred during its relatively short working life. Unfortunately, for those

readers who were hoping to find out more about the day-to-day operation of the inclined plane, for whatever reason, there is a dearth of documented information available, whether from the Minute Books of the Grand Junction Canal Company (GJCC) or other sources.

★ ★ ★ ★ ★

The Foxton Inclined Plane and its benefits were expounded by Gordon Thomas, its lead designer and the Engineer to the GJCC, in a paper written after one year of operation and entitled 'Surmounting of Great Ascents, the 'Thomas' Canal Barge Lift'. This was compiled for presentation at the 9th International Navigation Congress at Dusseldorf in Germany, in 1902. Below is a short extract from the paper, which gives details of the operating times for the inclined plane, its capacity to transfer laden boats and the cost of its operation:

> *'The time occupied for the operation of passing two boats in each direction is twelve minutes, as compared with one hour and fifteen minutes, the time taken in passing a single boat, or one hour and twenty minutes for a pair of boats in either direction, via the existing locks.*
>
> *The Lift is capable of passing from 190 to 200 ordinary canal boats in 12 hours of continuous working, and the whole plant can be worked by three men.*
>
> *With regard to the cost of working, the duty, taking 15 minutes intervals between the operations, is 6,000 tons per day of 12 hours, and the cost of dealing with this tonnage, based on the actual experience of the past twelve months is about £1. 4. 6 per day, including coal, stores and labour, which is equivalent to about one twentieth of a penny per ton.'*

Approximately four years later, Gordon Thomas wrote a similar paper on the same subject, entitled 'The 'Thomas' Lift Constructed at Foxton, Leicestershire, by The Grand Junction Canal Company'. This was possibly written for presentation to the Royal Commission on Canals & Inland Waterways, at which Thomas gave evidence on four separate occasions, firstly in November 1906 and subsequently in May, June and July 1908 (see Chapter 9). The following extract, which is very similar to the one above, also gives details of the operating times for the inclined plane, its capacity to transfer laden boats and the cost of operation:

> *'The time occupied in passing one or four boats simultaneously by this Lift is eight minutes, as against one hour taken by the passage of a single boat by means of the ten narrow locks formerly in use.*

The capacity of the Lift, allowing twelve minutes for each operation, and passing 70 tons in both directions, is 8,400 tons per twelve hours, or, approximately, 2,500,000 tons per annum of 300 working days.

The cost of dealing with this tonnage, based on the experience of the last six years, inclusive of coal, oil, stores and labour, would be .05d. or one twentieth of a penny per ton. The whole of the plant is operated by three men.'

The ratings for the inclined plane from the above extracts make impressive reading, especially when comparisons are made to the use of the old locks. On the assumption that these figures, or at least figures similar to these, had been available as predictions in 1897, then it is not surprising that the GJCC chose to proceed with the construction of the Foxton Inclined Plane. The statements by Gordon Thomas do not appear to have been just optimistic predictions but were seemingly based upon actual records, the first extract relating to just the first year of operation, whilst the second covered some six years of working. On these

LEFT: A group photograph thought to be at Foxton Bottom Lock, most likely of the Board of the GJCC, circa 1905. COURTESY THE FOXTON INCLINED PLANE TRUST Gordon Thomas is standing in the middle wearing the light coloured jacket, with cousin Barnabas Thomas on his right and Thomas Holt to his left.

BELOW: Part of what is believed to be the opening ceremony on 10th July 1900. COURTESY THE FOXTON INCLINED PLANE TRUST A posed photograph with everyone present, including the boat crews in traditional clothing, looking at the camera. The two horse-drawn narrowboats going into the right-hand caisson, prior to descending, are Marsworth and Langley belonging to Fellows, Morton & Clayton. Note the Union Jack flying from a temporary pole mounted on the gantry of the guillotine gate of the left hand aqueduct. Gordon Thomas appears to be standing on the far right of the onlookers, the others most likely being GJCC Board members.

Part of what is believed to be the opening ceremony on 10th July 1900. COURTESY THE FOXTON INCLINED PLANE TRUST
The caissons, each carrying two narrowboats, are crossing mid-way on the inclined plane.

facts alone, it would have appeared that the plane had a bright and potentially long future.

The similarity of structure of the two extracts gives the impression that the later one was an updating of the earlier. On this basis, it is of interest to make comparisons between the two, to see the extent that the greater period of operation of the inclined plane caused Gordon Thomas to alter his findings. For example:

• Both papers use the phrase '*the time occupied in passing*', which either could refer to just the time of travel of the caissons up and down the inclined plane, or the whole time taken, including loading and unloading the boats from the caissons. On the basis that the stated speed of travel of the caissons was 0.75 feet per second and the length of the plane was

Part of what is believed to be the opening ceremony on 10th July 1900. COURTESY THE FOXTON INCLINED PLANE TRUST
The two narrowboats coming out of the left-hand caisson have just ascended the inclined plane.

A view of the lower canal basin, looking southwards, soon after the opening of the inclined plane, circa 1901. COURTESY THE FOXTON INCLINED PLANE TRUST
Two narrowboat and butty pairs, one unladen and one fully laden (the latter already inside the right hand caisson) await their turn to ascend the incline. The incline and the surrounding earthworks all still look fresh and new, so this picture cannot have been taken long after opening.

nominally 300 feet, it seems most likely that the times quoted relate to just the time of travel. Whichever applies, however, it is of interest to note that, over the intervening four year period, the time taken for this procedure was reportedly reduced from 12 minutes to 8 minutes, which possibly reflects the increased expertise of the lift attendants and engineer
• The papers agree that the inclined plane is operated by just three men, although other authors have referred to a minimum of four operators being needed. The three men, presumably two lift attendants and an engineer, would have been kept very busy in periods of high volumes of traffic. It seems reasonable to assume that any routine maintenance and minor repairs would have been carried out by other personnel
• When it came to establishing the cost of working the inclined plane, Gordon Thomas again quotes a noticeably shorter time between operations after five years of operation – just 12 minutes – than he did for the same operation after just one year of operation – 15 minutes. Again, this possibly reflects the increased expertise of the operators

A 'mud hopper' at the top of the inclined plane, circa 1905. COURTESY THE FOXTON INCLINED PLANE TRUST
Two people seem to be manhandling a plank over the aqueduct but the purpose is unclear. Whatever it is, it seems to be generating a lot of interest. The guillotine gate on the right hand aqueduct is partially raised, suggesting that a boat has just gone into the caisson or is about to come out.

• The theoretical capacity of the inclined plane over a 12 hour day, based on the above two operating times, increased over the five year period between the two papers by 2,400 tons
• Rather oddly, given the above change in theoretical capacities, the quoted cost of operating the inclined plane remained unchanged; that is 'one-twentieth of a penny per ton'. One might have expected the cost per ton to have reduced in response to the increased tonnage capacity after six years of operation (a simple calculation suggests that the operating cost should have reduced to nearly one thirtieth of a penny per ton). It is possible, however, that the increased cost of coal, spare

parts and labour had effectively cancelled out the financial benefits of more efficient working of the inclined plane.

Also, at first sight, it might seem rather strange that, in both papers, Thomas refers to the high theoretical annual tonnages rather than the actual tonnages, based on either one or six years operation. Reference to historical records, however, reveals that the actual annual tonnage passed through the inclined plane in 1906 amounted to just 36,300 tons, well below the capacity quoted in the 1906 paper of 2,500,000 tons. The decision by Gordon Thomas to refer to the theoretical, rather than the actual, capacities in the 1906 paper would make sense if it had been written with the intention of extolling the virtues of the inclined plane, presumably to the Royal Commission on Canals & Inland Waterways.

★ ★ ★ ★ ★

So much for the theory, now for the reality of the situation. The Foxton Inclined Plane was formally opened to traffic on 10th July 1900. Although contemporary records are unavailable, it would not be unreasonable to assume that, as for other similar events on the canals, formal celebrations were held to mark the opening. These would most likely have included a flotilla of boats arriving at the top of the inclined plane, with the first boat, perhaps the GJCC steam tug *Gadfly*, carrying local dignitaries, together with GJCC Board members and Gordon Thomas. The second boat may well have contained a brass band to provide appropriate music for the occasion, whilst subsequent boats may have been carrying other guests. Laden working boats, possibly owned by Fellows, Morton & Clayton, would most probably have been part of the flotilla. With much pomp and ceremony, the flotilla would then possibly have descended the inclined plane, with the lead boats most likely carrying the invited guests on to Market Harborough for a celebratory meal and formal speeches at one of the hotels in the town.

★ ★ ★ ★ ★

With respect to the day-to-day operation of Foxton Inclined Plane, it seems most likely that, for various reasons, it was the intention of the GJCC to operate it only during daylight hours. This conclusion is based upon the repeated reference to twelve hours of operation in the extracts earlier in this chapter from Thomas' two papers. In reality, however, it is likely that the inclined plane was operated for more than twelve hours a day in the summer months and less than 12 hours a day during the winter. The conjecture about daytime working is consistent with the poor quality paraffin lamps that were provided in the buildings of the inclined plane, the lack of any electrical lighting to the site in general and the use of horse-drawn boats only at the turn of the century, which also only tended to work during the daytime.

It is of interest that, once night-time traffic through Foxton became necessary following the introduction of fly-boats drawn by steam tugs, around 1908, the GJCC elected to refurbish the locks rather than adopting night operation of the inclined plane. Presumably, this decision would have been driven almost entirely by cost; apart from the initial cost of refurbishing the locks, there were little or no running costs to the GJCC, as the boat crews carried out the locking. Conversely, night-time operation of the inclined plane would generally have incurred the canal company higher costs for coal to operate the steam engine and for lighting, as well as employing the lift attendants and engineer.

On the basis of daytime working, it seems reasonable to assume that, at the end of each day, the fire in the boilers would have been 'banked up' by the engineer, with the intention of keeping them alight overnight. By this means, the time taken to get the engine in steam the next morning and the inclined plane back in operation would have been minimised.

Foxton Locks circa 1905.
COURTESY THE FOXTON
INCLINED PLANE TRUST
This photograph seems to show the locks out of operation, with the lock gates open. It was most probably taken during the heyday of the inclined plane, when the plan was to abandon the locks.

The typical operation of the inclined plane after steaming-up would have been as described in the step-by-step process set out below, for which the starting position has been taken as follows:

• One caisson at the top of the plane linked up to the corresponding aqueduct, with the gate on the aqueduct and that on the caisson both fully raised. Leakage is prevented at the interface between the caisson and aqueduct by means of the hydraulic rams at the other end of the caisson that jack it longitudinally against the sealing face on the aqueduct
• The other caisson is at the bottom of the plane immersed in the lower canal basin, with the gate leading to the canal fully open
• The presence of three operatives on site, as stated by Gordon Thomas in his 1902 paper. Presumably, one would be working in the boiler house, with a lift attendant at the top of the plane and another at the bottom

Step 1 – Under this starting condition, canal boats were able to enter unimpeded into the caissons, whether from the lower canal basin or the upper canal arm. The boats would then have been tied up by the boatmen to bollards along the edges of the caissons, in readiness for when they started moving.
Step 2 – With the boats safely on board, the lift attendants would then lower the three gates, one on the lower caisson, one on the upper caisson and the corresponding one on

A problem circa 1905, which
was not recorded in the GJCC
Minute Book. COURTESY THE
WATERWAYS TRUST
The plinth of one of the main
pulleys for the hauling ropes
at the top of the inclined plane
has shattered, with the large
fragment of the casting that
has broken away to the left of
the picture. Thomas Holt, the
Area Engineer for the Leicester
Section, is squatting behind the
damaged pulley. The winding
house is in the left background
and one of the aqueducts with
its guillotine gate is in the right
background.

the aqueduct. This was achieved by means of levers on the fixed stanchions in the control
cabins, which controlled the operation of the 'jiggers'. Again from his control cabin, the
upper lift attendant would also release the pressure from the sealing face between the upper
caisson and the aqueduct by relaxation of the hydraulic rams.

Step 3 – The lift attendants would then disconnect the flexible pipework from the fixed
stanchions, in their respective control cabins, which linked the 'jiggers' for the caisson gates
with the hydraulic accumulator in the boiler room. Subsequently, the lift attendant at the
bottom would inform his colleague at the upper level, by means of a telegraph system, that
the lower caisson was ready to be moved.

Step 4 – The upper lift attendant would then walk across into the winding house to operate
the engine, thereby setting the hauling drum in motion, which in turn would instigate the
downward movement of the upper caisson simultaneously with the upward movement of
the lower caisson. Presumably, a gradual acceleration of the caissons from standstill up to
the normal running speed of nominally 0.75 feet per second would have been achieved by
means of a regulator.

Step 5 – When the caissons reached the end of their travel, they would have been brought
to a halt by the upper lift attendant, still in the winding house. Again, it is assumed that a
regulator would have been used so as to bring the caissons to a smooth stop. The upper lift
attendant would know when to begin deceleration, by observing the upper caisson from
his position in the winding house and by means of a reference mark on the winding drum.
The upper caisson would have been prevented from being over-driven by wooden stops
on the rails, whilst the lower caisson would come to rest against the walls in the lower canal
basin. (The procedure for decelerating and stopping the caissons might have been made
easier for the upper lift attendant by the use of a piece of brightly coloured cloth, tied at the
appropriate position onto the hauling ropes).

Step 6 – The lower lift attendant, now in the other lower control cabin, would then
connect the flexible pipework between the hydraulic accumulator and the lower caisson. He
would then operate the 'jigger' to raise the caisson gate, thereby allowing the canal boats to
exit and continue their journeys either northwards towards Leicester or eastwards to Market
Harborough. In parallel with this, the upper lift attendant would make his way to the other
upper control cabin, from where he would connect the pipework between the accumulator

VIEW OF LOW WATER LEVEL FOXTON CANAL LIFTS

Maintenance of the caissons, 1905. COURTESY THE FOXTON INCLINED PLANE TRUST
It would appear that replacement axles and wheels are being fitted to the caisson. In 1901, the GJCC took the precaution of agreeing the purchase of a spare axle and wheel set from J.&H. Gwynne, at a cost of £60. Other maintenance jobs are seemingly being carried out at the same time, including the replacement of the seals to the guillotine gate of the caisson.

and the upper caisson. He would then operate the hydraulic rams forcing the caisson onto the sealing face of the adjacent aqueduct making a water-tight seal. The connection of the wheels with the axles was designed so as to allow small but sufficient movement of the caisson longitudinally across the plane. Finally, the upper lift attendant would then operate the gate 'jiggers' to raise the gates on the caisson and aqueduct, allowing any canal boats to continue their journey southwards towards Watford. A safety mechanism prevented the caisson gates from being raised prior to the water-tight seal between the caisson and aqueduct having been made. The whole process could then be started over again.

According to Gordon Thomas, the time taken for the whole operation from loading to unloading was just 12 minutes, with nominally 8 minutes travelling time.

★ ★ ★ ★ ★

Within a month of opening, most likely in recognition of his hard work and outstanding achievements, the GJCC authorised Gordon Thomas to attend the 8th International Congress of Navigation in Paris, where, no doubt, there was much talk of the new inclined plane in England. It is likely that, during his time in Paris, he was persuaded to write a paper on the Foxton Inclined Plane, also referred to as the 'Thomas Lift'. This paper, already referred to above, was subsequently presented by Thomas at the 9th International Congress, which was held in Dusseldorf, Germany.

According to Charles Hadfield in *The Canals of the East Midlands*, the GJCC wrote to Fellows, Morton & Clayton in August 1900, to express their concern about the traffic on

The inclined plane viewed from below, circa 1905. COURTESY THE WATERWAYS TRUST One of the caissons is making a descent in the background laden with boats, whilst Bulbourne, a GJCC working boat, carrying a portable steam engine mounted on boards positioned across the hold, is moored up in the foreground in the lower canal basin.

A contemporary postcard view of the Foxton Inclined Plane from the Upper Canal Arm, circa 1903. COURTESY THE WATERWAYS TRUST The winding house, the accumulator house and the chimney are are on the left and the aqueducts and a caisson are on the right. It appears that a barge is being moved out the right caisson whilst the gates are raised.

the Leicester Line, advising that, despite their hopes, '*the through trade, especially of Coal, had decreased considerably*'. It should be noted that it was with the persistent urgings and assurances of increased traffic from the carriers that the GJCC had decided that the two bottlenecks posed by the flights of narrow locks at Foxton and Watford should be removed. Unfortunately, the historical records are not available to show this decline in through traffic in the years leading up to the opening of the Foxton Inclined Plane.

On 10th October 1900, the GJCC Minute Book records that the inclined plane had been working satisfactorily and states that, in recognition of this, a further payment of £2,119

The bottom locks at Foxton, circa 1905. COURTESY THE WATERWAYS TRUST
The locks are clearly in a state of neglect, presumably after the diversion of all the traffic through the inclined plane. All the paddles appear to be raised, suggesting that the water in the locks has been drained down.

10s 0d had been made to J. & H. Gwynne for the supply and erection of the steelwork and mechanical components of it.

By the beginning of 1901, the GJCC were taking advantage of the presence of the inclined plane to carry out repairs to the flight of locks at Foxton, which were presumably in poor condition. The Minute Book for 27th March 1901 records that Gordon Thomas had advised that the cost of these works, excluding the works to the side ponds, would not exceed £500. Unfortunately, no other details of the repair works are available.

In November of the same year, Barnabas Thomas, who had been the Resident Engineer on site for the inclined plane works, was formally appointed as an employee of the GJCC within the Engineer's Department, working for his cousin, Gordon Thomas.

That same winter, there was something of a crisis due to a lack of water in the summit section of the Grand Union Canal, with water levels being 2 feet 9 inches below normal. As a result, this part of the canal had to be closed to traffic for several weeks and, soon after, the GJCC decided to carry out urgent repairs to the leaky narrow locks at Watford. It was around this time that the Company called a halt to the works to widen the narrow locks at Watford and effectively abandoned their long-term goal of opening up the whole of the route between the East Midlands and London to barge traffic.

After that, the Minute Books make only passing reference to the operation of the inclined plane. For example, it is recorded that, in June 1905, the GJCC purchased a spare axle and set of wheels for the inclined plane from J. & H. Gwynne at a cost of £60. The requirement for J.&H. Gwynne to make these items available for future purchase had been a condition of the final payment in their contract, in February 1901.

Although not recorded in the Minute Books but possibly as referred to in the extract from *The Inland Waterways of England* by L.T.C. Rolt at the start of this chapter, problems were encountered with the rails on the inclined plane. By all accounts, the weight of the caissons caused localised flexing of the rails under the wheels, which, in time, led to the failure of the coach screws that had been used to fix the rails onto the timber sleepers. The ensuing repairs necessitated the inclined plane being taken out of operation for several days at a time. Some,

An inspection boat on the inclined plane, circa 1907. This sequence of six photographs, probably taken by Thomas Millner, is thought to be either a routine inspection of the Grand Union Canal by the Board of the GJCC or possibly the inspection by the Royal Commission into the Canals and Inland Navigations of the United Kingdom, on 26th July 1907. If the latter, then the boat used was Blisworth, *a GJCC working narrowboat which had been especially modified for the purpose.*

The photographs have been put together in a sequence that suggests that the inspection boat first ascended the inclined plane and then at some stage went back down again. It could, of course, have been the other way around. The bearded gentleman in a bowler hat is Thomas Holt. Gordon Thomas would almost certainly have been in attendance but has not been identified in the pictures.

TOP: **The inspection boat and caisson in the lower canal arm waiting to ascend the inclined plane.** COURTESY THE WATERWAYS TRUST *The inspection party are all seated in the horse-drawn boat, with crew members at the tiller and the bow.*

CENTRE: **The boat about to exit the left hand caisson at the top of the plane.** COURTESY THE FOXTON INCLINED PLANE TRUST *The raised umbrella on the boat suggests that it is raining. A uniformed lift attendant is on the right of the group on the aqueduct, whilst Thomas Holt is on the left of the group. The other man on the aqueduct seems to be a boat crew member and appears to be coiling up the bow-rope.*

BOTTOM: **The inspection boat coming out of the caisson.** COURTESY THE FOXTON INCLINED PLANE TRUST *In the foreground, the crew member throws the bow-rope over the aqueduct to the waiting lift attendant on the other side. Close examination reveals that a rope is simultaneously being thrown from the stern of the boat, to his colleague. Perhaps the intention is to pull the boat across the aqueduct to get past a moored barge waiting to enter. There seems to be a third uniformed lift attendant present, which suggests that the members of the inspection team were of some importance.*

The inspection team and boat part way down the inclined plane. COURTESY THE WATERWAYS TRUST
It is interesting to note that, in the first three photographs, with the boat having come up the plane, there may be up to 15 members in the inspection party, whilst in the last three photographs, the team seems to have been reduced to just 5 or 6 strong. This rather suggests that the ascent and descent may have been several hours apart and hence part of a longer inspection trip.

The inspection boat in the caisson, which is entering the lower canal basin. COURTESY THE FOXTON INCLINED PLANE TRUST
There is a horse and boatman in the right background on the far towpath, presumably waiting for the narrowboat behind the caisson to go up the inclined plane. There also appears to be another horse and boatman on the towpath in front of the bridge abutment, presumably waiting for the inspection boat. A crowd of onlookers are watching from the bridge in the background.

The inspection boat exiting the caisson into the lower canal basin. COURTESY THE WATERWAYS TRUST
Note that the other narrowboat, behind, is about to enter the caisson, whilst a horse waits for one or other of the boats on the far towpath. The crew member at the stern has pushed the tiller hard left.

A view of the top lock looking down the Foxton flight, with the boiler house and winding house at the top of the inclined plane on the right, circa 1907. COURTESY THE FOXTON INCLINED PLANE TRUST
Note this was taken before the refurbishment of the locks, for nighttime working, commenced in 1908. It is interesting to contrast this picture with the similar one opposite, taken after the refurbishment

Foxton Locks.

if not all, of the original softwood sleepers were replaced by hardwood, whilst the coach screws were replaced by bolts that passed right through the sleepers.

In November 1908, the Minute Book recorded the decision to fully reinstate the locks at Foxton as follows:

A view of the top locks at Foxton, circa 1908. COURTESY THE WATERWAYS TRUST
Again, the locks are clearly in a state of neglect but the jib of a crane is visible on the horizon between the two lock cottages, indicating that some works are under way.

'*It has been considered desirable with a view to passing traffic at night when the Lift is not in operation to reinstate the Foxton Locks at a cost of about £1,000, which includes the cleaning out of the side ponds etc ...*'

One can read into this that, since the opening of the inclined plane, the locks at Foxton

FOXON. LOCKS.

Foxton Locks, with the winding house, boiler house and chimney of the inclined plane on the right, circa 1910. COURTESY THE FOXTON INCLINED PLANE TRUST

The locks soon after their refurbishment and in readiness for night-time working, although this did not commence until a year or so after the closure of the inclined plane to traffic in November 1910. The all white balance beams are thought to have been painted thus to make them more visible during night working. This is the only known photograph which shows the beams in this condition, so it is a matter for conjecture as to how long they remained like this. The refurbishment of the locks took two years and, by all accounts, cost significantly more than the original estimate of £1,000.

An atmospheric view of the lower canal basin, with laden narrowboats and crews waiting to ascend the inclined plane at Foxton, circa 1905. COURTESY THE FOXTON INCLINED PLANE TRUST Note that one of the caissons is clearly visible in the background and also the 1899 date on the bridge. The woman on the stern of the left hand boat has a young child on her lap and all seem quite smartly attired, the women in typical waterways dress. Neither of the names on the nearer two narrowboats are clear; that on the left is HARRO... whilst the one on the right begins with an A.

A busy scene in the lower canal basin, looking back towards the Leicestershire & Northamptonshire Union Canal, circa 1905. COURTESY THE FOXTON INCLINED PLANE TRUST
This photograph was probably taken on the same occasion as the previous picture, although a little later because some of the boats seen in the background of that view have now departed up the incline.

had been generally out of operation, with the result that, after eight years or so, they were no longer in working condition. As the inclined plane only operated during daylight hours, the most likely explanation for the reinstatement works to the locks is that the volume of craft requiring passage at night was on the increase and that the condition of the locks was becoming an issue. Perhaps, in making the decision to repair the locks, the GJCC were anticipating the eventual demise of the inclined plane. By all accounts, the repairs to the locks took two years to complete and ended up being significantly more costly than the originally allocated £1,000.

Another problem occurred with respect to the inclined plane during the cold winter of 1908-9, when the hydraulic system that was used to operate the guillotine gates on the caissons and aqueducts became frozen, resulting in the fracturing of five of the hydraulic rams, or 'jiggers'. The Minute Book on 13th January 1909 recorded the reason for the problem as follows:

'… the damage being due to an insufficient quantity of glycerine being mixed with the water used for the hydraulic circulation.'

Gordon Thomas was authorised to purchase and install two new rams, and was required to get approval from the Board if any of the other rams needed replacing. As there was no further reference to this in the Minute Book, it seems reasonable to assume that the other rams were able to be repaired. The minute concludes as follows:

'The Engineer was also instructed to censure the man in charge of the Lift for not carrying out his instruction, and that printed instructions should be posted in a conspicuous place in the Engine Room with a view to preventing a similar accident occurring in the future.'

By October 1910, the low volumes of traffic on the Leicester Section of the canal and the cost of keeping the inclined plane in operation were causing the GJCC serious concern, to the extent that they were considering temporarily closing the canal at night and taking the inclined plane out of service. Just a few weeks later, on 9th November 1910, presumably

THE NEW LIFTS FOXTON CANAL.   M.C.P.L.

A view up the inclined plane from across the lower canal basin circa 1910. COURTESY THE FOXTON INCLINED PLANE TRUST
One of the caissons is in the left foreground, partially submerged in the basin, whilst the other is at the top of the incline. Note the vegetation growth on the plane, which rather suggests a lack of general maintenance. This would support the 1910 date, with the adjacent lock flight being refurbished and brought back into operation.

with the refurbished locks by then in full working order, the final decision was made to close the inclined plane. The decision was recorded in the Minute Book as follows:

> 'The Sub-committee have given the instructions for the Lift to cease working after a fortnight's notice, and the Locks to be utilised, and with regard to keeping the section between Aylestone and Foxton open at night time, Mess'rs Fellows Morton & Co. have been informed that the Company cannot see their way to do this but will delay such closing for a reasonable period to enable them to reorganise their working arrangements …'

And so, after a little over ten years of service, presumably with the various components still in good working order, the operational life of the Foxton Inclined Plane was at an end. However, some sources suggest that the inclined plane may have been brought back into service a few times thereafter but the particular reasons for this, if it did happen, are not known.

★ ★ ★ ★ ★

It almost goes without saying that the Foxton Inclined Plane was not a commercial success. After many years of development, design and then construction, the inclined plane only remained in service for ten years, a woefully short period of time given the relatively high cost of construction. In stark contrast to this, the Anderton Boat Lift was opened for service in 1875, was refitted to electrical operation in 1908 and was only closed in 1983, giving a total operational life of over 100 years.

The reason for the demise of the Foxton Inclined Plane can be seen by examination of the annual tonnage of cargo passing through it between 1905 and 1910, and then through the locks thereafter, as set out in **Table 8.1** and the bar chart below. Unfortunately, the tonnages for the years leading up to the opening of the inclined plane and for the first four years of its operation are not available.

By reference to the figures highlighted in bold in the table, the actual annual tonnage through the Foxton Inclined Plane can be seen to be only a fraction of the theoretical capacity of 2,500,000 tons as quoted by Gordon Thomas in his 1906 paper. Based on the six year period of records available for the inclined plane, the average annual tonnage passed was nominally 35,500 tons, which would have resulted in a cost of operation closer to threepence per ton of cargo, rather than the original cost estimate of one-twentieth of a penny per ton. Making use of the actual average annual tonnage and allowing for the fact that, due to the narrow locks at Watford, it would have been almost entirely narrowboats using the inclined plane, then the average number of laden boats carried per day in a 300 day year would have been just three or four; presumably, a figure well below that which was needed to make the it financially viable. Again, contrasting this record with that of the Anderton Boat Lift, the typical annual tonnage that was conveyed by this structure during the same six year period was close to 200,000 tons.

After so much optimism, backed by major expenditure on the channel improvements to the Grand Union Canal and subsequently the construction of the Foxton Inclined Plane, what happened to the surge in traffic that was predicted by both the GJCC and Fellows, Morton & Clayton? Why was it that the GJCC's goal of completing the wide-beam inland waterway between the East Midlands and London faltered so soon after the opening of the inclined plane at Foxton?

By all accounts, the Foxton Inclined Plane was as much a technical triumph as was the Anderton Boat Lift. The historical records indicate that, for a project of such size, the inclined plane suffered only from relatively minor problems and time has revealed to us today that it is considered by many as a Victorian engineering masterpiece. The failure to generate the necessary traffic cannot, therefore, be blamed on its performance. The only explanation is the all-powerful railways that, since the middle of the 19th century, had been revolutionising transport in Britain. Unlike the Anderton Boat Lift, the Foxton Inclined Plane was part of a transport route that was competing head on with the railway companies. There was only ever going to be one winner. The GJCC had fought a long and hard battle over fifty or so years but, by the turn of the century, they were left with no choice but to bow to the inevitable. With the benefit of hindsight, it is evident that the Company made the wrong decision, just thirteen years earlier, to compete with the railways by proceeding with the construction of the Foxton Inclined Plane.

Gordon Thomas' views on the reasons for the demise of the inclined plane are recorded by Charles Hadfield (*The Canals of the East Midlands*) as follows:

'*Thomas himself, who of course had an interest in showing in his evidence before the Royal Commission that responsibility for failure lay outside the Grand Junction, blamed the bad condition of the railway-owned Cromford, and also of the Erewash, the desuetude of the Nutbrook, and the high tolls of the railway-owned Nottingham, in his evidence before the*

TABLE 8.1: TRAFFIC THROUGH FOXTON 1905-29	
DATE	TRAFFIC (TONS)
1905	33,400
1906	36,300
1907	31,400
1908	31,500
1909	39,700
1910	40,800
1911	41,500
1912	37,300
1913	36,700
1914	34,900
1915	23,500
1916	15,500
1917	16,700
1918	10,400
1919	12,900
1920	12,800
1921	8,200
1922	11,000
1923	7,600
1924	9,900
1925	12,500
1926	9,800
1927	10,000
1928	9,700
1929	7,200

The years relating to the inclined plane are given in bold

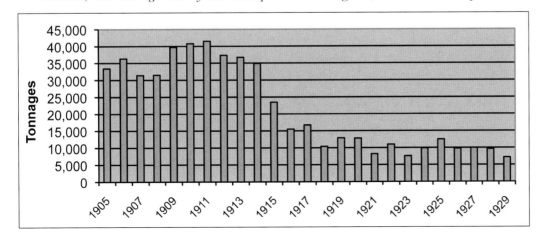

A view of Foxton from the canal, circa 1920. COURTESY THE FOXTON INCLINED PLANE TRUST
The Leicestershire & Nothamptonshire Union Canal at Foxton, with the inclined plane awaiting its fate on the skyline and the bottom of the flight of locks just visible through the bridge arch on the right. The canal continues to Market Harborough beyond the trees on the left. The caissons were parked out of sight lower down the plane.

Royal Commission. The plane itself was not at fault, for both Thomas and the company were sufficiently impressed with its usefulness to suggest to the Royal Commission in 1906 the building of others as part of a plan to enlarge several canals to 80-ton standard.'

Finally, I include a page from the October 1928 edition of the *Meccano Magazine* (right), with an article about the Foxton Inclined Plane. Although many of the details given in the text are clearly not correct, it nevertheless serves as an interesting observation from over eighty years ago on this spectacular but failed enterprise.

Sources For This Chapter

The Inland Waterways of England, L.T.C. Rolt, George Allen & Unwin Ltd, 1950

The Canals of the East Midlands, Charles Hadfield, David & Charles, 1966

'Surmounting of Great Ascents – The 'Thomas' Canal barge lift' – a professional paper written by Gordon Cale Thomas for the 9th International Navigation Congress in Dusseldorf, circa 1902

'The 'Thomas' Lift constructed at Foxton, Leicestershire by the Grand Junction Canal Company', a paper written by Gordon Cale Thomas circa 1904

Foxton: Locks and Barge Lift, by Peter Gardner & Frank Foden, Leicestershire County Planning Dept in association with the Leicestershire branch of the Council for the Protection of Rural England, 2nd ed. 1979

Foxton Locks and Inclined Plane – A Detailed History, compiled by members of the Foxton Inclined Plane Trust and published by Department of Planning & Transportation, Leicestershire County Council, circa 1986

October 1928 edition of the *Meccano Magazine*

The archives of the Foxton Inclined Plane Trust at Foxton

FROM OUR READERS

Contributions not exceeding 500 words are invited, with or without photographs or sketches for use as illustrations, and payment will be made for all articles published. The Editor takes no responsibility for the accuracy of statements contained in such articles, nor for the opinions of contributors.

The Mechanical Locks at Foxton

Some time ago I visited the once famous mechanical locks at Foxton, 10 miles from Leicester, which have now been standing idle for 15 years. At this place the Grand Junction Canal meets the Union Canal, one being 100 ft. higher than the other. In order that barges might be transferred from one canal to the other 10 locks were built. 50 years ago, but towards the end of last century traffic became so heavy that mechanical locks were installed in order to speed up the transfer. These were used until 1912, by which time road traffic had superseded waterways to such an extent that the locks did not carry sufficient traffic to pay for their upkeep.

At first sight the locks remind one of a giant Meccano funicular railway. Two huge iron tanks, each having 16 wheels, run on four pairs of rails up the slope from one canal to the other. These tanks are 7 ft. in depth, 15 ft. in width and 70 ft. in length. Each weighs 200 tons when empty, and holds 100 tons of water.

Four 4 in. steel cables are fastened to each tank, and pass round large pulley wheels at the top of the slope to a 5 ft. winding drum. This drum has a massive gear wheel, 10 ft. in diameter, which engaged a worm wheel driven by a single-cylinder steam engine.

One of the tanks of the mechanical locks at Foxton with the far gate raised

When a barge was to be brought up, one of the tanks was run into the water at the bottom, the barge was towed in, and the end closed. The tank was then hauled up the rails to the top, the journey taking about five minutes.

At the top the tank fitted closely against another fixed tank that joined the main canal, and when the intervening doors were opened the barge was towed out into the canal. In this manner one barge could be taken up and another down at the same time, the weight of the rising tank being partially balanced by the weight of that going down. The use of this method resulted in the saving of half an hour in comparison with the old lock system.

The machinery and tanks have been regularly cleaned and kept in good order, as they are valuable, but work has now been commenced on the demolition of the apparatus. The huge chimney that was a familiar landmark for many years has already been felled, and the boiler house is being dismantled.

G. W. WESTON (Foxton).

From Greenock to Glasgow

I had a very interesting trip up the Clyde recently when I crossed from Ireland to Glasgow. The boat on which I sailed reached Greenock at about seven o'clock, where we stopped for about an hour putting off passengers and cargo. At about eight o'clock we started again, just as the sun rose over the hills, flooding the river in golden, sparkling light. Ten minutes later we passed a sewage ship, of which Glasgow has two. From the outside one would never guess what they are, as they look so clean and tidy.

About a mile higher up from Greenock on the opposite side a number of small "tramps" were collecting sand for the new docks at Glasgow. Later we came to Dumbarton Rock, which towers high above the river. This rock rises almost vertically from perfectly flat ground to a height of about 300 ft.

The nearer we got to Glasgow the more interesting things became. Speed had to be reduced to about five knots so as not to disturb other ships by the wash. We passed one large dockyard where two destroyers were in course of construction, H.M.S. "Canberra," and H.M.S. "Australia." I was greatly struck by the large number of dredgers at work up and down the river. These do not hold the mud themselves, but deposit it in hoppers moored alongside. Most of the dredgers are of the bucket type, the buckets tipping the mud down a shoot into the hopper. When one of these is full it goes off to be emptied, while another takes its place. Of course it is very important always to have the channel clear, and it is only by constant dredging that the way to the docks is kept clear for large vessels.

At about nine o'clock we reached Merklands, where we stopped to put off cattle, which took about three-quarters of an hour. Merklands is a suburb of Glasgow and contains the cattle market of the great city. Between there and Glasgow we passed several large cargo boats, but no passenger boats. Half-an-hour later we moored alongside the quay at Glasgow, where everybody disembarked and the busy work of unloading the cargo was started. Then the crew, having washed down and cleaned up, obtained a well-earned rest. Most of the passengers disappeared at once, but I was very reluctant to leave the fascinations of the water front, where boats that had brought cargoes from many foreign countries were to be seen.

A. WELCH (Rutland).

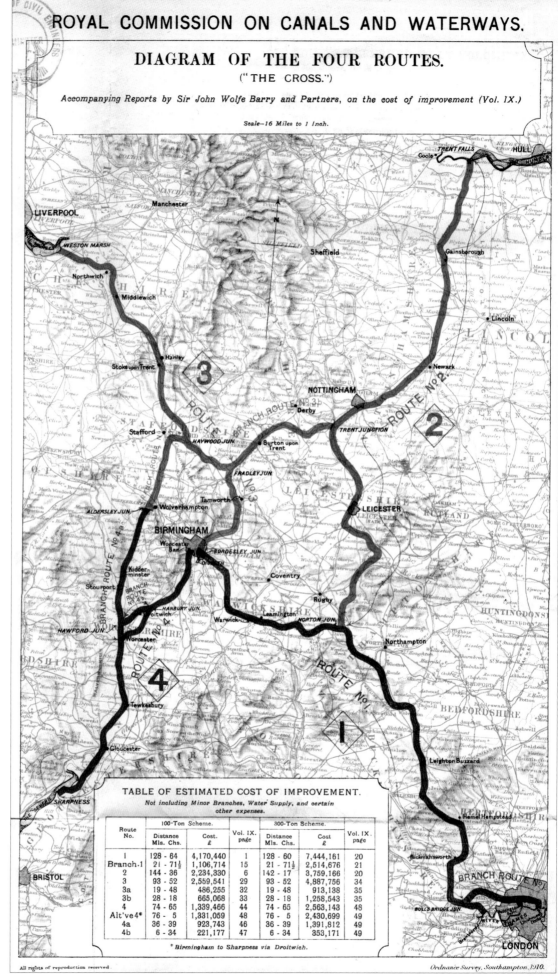

ROYAL COMMISSION ON CANALS AND WATERWAYS.

DIAGRAM OF THE FOUR ROUTES.
("THE CROSS.")

Accompanying Reports by Sir John Wolfe Barry and Partners, on the cost of improvement (Vol. IX.)

Scale—16 Miles to 1 Inch.

A relief plan of the proposed arterial canals forming 'The Cross'. From Vol. IX of the Reports of the Royal Commission into the Canals and Inland Navigations of the United Kingdom, March 1910. COURTESY THE INSTITUTION OF CIVIL ENGINEERS The four proposed arterial canals form a cross straddling England, with Birmingham at its centre and London, Hull, Liverpool and Bristol at the four extremities. The table at the bottom of the plan gives the mileages and estimated costs of the proposed arterial canals.

TABLE OF ESTIMATED COST OF IMPROVEMENT.
Not including Minor Branches, Water Supply, and certain other expenses.

Route No.	100-Ton Scheme.		Vol. IX. page	300-Ton Scheme.		Vol. IX. page
	Distance Mls. Chs.	Cost. £		Distance Mls. Chs.	Cost £	
1	128 - 64	4,170,440	1	128 - 60	7,444,161	20
Branch 1	21 - 71½	1,106,714	15	21 - 71½	2,514,676	21
2	144 - 36	2,234,330	6	142 - 17	3,759,166	20
3	93 - 52	2,559,541	29	93 - 52	4,887,756	34
3a	19 - 48	486,255	32	19 - 48	913,138	35
3b	28 - 18	665,068	33	28 - 18	1,258,543	35
4	74 - 65	1,339,466	44	74 - 65	2,563,143	48
Alt've 4*	76 - 5	1,331,059	48	76 - 5	2,430,699	49
4a	36 - 39	923,743	46	36 - 39	1,391,812	49
4b	6 - 34	221,177	47	6 - 34	353,171	49

* Birmingham to Sharpness via Droitwich.

Ordnance Survey, Southampton, 1910.

CHAPTER 9
1906 TO 1911
THE ROYAL COMMISSION
AND 'THE CROSS'

'Conducted as they are, lacking capital even for maintenance in many cases, without any general system of management or unity of purpose, exposed to the active and keen competition of the railways here and to the more killing indifference of railway proprietors there – suffering from this accumulated weight of adverse influences, the canals will be slowly strangled. Their present condition is little better than lingering death.'
Extract from an article in The Westminster Gazette, *20th December 1909*

There are rare moments during the course of historical research when, almost out of the blue, a completely unexpected event comes to light that brings with it a whole new area of understanding, hitherto unimagined. So it was for me when I stumbled upon the work of the Royal Commission into the Canals and Inland Navigations of the United Kingdom during my research for this book at the National Archives at Kew. I never, for one moment, imagined that so much time and money had been spent investigating the state of the country's inland waterways at the beginning of the 20th century and I certainly had no idea that it had recommended such a grandiose scheme for the modernisation of the waterways. Needless to say the recommendations were not accepted.

But why, you may ask, does the work of the Royal Commission appear in a book about the Foxton Inclined Plane? Its inclusion here is mainly due to the fact that Gordon Thomas, the Engineer to the Grand Junction Canal Company (GJCC) and the lead designer of the Foxton Inclined Plane, was a key witness to the Royal Commission. In all, he gave evidence on four separate occasions, over a period of eighteen months; firstly on 6th and 7th November 1906, then on 12th May 1908, followed by 16th and 17th June, and finally on 14th July 1908.

The other reason that this chapter has been included is that the Royal Commission's recommended scheme, referred to in the chapter title as 'The Cross', involved the development of the Leicester Branch of the Grand Junction Canal. Furthermore, the Foxton Inclined Plane was seemingly used as a template for numerous inclined planes that the Royal Commission proposed, to replace existing lock structures on the various canals that made up 'The Cross'.

What I hope to achieve in this chapter is to review the evidence given by Gordon Thomas, insofar as it may be relevant to the story of the Foxton Inclined Plane, and by so doing give an insight into the work and findings of the Royal Commission.

★ ★ ★ ★ ★

The Royal Commission was appointed on 5th March 1906, under the reign of King Edward VII, and met over a three year period. It took evidence from over 200 witnesses, representing different parts of industry with interests in the future of the country's transport system. Ughtred James, Baron Shuttleworth, was appointed as Chairman, with nineteen other members including three barons

The front cover of Vol. IX, of the Reports of the Royal Commission into the Canals and Inland Navigations of the United Kingdom. *COURTESY THE INSTITUTION OF CIVIL ENGINEERS Issued on 24th March 1910, Vol. IX reported on the cost of improving canal routes connecting the Midlands with the estuaries of the Thames, Humber, Mersey & Severn.*

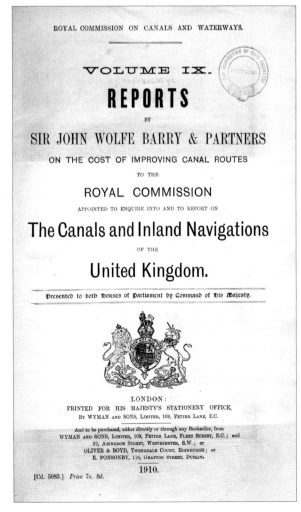

ROYAL COMMISSION ON CANALS AND WATERWAYS.

VOLUME IX.

REPORTS

BY

SIR JOHN WOLFE BARRY & PARTNERS

ON THE COST OF IMPROVING CANAL ROUTES

TO THE

ROYAL COMMISSION

APPOINTED TO ENQUIRE INTO AND TO REPORT ON

The Canals and Inland Navigations

OF THE

United Kingdom.

Presented to both Houses of Parliament by Command of His Majesty.

LONDON:
PRINTED FOR HIS MAJESTY'S STATIONERY OFFICE,
BY WYMAN AND SONS, LIMITED, 109, FETTER LANE, E.C.

And to be purchased, either directly or through any Bookseller, from
WYMAN AND SONS, LIMITED, 109, FETTER LANE, FLEET STREET, E.C.; and
32, ABINGDON STREET, WESTMINSTER, S.W.; or
OLIVER & BOYD, TWEEDDALE COURT, EDINBURGH; or
E. PONSONBY, 116, GRAFTON STREET, DUBLIN.

1910.

[Cd. 5083.]   *Price 7s. 8d.*

and three knights of the realm. The Commission's brief, as set out by the government of the time, was as follows:

> *'We have deemed it expedient that a Commission should forthwith issue to enquire into the Canals and Inland Navigations of the United Kingdom, and to report on:*
> *(1) Their present condition and financial position*
> *(2) The causes that have operated to prevent the carrying out of improvements by private enterprise, and whether such causes are removable by legislation*
> *(3) Facilities, improvements and extensions desirable in order to complete a system of through navigation by water between centres of commercial, industrial, or agricultural importance, and between such places and the sea*
> *(4) The prospect of benefit to the trade of the country compatible with a reasonable return on the probable cost*
> *(5) The expediency of canals being made or acquired by public bodies or trusts, and the methods by which funds for the purpose could be obtained and secured; and what should be the system of control or management of such bodies or trusts'*

The Commission was empowered to call before them witnesses, to examine any documents and to visit any site or premises that it considered would assist in fulfilling the brief.

By inference from the brief but also as dealt with so succinctly in the extract from the *Westminster Gazette* at the head of this chapter, the organisational, physical and financial conditions of Britain's inland waterways were, by the end of the 19th century, in a parlous state and most likely in terminal decline. The setting up of the Royal Commission was not too soon and, with the benefit of hindsight, turned out to be bolting the stable door well after the horse had fled.

The findings of the Royal Commission were published over a six year period between 1906 and 1911, and consisted of eleven volumes, as set out below:

Vol. I Pt I: *First Report* (issued 26th November 1906)
Vol. I Pt II: *Minutes of Evidence, Appendices and Map* (issued 26th November 1906)
Vol. II Pt I: *Second Report* (issued 30th October 1907)
Vol. II Pt II: *Minutes of Evidence, Appendices and Map – Ireland* (issued 30th October 1907)
Vol. III: *Minutes of Evidence, Appendices and Map – Ireland* (issued 28th February 1908)
Vol. IV: *Canal Returns* (issued 22nd June 1908)
Vol. V Pt I: *Third Report* (issued 12th October 1909)
Vol. V Pt II: *Minutes of Evidence and Appendices* (issued 12th October 1909)
Vol. VI: *Foreign Inquiry – Reports on the Waterways of France, Belgium, Germany and Holland*, by W.H. Lindley MInstCE (issued 16th October 1909)
Vol. VII: *Fourth and Final Report of the Commission – England and Wales and Scotland* (issued 28th December 1909)
Vol. VIII: *Appendices to the Fourth and Final Report of the Commission – England and Wales and Scotland* (issued 28th December 1909)
Vol. IX: *Reports on the Cost of improving Canal Routes connecting the Midlands with the Estuaries of the Thames, Humber, Mersey & Severn*, by Sir John Wolfe Barry & Partners, together with other Papers, Plans & Sections (issued 24th March 1910)
Vol. X: *Reports on the Water Supply of Canal Routes* by R.B. Dunwoody Assoc. MInstCE, FRGS, to the Water Supply Committee of the Royal Commission into the Canals & Inland Navigations of the United Kingdom (1911)
Vol. XI: *Final Report on the Canals & Inland Navigations of Ireland* for the Royal Commission into the Canals & Inland Navigations of the United Kingdom (1911)

Volumes I, II and III contain the verbatim evidence given by the various witnesses, generally on a question and answer basis. Volume III contains the evidence given by Gordon Thomas, by reference to which the following summaries have been written.

Summary of Evidence given by Gordon Thomas on 6th-7th November 1906

Gordon Thomas was first called by the Commission to give evidence on behalf of the GJCC over a two day period in November 1906. The first of these days was generally taken up dealing with the situation that existed at the time, with Thomas being asked about the extent of the canal system that was in the ownership of the GJCC. The second day was taken up with his proposals for major improvements to the canal system as a whole.

He began by describing the main cross country routes in existence at that time, of which the Grand Junction Canal and its branches were significant elements. Questioning by the Commission prompted answers from him that singled out the flight of seven narrow locks at Watford as the only restrictions to wide barges on two of these main through routes. With respect to the route between London and the coalfields of the East Midlands, Thomas advised that the mileage from Brentford, in London, to Langley Mill, on the Cromford Canal, was 167¾ miles and that it contained 150 wide locks, with just seven narrow locks – those at Watford on the Leicester Branch. With respect to the route from the River Humber to London, the total distance from Brentford to Trent Falls, where the River Trent meets the River Humber, was 247 miles, with 142 wide locks and the same seven narrow locks at Watford.

By 1906, the Leicester Branch, as Gordon Thomas referred to it, comprising the old Leicestershire & Grand Union Canal and the old Grand Union Canal, had been in the ownership of the GJCC for twelve years. Since the purchase, completed in 1894, major refurbishment works of the two canals had been carried out and the Foxton Inclined Plane had been built, thereby removing one of the restrictions to wide barges. The combined cost of the canal improvement works and the construction of the inclined plane was identified by Thomas as £86,767. When asked why the GJCC had not, by that time, removed the bottleneck posed by the narrow locks at Watford similarly, he bluntly replied:

'It has not been thought expedient for the Grand Junction Canal Company to widen these locks.'

On a subsequent day of giving evidence, Thomas expanded on this answer. He advised that, with the conditions which existed at that time on the various canals comprising the through route between the East Midlands and London, and with the tunnels generally being unable to accommodate two-way working by wide barges, the GJCC had concluded that the most appropriate vessels were narrowboats.

It is not clear, however, to what extent Thomas agreed with the GJCC's decision not to improve the Watford Locks. As the main protagonist for the Foxton Inclined Plane, he might well have been disappointed not to be allowed to continue with the improvements on the Leicester Branch, as originally intended with the construction of another incline at Watford. On the other hand, as the Engineer to the GJCC, he would have been in regular contact with the Board and hence would have been aware of the commercial factors that led to the decision.

Thomas explained to the Commission that, after the purchase of the Leicestershire & Northamptonshire Union and the Grand Union canals, through traffic on the Leicester Branch had not picked up as had been hoped. He put this down principally to the poor condition of the Cromford, Erewash and Nutbrook canals, which linked the East Midland coalfields to the rest of the canal system southwards. Significantly, by that time several canals, including the Cromford and the Ashby, were already in the ownership of railway companies.

Gordon Thomas provided figures to illustrate the gradually increasing adverse effects of the development of the railways on the finances of the GJCC during the 19th century. In 1838, the year that the railways first began carrying freight, through traffic on the Grand Junction Canal amounted to 202,134 tons, giving revenue of £93,697. The volume of through traffic on the canal grew steadily over the following years, to reach 294,257 tons in 1845 but, due to the need to reduce tolls to remain competitive, the revenue had declined by nearly half to just £48,695. By 1846, the year when railways first began to gain control of various canal routes, through traffic had fallen to 229,000 tons and revenue to £36,000.

The GJCC started operating as a carrier in 1847, which brought about a brief recovery in through traffic to 253,141 tons, whilst the revenue increased to £39,700. Thereafter, however, increasing railway competition and other factors forced the lowering of canal tolls to chase the ever dwindling tonnage of through traffic. By 1870, it had slipped to just 135,657 tons, with revenue of £14,379.

Income from local traffic on the Grand Junction Canal had also suffered against the growing competition from railways. In 1838, the local traffic amounted to some 750,000 tons, which provided revenue of £58,857. By 1905, the local traffic had more than doubled to over 1½ million tons but the revenue had remained relatively static at £53,773, which again was a function of reduced tolls needed to compete with the railways.

The first day of Gordon Thomas' evidence ended with him advising what he thought were the main trading problems encountered by the Grand Junction Canal, during the latter part of the 19th century:

> 'First, the diversity of interests on the through routes; second, the railway control of intermediate links, and canals in the distributing and collecting areas of the traffic; a further cause is the deteriorated and imperfect condition of many of the canals forming links in the through routes between the originating or collecting areas of traffic to London.'

When asked whether statutory powers existed to ensure that railway companies maintained their waterways in good working condition, Thomas answered:

> 'Yes, I believe in all cases there are statutory powers relating to the proper upkeep of the canals owned by the railways.'

Finally, in response to a request for his views on what had prevented these powers from being used, Thomas responded:

> 'There is very great difficulty in getting the proper authorities to move in the matter: there is the expense – an expense which independent canals hardly feel justified in going to, owing to the uncertainty engendered by conflicting interests of canals forming through routes.'

Not surprisingly, in many cases it suited the railways companies to allow their canals to fall into disrepair.

The subject matter on the second day of Thomas giving evidence, on 7th November, moved on to what he considered could, and perhaps should, be done to improve the through routes associated with the Grand Junction Canal. He prefaced his responses, however, by saying that:

> 'In what I may say under that head I wish the Commission to understand that I do not have the imprimatur of my board to put these views forward as coming from them, but merely as an engineer with special knowledge of the routes dealt with for the information of the Commission.'

By this means he was making it clear that the proposals he was about to submit were his own personal ideas and not necessarily those of the GJCC.

Thomas firstly advised that it was crucial for the main arterial canal routes to be amalgamated under the jurisdiction of a single authority, in order to achieve administrative and operational efficiencies. He then proposed that the canals between Liverpool and London, and Hull and Bristol should be the first to be amalgamated and improved. He considered that by this means, major increases in through traffic would be achieved. (His proposal was effectively what the Commission subsequently recommended and referred to as 'The Cross')

Thomas stated that, in his opinion, the preferred vessels for Britain's improved waterways were either 80 ton wide barges or breasted pairs of 40 ton narrowboats. The improved routes would be capable of accommodating trains of three wide barges or three breasted pairs of narrowboats, that is to say six narrowboats in total; anything longer than this would be unwieldy. Narrowboats would most likely remain the preferred vessel of many of the carriers, on the basis that narrowboats worked singly would be able to navigate the narrower unimproved waterways or feeder canals, and would be better suited to loading and unloading at many of the existing wharves.

Thomas proposed that the four main arterial routes should be improved to provide a rectangular section of waterway, measuring 45 feet in width with a depth of water of 7 feet. This size of waterway would provide a 5 to 1 ratio between the cross sectional area of the waterway and the wetted cross sectional area of the proposed 80 ton wide barge or breasted pairs of 40 ton narrowboats. Thomas emphasised that this ratio was necessary to achieve an optimum maximum speed of 3mph for laden trains of boats and 5mph for unladen trains.

The canals would also be straightened in places, thereby effecting significant reductions in the overall mileages, whilst many of the locks would be replaced by inclined planes similar to that at Foxton. The remaining locks would be replaced by 'tandem' or parallel pairs of locks, one of which would be 253 feet in length in order to accommodate the train of three barges, whilst the other would presumably be nominally 80 feet in length to accommodate single barges.

The route between Brentford and Langley Mill, that is the route from London to the coalfields of the East Midlands, which included the Leicester Branch, would be reduced in length from 167¾ miles to 152½ miles at a cost of nominally £4.3 million, or £28,144 per mile. The existing 157 locks would be replaced by twelve inclined planes and seventy 'tandem' locks. All overbridges would need to be rebuilt with a waterway width of 32 feet. The Foxton Inclined Plane would require relatively minor modifications to accommodate the larger boats, whilst the locks at Watford would be replaced by one of the proposed inclined planes. The route between London and Birmingham would be similarly improved.

Gordon Thomas predicted that significant savings in travel time could be achieved, which would enable toll rates to be reduced, thereby attracting more traffic onto the canal system. He suggested that, on the Birmingham to London route, the time for lockaging would be reduced from 15 hours to 10 hours for single barges or breasted pair of narrowboats and from 60 hours to 10 hours for a train of boats.

With respect to income and expenditure associated with these new improved canals, Thomas told the Commission that his overall proposals would affect nominally 300 miles of canal, at a total construction cost of just under £8 million, with annual management costs of £72,000 and annual operating costs of £45,000. On the income side, the improved canal system would generate nominally 4 million tons of through traffic each year, thereby providing annual revenue of £583,333. Furthermore, local traffic could be effectively doubled to 4 million tons, with annual revenue of £100,000.

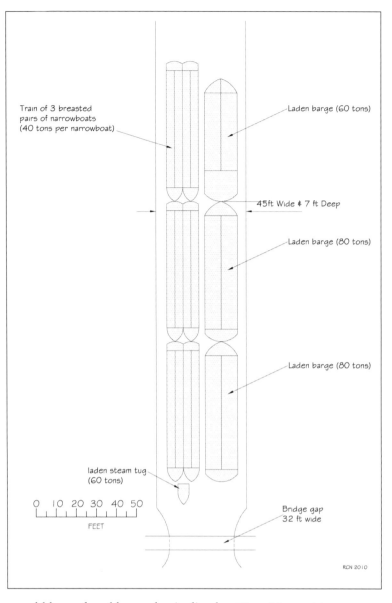

Plan of the arterial waterway as proposed by Gordon Thomas in his evidence to the Royal Commission on 7th November 1906.

DRAWING PREPARED BY THE AUTHOR AND ROSS NORVILLE *The preferred vessels for Britain's improved waterways were either to be 80 ton wide barges or breasted pairs of 40 ton narrowboats.*

★ ★ ★ ★ ★

A letter from Gordon Thomas to Thomas Millner revealed that, on 26th July 1907, between the first and second sessions of him giving evidence, the Royal Commission made an inspection of the Grand Junction Canal, which presumably included the Foxton Inclined Plane. The boat *Blisworth* was modified especially to convey the Royal Commission members, presumably in some comfort, along the canal. If this inspection did include a visit to the inclined plane, then it is likely that it is this event which is recorded in the photographs on pages 122-23.

Summary of Evidence given by Gordon Thomas on 12th May 1908

About eighteen months after first giving evidence, Gordon Thomas was again summoned to appear before the Royal Commission.

He began by providing further explanatory details of data submitted earlier by him to the Commission. He described the disproportionate tolls that were being charged by the canal companies making up the various through routes and made the point that the GJCC's share of any through toll was generally less than other canals, particularly those owned by the railway companies. He repeated his earlier statement regarding the general poor condition of railway owned canals, with particular emphasis this time on the Ashby Canal which was, by then, owned by the Midland Railway Company. This canal was an important feeder from Measham Colliery.

Thomas went on to present the results of various experiments that he had organised the previous year on the Grand Junction, which had the objective of identifying the optimum speeds of canal boats pulled by steam tugs. As stated previously by him, the optimum speed increases as the cross sectional area of the canal increases. By way of illustration, he advised that with a ratio between the area of the canal and the wetted area of the boat of 7 to 1, a horse could pull a 50 ton vessel a distance of 25 miles in a day. However, with a reduced ratio of 3½ to 1, the horse with its 50 ton load could manage just 14 miles in a day.

Thomas then presented the results of the experiments with steam tugs, pulling various configurations of narrowboats and barges. Hence, with a ratio of areas of 8 to 1, an optimum speed of 5mph was achievable, whilst with a ratio of 5 to 1, the speed fell away to 3mph and with a ratio of just 3½ to 1, the speed was just 2mph. Thomas further reported that the results of similar experiments carried out by the Prussian Government in Charlottenburg were generally consistent with his findings.

The day concluded with Thomas stating that, in his opinion, the narrowboat, with a width of nominally 7 feet, was the vessel most suited to Britain's waterways; it could travel at faster speeds with less power than wide barges and was capable of navigating branch canals as well as working in breasted pairs on the improved main lines. He considered that narrowboats carrying 40 tons of freight and barges laden with 80 tons of freight would both be suited to his proposed arterial waterways.

Tabulated results of experiments carried out by Gordon Thomas into optimum boat speeds with different waterway sizes. DRAWING PREPARED BY THE AUTHOR AND ROSS NORVILLE This evidence was presented to the Royal Commission on 12th May 1908.

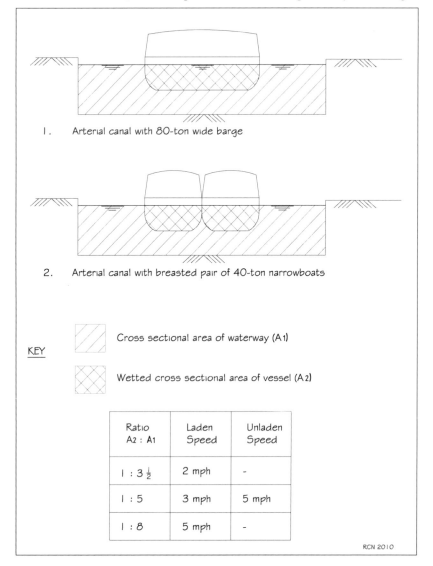

1.   Arterial canal with 80-ton wide barge

2.   Arterial canal with breasted pair of 40-ton narrowboats

KEY

▨   Cross sectional area of waterway (A1)

▧   Wetted cross sectional area of vessel (A2)

Ratio A2 : A1	Laden Speed	Unladen Speed
1 : 3½	2 mph	-
1 : 5	3 mph	5 mph
1 : 8	5 mph	-

RCN 2010

Summary of Evidence given by Gordon Thomas on 16th-17th June 1908

The evidence given by Thomas on these two days related, again, to his proposed improvement scheme for the canals that link Birmingham with London, and the River Humber to London. He repeated his earlier statement that trains of six narrowboats, in breasted pairs or trains of three barges line-ahead travelling at 3mph, was the optimum arrangement. In the case of a train of barges, the gross weight of the laden steam tug boat would be 60 tons, whilst the gross weight of each of the two wide butty boats would be 80 tons, giving a total tonnage of 220 tons.

Thomas stated that the canals making up his proposed arterial waterways, of which the Grand Junction Canal, including the Leicester Branch, was a part, also included the Leicester Navigation, the Loughborough Navigation and the Warwick canals, together with parts of the Oxford, the Stratford, the Worcester & Birmingham, the Birmingham and the Coventry canals. Presumably, the so-called feeder canals would have included the Erewash, the Cromford, the Nutbrook, the Nottingham and the Ashby canals.

Thomas reiterated that he did not favour an alternative proposal put forward by John Saner, which incorporated a basic vessel size of 350 tons. To accommodate this size of boat, he advised that the canals would need to be widened to 95 feet in order to achieve the proposed 3mph speed.

On the second day, the questioning by the Commission initially continued to address the proposed improvements but subsequently moved on to challenging Thomas's economic justification of his proposals, when compared to the transport of freight by rail. He was adamant that canal transport would be more efficient, despite the fact that his submission had suggested that only eleven men would be required for a 440 ton railway train, whilst eighty-eight men would be needed to work the equivalent tonnage by barge trains. Clearly, the members of the Commission were not convinced by his argument but when they pushed Thomas harder on the matter, he resorted to the following bold assertion:

> 'It is an undoubted fact that when you are comparing the cost of conveyance by canal with railway, the canal is cheapest.'

Summary of Evidence given by Gordon Thomas on 14th July 1908

The final day that Thomas was called in front of the Commission was taken up with what can best be described as a cross-examination. Initially, he was closely, almost at times aggressively, questioned with respect to his preference for a 45 foot rectangular waterway, with trains of 80 ton or 100 ton barges. However, despite various attempts by the Commissioners to convince him that a larger boat on a larger waterway would be more economical, Thomas doggedly stuck to his original proposals.

The cross-examination then shifted to challenging the GJCC's management of the Wendover Arm, which had suffered from leakage problems for an extended period of time. After a while, the Commission altered its line of attack onto the Company's management of the Buckingham Arm, the last 1¼ miles of which were badly silted up, thereby preventing fully laden boats from accessing the quay at Buckingham. However, on both of these subjects, which seem to have had little relevance to the main purpose of the Commission, Thomas staunchly defended his employer's position.

★ ★ ★ ★ ★

Although Gordon Thomas had no further input, the Commission continued to question various expert witnesses and to consider all the evidence presented to reach its conclusions regarding the future of Britain's canal network.

A Board of Trade document dated March 1911 provides a reasonably concise summary of the findings of 'a majority' of the members of the Royal Commission:

> 'The first and 'most urgent' step is the appointment of a Waterway Board, composed of three

A detail from the relief plan showing the proposed arterial routes ('The Cross'). From Vol. X of the Report of the Royal Commission into the Canals and Inland Navigations of the United Kingdom, *March 1910.*
COURTESY THE INSTITUTION OF CIVIL ENGINEERS
An enlargement showing the junctions connecting the four proposed canals in and around Birmingham.

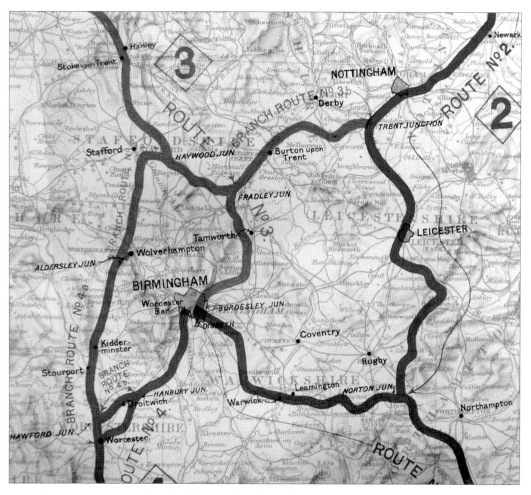

or five commissioners, who should be paid and give their whole time to the work. Their duties would be to review the whole situation, and present to Parliament schemes for the acquisition and improvement of canals on business principles.

It is proposed to invest in the Board, either on its constitution or at an earlier date, four main waterway routes, to be acquired by State aid, connecting the Birmingham district with the Thames, Humber, Severn and Mersey; and suggestions are made as to the lines on which the Board should develop these waterways. The improvements recommended would enable 100-ton barges to go anywhere on the four main routes, and 300-ton barges, or even larger boats, to work on certain sections.'

The recommendations by the Commission are almost identical to those originally proposed by Gordon Thomas on 7th November 1906, seemingly only differing in relatively minor details. Notwithstanding this, the recommendations are radical; to put them in a modern day perspective, they could be considered to be equivalent to the introduction of motorways to Britain's congested road system, or the construction of the TGV network in France, in the 20th century.

As can be seen from the above extract, the 'majority report' proposed four routes for the major improvements that radiated outwards from Birmingham, hence 'The Cross'. These reached out to London in the south east (Route 1); Hull in the north east (Route 2); Liverpool in the north west (Route 3); and Bristol in the south west (Route 4). The total estimated costs of 'The Cross' for the 100 ton scheme was nominally £15 million, whilst for the 200 ton scheme it was nominally £27 million.

Ironically, given the adoption of most of Gordon Thomas's proposals, the Commission eventually selected a shortened route for the new arterial canal through the Market Harborough area of the Leicester branch that bypassed the Foxton Inclined Plane. The plane, however, was to be retained to provide access to the Market Harborough Arm. In the

Commission's own words:

'With the exception of a deviation about three-quarters of a mile long at Theddingworth, there are no works of importance until the Foxton Incline is reached. From here onwards for the next six miles many alternative schemes were considered, and eventually we decided upon an important deviation nearly five miles long, leaving the existing canal on the high level above the Foxton Incline, following the high ground for a distance of nearly four miles, until in the neighbourhood of Kibworth it drops about 107 feet by means of two inclined lifts and joins the existing canal a little beyond Crane's Lock. By this deviation a distance of a mile-and-three-quarters would be saved. Two new lifts would take the place of the Foxton Incline, the four Kibworth Locks and Crane's Lock; and the Saddington Tunnel would be avoided altogether. It would be necessary, however, to maintain the Foxton Incline in order to give access to the Market Harborough Branch, which leaves the main canal at the foot of the incline.'

A detail from the relief plan showing the proposed arterial Routes 2 in the vicinity of Foxton. From Vol. VIII Appendices to the Fourth and Final Report of the Royal Commission into the Canals and Inland Navigations of the United Kingdom. COURTESY THE INSTITUTION OF CIVIL ENGINEERS
The lighter coloured lines (red on the original) show the existing canals, whilst the black lines show the proposed improved routes. Note that the Foxton Inclined Plane is shown as being bypassed by a new canal route; it would now only provide a link down to the Market Harborough Arm.

The relatively unbiased reporting of the press into the findings of the Royal Commission is of interest, as can be seen from another extract from the article in the *Westminster Gazette* on 20th December 1909:

'Whatever view may in the end be taken of its recommendation, the final report of the Royal Commission on Canals and Inland Navigations, which is issued today, is a document of real significance to the national life, and one that will neither be accepted nor dismissed without big consequences. To anybody who reads the Report it must become clear that the issue presented is no less than the continued existence or the almost complete disappearance of the network of inland waterways which traverses the greater part of England in every direction.'

It should be noted that the Royal Commission's recommendations were not supported by all of the Commissioners; three of them chose not to sign up to the 'majority report', each issuing their own written statements. Also, three of the sixteen members that signed the report only did so with reservations.

In addition, there were many public detractors to the Commission's recommendations. Many saw the proposals as interfering with the free market in favour of the inland waterway system and, hence, militating against the interest of the railways. Edwin Pratt was particularly vociferous in condemning the proposals. As early as 1906, before the Commission began work, he set out his views in his book entitled *British Canals: Is Their Resuscitation Practicable.* He quotes from a letter by Mr Joseph Sanders, dated 1825, that was written on the subject of the proposed Liverpool to Manchester Railway but was also very applicable to the debate on the future of the canals in 1906:

'Canals have done well for the country, just as high roads and pack-horses had done before canals were established: but the country has now presented to it cheaper and more expeditious *means of conveyance,* [the railways] *and the attempt to prevent its adoption is utterly hopeless.'*

Edwin Pratt seems to be even more opposed after the publication of the findings of the Commission. He gives vent to his frustration in 1910, in his book entitled *Canals and Traders – The Argument Pictorial as applied to the Report of the Royal Commission on Canals and Waterways:*

> *'A more lame and impotent conclusion has surely, never yet been arrived at, after so prolonged an inquiry, by a body dignified with the title of a Royal Commission.'*

★ ★ ★ ★ ★

As we now know, for whatever reason, the recommendations of the Royal Commission were not adopted by the government of the day. As a consequence, Britain's canal system continued its inexorable decline into commercial oblivion in the face of overwhelming competition, firstly from the railways and then the road system. This decision by the government seems to have been the last nail in the coffin for the Foxton Inclined Plane and any prospects of a second one at Watford. Within a year of the publication of the Commission's findings, the GJCC had decided to cease working the inclined plane, with all traffic being diverted back to the refurbished narrow flight of locks. And so it was that, after just ten years in service, the Foxton Inclined Plane, which was arguably Gordon Thomas' glimpse of a canal system fit for the 20th century, came to what seemed to be a premature and undignified end.

★ ★ ★ ★ ★

Personally, I am very ambivalent about the outcome of the Royal Commission and the government's decision. The romantic canal enthusiast in me would be disappointed, believing, as many do, that a wonderful opportunity to modernise the waterways for future generations was missed. However, the engineer and pragmatist in me would probably be accepting of the inevitable decline of the canal system, on the basis that it was unfit for the modern world of commerce. I certainly have some sympathy with the views of Edwin Pratt and many others like him, who rejected the Commission's proposals for what would have effectively been nationalisation of the waterways. The last words in this chapter are from an article in *The Times Engineering Supplement,* 13th April 1910:

> *'It is the pace that kills the canals, rapid transit, in general, is essential for through traffic, and rapid transit of barges over long, narrow routes is in this country so obviously impracticable that it is difficult to find justification for the cost of collecting the elaborate details which the Royal Commission in volume after volume of Blue-books is continuing to accumulate as testimony to that effect.'*

Sources For This Chapter

The reports of the Royal Commission appointed to enquire into and report on the Canals and Inland Navigations of the United Kingdom, dated 1906 to 1911 and available at the National Archives, Kew

'Foxton Revisited – The Inclined Plane in Context', David Turnock, *Journal of the Railway & Canal Historical Society,* Vol. 34, Pt 1, March 2002

Article from the *Westminster Gazette,* 20th December 1909

British Canals: Is Their Resuscitation Practicable?, Edwin A. Pratt, John Murray, 1906

Canals and Traders – The argument pictorial as applied to the Report of the Royal Commission on Canals and Waterways, Edwin Pratt, P.S. King & Sons, 1910

Article from the *Times Engineering Supplement,* 13th April 1910.

Report by the Board of Trade dated March 1911, available at the National Archives, Kew

Letter by John Sanders dated 1825 and quoted in Pratt, 1906

Copybooks and letters from the Grand Junction Canal Company's Northern District Engineer's office at Blisworth, held at the Northamptonshire Record Office

CHAPTER 10
1910 TO 1975
THE DECLINE OF THE
FOXTON INCLINED PLANE

'In a similar house at the top of the lock ladder, about 80 feet up the hill, lived George, who had lost a leg in an accident at the lift. I went to call on him to ask him about the remains of the lift. "They've taken it all away now", he said. "That's where the power house used to be, yonder – I used to keep a bright wheel there when I was younger. There's a bit of the chimney left over there, but it's no good to anyone."

Deciding to explore, I crossed the lock from George's house to a wild piece of weedy land, crowned with bushes where the mechanical lift had operated. The system was designed on the principle of the twin lifts on cliff faces at seaside towns … The whole thing was closed in 1911, chiefly because it proved too expensive. "For several years now", George told me, "wheels, engine parts, bricks, nails and chains have been disappearing." Today the only monument to an ingenious engineer is a dock which has become a backwater and a hillside so overgrown with pine trees that no one could guess that it was once crowned with strange mechanical shapes.'
From Canals, Barges and People *by John O'Connor*

I n this chapter, I will deal with the deterioration of the condition of the Foxton Inclined Plane, from the time of it being taken out of regular operation by the Grand Junction Canal Company (GJCC) in 1910, to the time when interest began to be shown in the preservation of what remained of the structure in the mid 1970s.

★ ★ ★ ★ ★

The extract at the top of the chapter is a first-hand account of how, over a period of some forty or so years, the Foxton Inclined Plane fell into disrepair, initially through disuse, then neglect and finally when it was dismantled, with the parts being sold for scrap. It should be noted, however, that the reference to the hillside being overgrown with pine trees is probably more poetical than factual, as I have been reliably informed that the tree cover was mainly deciduous, principally Ash.

The George referred to was George Durran. He began work as an employee of the GJCC at the end of the 19th century and worked for a time on site during the construction of the inclined plane. In October 1909, whilst working as a carpenter on the Leicester Branch of the canal, George was involved in an accident, which is most likely when he lost his leg. After the inclined plane was closed in November 1910, George was appointed as a lock-keeper on the Foxton Locks, a position he held until 1947, at which stage he presumably retired.

L.T.C. Rolt also makes reference to George Durran in his book *Narrowboat*, recounting a journey when he took his boat, *Cressy*, down the Foxton Locks in 1939:

'As we journeyed on, the hills became more gentle of contour and covered with woodland, to fall away altogether just before noon when we sighted the whitewashed cottage which I knew marked the top of Foxton Locks.

George Durran, lock-keeper (left) and Ted Boswell, carpenter, standing in front of a Grand Junction Canal Company working boat or 'work flat', circa 1930.
COURTESY THE FOXTON INCLINED PLANE TRUST

George Durran and his dog, sitting on the steps of what is believed to be the bridge over the lower lock at Foxton, circa 1930. COURTESY THE FOXTON INCLINED PLANE TRUST Presumably, at this stage, George was employed here as lock-keeper.

The descent of Foxton is greater and even steeper than the ascent at Watford, there being no less than five pairs of staircase locks having a combined fall of seventy-five feet. So abrupt is the change of level that when we first sighted the summit lock, the long beams with their white painted ends stood out boldly against the open sky until, on closer approach, a wide expanse of the Leicestershire plain came into view below. The paddles of these locks were extremely heavy, and we were assisted on our way down by the lock-keeper, who had a windlass with an extra long crank, made especially for the purpose. He was a most kindly and helpful old man, having only one leg, but with the aid of a single crutch he made his way about the locks with most remarkable agility and speed, balancing himself dextrously on this solitary foot when he wound up the paddles.'

Rolt goes on to describe what he saw of the remains of the inclined plane, as follows:

'All that we saw of it [the Foxton Inclined Plane], *apart from two short backwaters that connected the canal to it, was a steep ramp of crumbling concrete up the face of the hill overgrown with briars, and, on the summit, the ruins of the engine-house* [boiler house].'*

A family crew bow-hauling a boat into the top lock of the Foxton flight, circa 1909. COURTESY THE FOXTON INCLINED PLANE TRUST The winding house and one of the aqueducts can be seen in the background.

★ ★ ★ ★ ★

To summarise where we have got to in the story of the Foxton Inclined Plane, in 1908 the GJCC made the decision to reinstate the flight of narrow locks at Foxton, so that they could be used by boats at night-time, between 6pm and 6am, when the inclined plane was not operating. In 1909, the Royal Commission into the Canals and Inland Navigations of the United Kingdom, after three years of investigations, published a majority report recommending 'The Cross', which was a comprehensive modernisation of Britain's ailing canal system. If implemented, the scheme would have given the Foxton Inclined Plane a role, albeit very much secondary, connecting one of the proposed arterial canals to the Market Harborough arm. The Commission's recommendations, however, were not taken up by the Government of the time and the canal system in general continued its inexorable decline. In November 1910, the short working life of the Foxton Inclined Plane, a truly remarkable engineering structure, came to rather an ignominious end. By all accounts, the three men who were employed to operate the inclined plane were transferred to work on the locks.

New Lifts, Foxton.

After 1910, there is very little reference to the Foxton Inclined Plane in the Minute Books of the GJCC and other documents. The impression given by the records was that the structure was working one day and the next it was not. However, some sources suggest that, in the years immediately after its reported closure, the inclined plane may have been brought back into operation intermittently, possibly when the locks were undergoing some form of repair. By reference to historic photographs of the inclined plane after closure, the caissons were parked mid-way down the slope, in very similar positions to those in which they were first fabricated ten years earlier in 1900.

According to Gardner & Foden (*Foxton: Locks & Barge Lift*), the steelwork and machinery of the inclined plane was painted regularly and maintained in working order up until the beginning of the First World War but, from 1914 onwards, no further works were undertaken in this respect. Apparently the driving force behind these maintenance works during the early years of closure was Gordon Thomas, the lead designer and hence advocate of the inclined plane. They suggest that once Thomas disappeared from the scene in 1916 (see Chapter 11), the maintenance of the moth-balled inclined plane seemed to lapse. This situation would have been exacerbated by the retirement, two years earlier, of Thomas Holt, the Area Engineer for the Leicester Section and then by the prolonged absence through ill-health of Thomas Millner, the Northern District Engineer, soon after he had taken on the duties of Gordon Thomas. So within a period of around two years, three key players in the management of the Grand Junction Canal and, more specifically, the Foxton Inclined Plane had departed the scene.

★ ★ ★ ★ ★

During the First World War, the canals played a secondary role, in terms of transport, in Britain's war effort. This may have been to some extent due to the fact that many able-bodied men left their employment on the canals to take up military service, whilst yet more went to work in munitions and other factories where higher wages were being paid.

A view up the inclined plane from the lower canal basin circa 1913. NEIL PARKHOUSE COLLECTION
An interesting postcard view which belies its caption, because it shows the Foxton Inclined Plane after it had been abandoned. The two caissons are parked in their final resting place, mid-way down the plane, which is already heavily overgrown with low vegetation, whilst several sections of rails are dislodged or missing altogether. The condition of the rails may suggest that reports of the lift being brought back into use on occasion in the years after closure could be fanciful, whilst the reeds growing in the lower basin are a clear indication that the water here had not been disturbed for some time.

A narrowboat laden with coal making its way up the locks at Foxton, circa 1918. COURTESY THE FOXTON INCLINED PLANE TRUST *A group of sightseers pose to have their photograph taken with a narrowboat and its crew heading up the lock flight. The owners' name can just be made out on the side of the boat as Atkins & Son. The cabin looks to be too small to house an engine, so this is either a 'butty' or a horse-drawn boat. The photograph was taken by a Mr Ernest Jacques of Leicester.*

The canal companies continued to be managed independently during the war but with the British Government favouring the use of faster forms of transport, that is to say railways and roads, the canal system as a whole suffered significant reductions in traffic volumes. The major downturn in traffic volumes on the Leicester Section, that coincided with the onset of war in 1914 and generally continued thereafter, are shown in **Table 8.1** and its accompanying bar chart (page 129).

It is not unreasonable to assume that the diminishing traffic volumes during the war would have served to confirm to the GJCC that its decision to close the Foxton Inclined Plane in 1910 had indeed been the right one.

During the latter part of the war, it seems likely that the main elements of the inclined plane were left unprotected against the weather, whilst some of the smaller, more useful items may have been taken away for use elsewhere on the canal system.

Somewhat belatedly, in 1917, the Government took a more hands-on interest in the country's canals, with the setting up of the Canal Control Committee, which was answerable to the President of the Board of Trade. The purpose of the Committee was to co-ordinate traffic between canals and to help improve working conditions and staffing. One obvious benefit of the Committee was that canal companies were given a guaranteed income at pre-war rates for several years. Unfortunately, the setting up of the Committee seems to have been too little too late (as indicated by the bar chart on page 129), with traffic volumes on the waterways failing to recover to their pre-war volumes.

A letter from the then Engineer, William Yates, to Thomas Millner, dated 4th March 1917, reveals that the Canal Control Committee wanted to know about the condition of the Grand Junction Canal and what would need to be done to return it to its pre-war condition. The Committee also wanted to know whether the GJCC had enough employees to enable the refurbishment works to be carried out.

The next reference to the Foxton Inclined Plane in the Minute Book was on 14th March 1917, when it was noted that a report had been received from William Yates, which addressed the deteriorating condition of the various elements of the structure, although no details were included. A few months later, on 8th August 1917, the Minute Book records that:

'The Chairman submitted a report dated 21st February last from the Engineer on the condition of the Foxton Lift, consideration of which had been deferred by the Sub-committee in view

of the canal being controlled by the Government. The Committee were of the opinion that in view of the Engineer's report showing that deterioration was going on, the large outlay that would be involved in putting the Lift in working order, also the diminishing traffic on the Leicester Section of the Canal, that the plant and machinery should be disposed of now prices are good, and the engine house pulled down.'

The Canal Control Committee, however, was not yet ready to accept that the inclined plane had no future role to play, for, on 10th October 1917, the Minute Book records that:

'An instruction has since been received that the Control Committee cannot give its consent to the sale at the present moment pending further enquiries being made as regards any anticipated increase in Coal Traffic from Nottingham to London in the event of the Foxton Lift being put into order and another lift or new locks being built at Watford.'

A letter from Thomas Millner, dated 11th October 1917, to John Bliss at Surrey Street, London, reveals that a representative of the Ministry of Munitions was to visit the Foxton Inclined Plane in a few days time. Whether this visit was related to the work of the Canal Control Committee or not is unclear. It is possible the man from the Ministry was assessing whether any of the metalwork of the redundant structure could be re-used for the war effort.

The Canal Control Committee, however, ceased to function on 31st August 1919, seemingly without a decision being made regarding the refurbishment or otherwise of the inclined plane, nor of the suggested improvements to the locks at Watford. Hence, from that time on, the GJCC was able to make its own decisions regarding the inclined plane. Consequently, on 9th November 1921, the Minute Book records that:

'The Chairman mentioned the question of disposal of the machinery and plant at Foxton Lift, which had been closed for traffic purposes since November 1910, but it was decided to defer consideration until better prices are ruling in the market.'

TOP: The abandoned inclined plane, circa 1920.
MIDDLE: The redundant left hand aqueduct, winding house and chimney, circa 1915.
BOTTOM: The redundant aqueducts circa 1920.
ALL COURTESY THE FOXTON INCLINED PLANE TRUST

Notwithstanding this, many of the associated structures were dismantled or demolished over a period of time by the GJCC, for use elsewhere. For example, the brick chimney of the boiler house was, according to Foden & Gardner, demolished in 1922, so that the bricks could be re-used elsewhere on the canal system. However, it should be noted that, contrary to this, the Foxton Inclined Plane Trust states that the chimney was demolished in 1927, a date that would make more sense given the extract from the Minute Book below, from September 1925.

ABOVE LEFT: The boiler house chimney being demolished in 1922 or 1927. COURTESY THE WATERWAYS TRUST
The procedure used was to remove a large part of the brickwork at the base, with timber props supporting the remainder of the chimney. Anything flammable to hand would then be piled around the props and set on fire. In time, this would burn away the timber props, leading to the collapse of the chimney. This process was wonderfully demonstrated on television in the early 1980s by the late Fred Dibnah.

ABOVE RIGHT: The boiler house circa 1927. COURTESY THE FOXTON INCLINED PLANE TRUST
The window frames and lintels were reused by the GJCC to refurbish a pumping station at Tring. Workmen are also working on the roof of the accumulator house, possibly removing the valuable lead.

In July 1924, Messrs Blackwell & Son of Northampton enquired whether the GJCC would be willing to sell the various components of the inclined plane for scrap purposes. Apparently, they were acting on behalf of a scrap metal dealer, Messrs Cox & Danks Ltd of Birmingham. After three months of protracted negotiations, however, the GJCC rejected an offer of £925 for the metalwork components of the inclined plane.

Just over a year later, on 30th September 1925, it was recorded in the Minute Book that:

> '*A report dated 7th instant from the Engineer was read recommending scrapping of the Foxton Lift unless there is an early prospect of it being put into use again. RESOLVED: that the matter be deferred for further consideration pending advice being obtained from the Company's Auditors Mess'rs Price Waterhouse & Co. on the subject.*'

After consideration of the auditor's report, the GJCC decided on 23rd December 1925 that:

> '*… the Select Committee be recommended to sanction dismantlement of the Lift, as recommended in the Engineer's report dated 7th September last, and that any amounts received by the disposal of machinery etc (including material removed to other Districts for maintenance work) be credited to the Leicestershire & Northamptonshire Union and Grand Union Canal Capital Account.*'

After a further three years or so of negotiations, the GJCC sold all the metalwork '*as and where it lies*' on the inclined plane, to Messrs Glaze & Whorton, of Wellington in Shropshire, for the relatively small sum of £250. This was significantly less than the offer made in 1924 but most likely reflected the state of the market and the difficulty of breaking up and removing the items from the site. The items taken for scrap would presumably have included the

LEFT: *The winding drum, believed circa 1928.*

BELOW: *Dismantling the caissons, circa 1928.*
The metalwork of the inclined plane was scrapped by Glaze & Whorton.

BOTTOM: *The boilers in the boiler house at the Foxton Inclined Plane, it is believed being scrapped circa 1928.*
ALL COURTESY THE FOXTON INCLINED PLANE TRUST

engine, the boilers, the caissons, the aqueducts, the ropes and most likely the rails. The removal of the various components is reported to have taken about six months to complete.

Again, according to Foden & Gardner, the timber sleepers were taken up by the GJCC over a period of time and used to repair lock gates, although one has to wonder whether they would have been any use after being in the ground for around eighteen years. Similarly, the mooring bollards from the caissons and lower basin were installed on the flight of locks, and the windows and the stone arch lintels from the boiler house were taken to Tring for re-use in the refurbishment of a pumping station. Most of the below-ground parts of the inclined plane, however, were left in place, which included the concrete foundations for the plane, together with the upper canal arm and the lower canal basin.

At some stage, the buildings associated with the inclined plane were also demolished, with just the rear wall of the boiler house remaining. It is not clear, however, whether this was done in 1927 by Glaze & Whorton, to facilitate the recovery of the metalwork items, or at some later time.

Over the next fifty years or so, the story of the Foxton Inclined Plane site can be summed up quite simply by one word – neglect. The whole area very

These five photographs show over-pumping of water at Foxton Locks during a period of shortages in the summit length, apparently in the 1930s. It is likely that these are similar to operations that were carried out by the GJCC during water shortages in 1901. Often, the Leicestershire & Northamptonshire Union part of the system was sacrificed to the main line of the Grand Junction Canal to the south, with water being pumped up to the summit over Foxton Locks and then let down through Watford Locks. COURTESY THE FOXTON INCLINED PLANE TRUST AND THE WATERWAYS TRUST

The pumping operation seems to have been carried out in two stages, firstly by means of a portable steam engine and pump from the bottom lock to the central pound half way up the flight of locks, and then boosted by means of a second portable steam engine and pump from the central pound to the summit.

OPPOSITE PAGE TOP LEFT: The first stage of the operation, with pipework and equipment in the bottom lock. A portable steam engine with a belt-drive to a pump can be seen top right, just under the bridge arch. A workman is bent over inspecting or possibly priming the pump. The ice-breaker Gordon Thomas is moored up in the lock as a working platform.

OPPOSITE PAGE TOP RIGHT: Looking down at the second portable steam engine and pump behind an empty lock.

OPPOSITE PAGE BOTTOM: The second portable steam engine, belted-up to a pump at the central pound. Note the variety of temporary wooden supports for the pipework and the pile of earth on the right, presumably silt removed from the central pound.

THIS PAGE TOP: The central pound looking uphill. It is temporarily drained of water and is being inspected by an inquisitive schoolboy. Note the temporary wooden cross supports to the pipework.

THIS PAGE BOTTOM: A view looking downwards, showing the pipework and temporary wooden cross supports in the central pound, and the towpath down to the bottom lock. The smoke from the portable steam engine at the bottom lock drifts across the horizon.

A motor-powered narrowboat waiting at the top lock of the Foxton flight, circa 1920.
COURTESY THE FOXTON INCLINED PLANE TRUST
The boatman is on the far side of the lock, whilst a family, perhaps in their Sunday-best, watch from the right bank. The lock is apparently being emptied in readiness for bringing the 'butty' up to join the 'motor' boat. It is likely that the photograph was taken from an upper window of the lock cottage.

rapidly returned to nature, with the plane becoming overgrown with shrubs and then trees, to the extent that what remained of it soon became all but invisible to the casual observer.

★ ★ ★ ★ ★

To close this chapter, the following article comes from the *Leicester Evening Mail* for Saturday 16th January 1932 and was written by M.E. Cherry. It was printed under the heading 'An Engineer's Dream That Came To Naught' and paints rather a sorry picture of the site of the inclined plane at Foxton at that time:

PROOF THAT TIME IS NOT MONEY

'In a few months nothing but a scarred hillside, a few mounds of earth like ancient ramparts will remain to remind the villagers of Foxton, near Market Harborough, how advanced civilisation tried to encroach upon their village, only to be ousted by the bargee.

For more than a century Foxton has been noted for its wonderful chain of locks – thirteen of them – by which barges laboriously climb the hill which divides the high level canal from the low. They have always been a source of interest to the anglers who fish the prolific waters there, and to the casual visitor.

BOLD EXPERIMENT

In 1907 when the craze, now world wide, for speeding things up was in its infancy, Foxton leapt into the news as the site of a bold experiment. A machine, simple in its principle, but immense in what it attempted, was erected by a canal engineer with the object of cutting out the locks.

It cost a quarter of a million, took three years to build, and its sole appeal was that it saved time at the expense of hard cash. The machine accomplished the same end as the locks, but it took seven minutes rather than an hour to do it.

Instead of passing through the long series of gates, the barge was floated into a huge tank, and drawn bodily up the hillside by steam power. When it reached the top it was floated out again.

MAYFLY EXISTENCE

It would be interesting to know how many barges were transferred from one level to another by this method, but the information is not available. It soon became evident that the amount of traffic carried did not warrant the expense of keeping the boilers constantly heated, and so after a mayfly existence of a mere decade the machine ceased to function and fell into disrepair.

Comparatively young people at Foxton will tell you how, in their childhood days, it was their delight to beg a lift up the hill of a willing bargee. Innocent amusement was provided at Sunday School treats by procuring a barge, and making a memorable trip at the expense of some benevolent churchman. Had the idea appealed to the bargee as much as it did to the children it would have been a great success.

But business has no room for sentiment. Foxton has proved that

The lower canal basin in a state of neglect, circa 1950.
COURTESY THE FOXTON INCLINED PLANE TRUST
The far bank was by this date overgrown with shrubs, whilst the timber decking had all but rotted away.

though time may be money it is sometimes cheaper to spend the former than the latter. And so the dream of a mechanical lock at Foxton was shattered. After lying idle for 10 years or more the great metal tanks and all the fitments were sold for scrap iron three years ago.

ANOTHER ATTEMPT
The engine house was allowed to stand derelict for a few more years but now that too is being broken up and its bricks and timbers are being removed as required, to be used elsewhere in the great canal reconstruction scheme now in progress.

Even so man has not yet finished with Foxton hill, and is not quite sure that time is not money.

Last year a scheme was advanced for building a new set of locks, eight in all, as compared with thirteen at the moment, by which barges can climb the hill in 40 minutes instead of an hour. It was brought before the Harborough Rural Council and duly passed, but the call for national economy has made the promoters move slowly for the time being.

And so those who visit the spot now will see the same locks the machine was built to supersede, lifting barges slowly and laboriously over the hill, while the bargees sit and smoke a contented pipe, and chat with the lock keeper. It is quite plain to see that they do not in the least mind the wait necessitated by passing through the locks. On the contrary, they seem to enjoy it.'

A very fitting and flowery summary of the life of one of the '*many strange freaks that the mechanical age has produced*', using the words of L.T.C. Rolt. Unfortunately, in typical journalistic fashion, the newspaper article is riddled with errors, which include the reference to thirteen, rather than ten locks, the construction cost of £¼ million rather than £40,000, and to ten years or so of the inclined plane lying idle rather than twenty five years.

Sources For This Chapter
The minutes of the Committee of the Grand Junction Canal Company held at the National Archives, Kew
The Canals of the East Midlands, Charles Hadfield, David & Charles, 1966
Canals, Inclines and Lifts, David Tew, Alan Sutton Publishing Ltd, 1984
The Illustrated History of Canal and River Navigations, Edward Paget-Tomlinson, Sheffield Academic Press, 1993
Foxton: Locks and Barge Lift, Peter Gardner & Frank Foden, Leicestershire County Planning Dept in association with the Leicestershire Branch of the Council for the Protection of Rural England, 2nd ed. 1979
Foxton Locks and Inclined Plane – A Detailed History, compiled by the Foxton Inclined Plane Trust, Department of Planning & Transportation, Leicestershire County Council, circa 1986
Canals, Barges and People, John O'Connor, Art & Technics Ltd, 1950
The Grand Junction Canal, Alan Faulkner, David & Charles, 1972
The *Leicester Evening Mail*, Saturday 16th January 1932
The Archives of the Foxton Inclined Plane Trust
Copy-books and letters from the Grand Junction Canal Company's Northern District Engineer's office at Blisworth, held at the Northamptonshire Record Office

Foxton Locks and the remains of the inclined plane, circa 1930. COURTESY THE FOXTON INCLINED PLANE TRUST
The overgrown remains of the inclined plane rise up behind the building on the left, which today is the Foxton Locks Inn.
The rowing boats tied up in front of it suggest that it was in use as an inn or tea house at this time. Note the horse partly
obscured by the lock-keeper's cottage on the right, which would seem to indicate that a horse-drawn boat is using the locks.

TABLE 11.1: SUMMARY OF THE INVOLVEMENT OF THE THOMAS FAMILY WITH THE GRAND JUNCTION CANAL COMPANY

DATE	DETAILS
1864	Hubert Thomas is appointed as Engineer to the Grand Junction Canal Company
c1866	Gordon Thomas is born to Hubert Thomas and Georgiana Thomas at their home in Watford, Hertfordshire
December 1882	George Herbert Thomas, Gordon's elder brother by two years, is granted 50 guineas by the GJCC as a testimonial on leaving its employment when the Slough Branch of the canal is completed
c1885	Gordon Thomas is employed in the Engineer's department of the GJCC under the tutelage of his father
1891	Gordon Thomas, together with his wife Mabel are living at 76 Canal House, Marsworth in Buckinghamshire
April 1891	Gordon Thomas is promoted to the post of Assistant Engineer, presumably to take over many of the responsibilities of his father who is technically still acting as the Engineer but has also taken on the roles of the Secretary and Clerk to the Company
December 1894	Gordon Thomas, at that time Assistant Engineer for the GJCC, oversees a major dredging campaign on the newly acquired Leicestershire & Northamptonshire Union Canal and the Grand Union Canal
December 1894	Messrs Thomas & Taylor, a consulting engineering practice based in Westminster in London, submit a Memorandum to Gordon Thomas on the subject of 'Balance Lift for Canals'
April 1896	Gordon Thomas, Barnabas James Thomas and Joseph Jex Taylor submit the first patent for the design of an inclined plane, broadly as constructed at Foxton. Barnabas Thomas is Gordon's cousin. Gordon is either the lead designer or co-designer of the Foxton Inclined Plane
November 1896	Gordon Thomas, Barnabas James Thomas and Joseph Jex Taylor submit the second, smaller patent for the design of an inclined plane, primarily relating to the curved upper section of the inclined plane
Spring 1898	Barnabas James Thomas is engaged by the GJCC to be the Resident Engineer for the construction works on site for the Foxton Inclined Plane
July 1898	The Engineer's office is relocated from the Bulbourne Depot to the GJCC's head office at Surrey Street in London. Gordon Thomas is required by the GJCC to move to London and is granted a housing allowance of £100 per annum
April 1900	Gordon Thomas' value to the GJCC is recognised by his promotion to the role of the Engineer to the Company, back-dated to June 1894
July 1900	Gordon Thomas is authorised by the GJCC to attend the 8th International Congress of Navigation in Paris
March 1901	Gordon Thomas' salary is increased to £800pa, back-dated to Christmas 1900, but his housing allowance is discontinued and he is not permitted to undertake any private practice without the consent of the GJCC
November 1901	Barnabas James Thomas is formally engaged by the GJCC within the Engineer's Department
1902	Gordon Thomas writes a paper on the Foxton Inclined Plane for the 9th International Navigation Congress in Dusseldorf
1904	Arguably the high point in Gordon Thomas' career, with the Foxton design being awarded a Gold Medal and a Diploma at the St. Louis Exhibition in America
November 1905	Hubert Thomas, by then the General Manager and Clerk to the GJCC, retires after a three month period of ill health, at about 66 years of age. Hubert has worked for the GJCC in various capacities for approximately forty years
November 1905	Whilst still acting as the Engineer, Gordon Thomas temporarily takes over his father's role as General Manager until such time as a permanent replacement is found. John William Bliss is subsequently appointed as Clerk to the Company
1906	Gordon Thomas writes a paper entitled 'The 'Thomas' Lift Constructed at Foxton, Leicestershire by the Grand Junction Canal Company', possibly for presentation to the Royal Commission on Canals and Inland Waterways. This seems to have been the first use of the term 'Thomas Lift'.
November 1906	Gordon Thomas represents the GJCC by giving evidence to the Royal Commission on Canals & Inland Waterways
May, June & July 1908	Gordon Thomas gives further evidence to the Royal Commission on Canals & Inland Waterways
March 1913	Sidney E.B. Thomas is appointed by the GJCC as a pupil to the Engineer, Gordon Thomas. It seems likely that Sidney and Gordon were related
30th November 1913	Barnabas James Thomas has his engagement with the GJCC terminated due to ill health

CHAPTER 11
1916 TO 1921
THE DOWNFALL OF THE ENGINEER

'The Sub-committee fully considered certain irregularities of the Engineer, Mr. Gordon C. Thomas, in connection with works carried out at Bells United Asbestos Co. works at Harefield in the years 1911, 1912 and 1913 in which the Company's plant and workmen were employed and charged in the Company's pay sheets and the accounts in respect of such works were made out in the Engineer's name and payments made to him and not accounted for or paid over to the Company.'

Extract from the minutes of the Sub-committee of the Grand Junction Canal Company at its meeting on 14th January 1916

Gordon Cale Thomas, Engineer to the GJCC 1895-1916 and lead designer of the Foxton Inclined Plane. COURTESY THE FOXTON INCLINED PLANE TRUST *A photograph taken during the construction of the Foxton Inclined Plane circa 1900, when Thomas was around 34 years old. He is sitting on the edge of one of the sumps for a safety rope pulley in the lower canal basin during construction, before it was filled with water. He is elegantly dressed in a white panama hat, bow tie and a light coloured, double-breasted suit, and is resting his arms on his shooting stick and was so attired, it seems, for a series of photographs of the construction that featured him and his wife, Mabel.*

The above extract, from the minutes of the Sub-committee of the Grand Junction Canal Company (GJCC), is the first intimation of the impending storm that was about to break over the head of the Company's respected Engineer of twenty-two years standing. It is worthy of note that the alleged malpractices by Gordon Thomas, referred to above, dated back some five years. One cannot help but wonder whether the malpractices had continued since that time and, if so, what the total of monies involved was.

It is not difficult to imagine the grief that these accusations would have caused to Hubert, Gordon Thomas' father, who, after a career spanning over forty years with the GJCC, had retired eleven years earlier due to prolonged ill-health. Hubert eventually died on 8th October 1916, less than one year after the first accusations against his son and coinciding almost exactly with the trial at the Central Criminal Court at the Old Bailey. Perhaps the death of Hubert Thomas was in some way caused by the stress of the court proceedings against Gordon.

★ ★ ★ ★ ★

This chapter wanders somewhat off the main subject of the book but the continuation of the story of the designer of the Foxton Inclined Plane and Engineer to the GJCC is worthy of telling. So, please allow me to indulge myself.

It is useful, at this stage, to remind ourselves of the extent and importance of the involvement of the Thomas family with the GJCC up until 1916 (**Table 11.1**).

One might reasonably conclude that Gordon Thomas' opportunity of employment with the GJCC first arose due to his father being their Engineer. Whether this was the case or not, from that stage onwards, any suggestion of nepotism influencing his career might be discounted, as the evidence strongly suggests that he rose through the ranks of the Engineer's department by dint of hard work and his undoubted abilities as a civil engineer. By the age of 28, he was effectively carrying out the duties of the Engineer for the GJCC and, by 1910, at the age of 44, Gordon Thomas had risen to the top of his profession, both within the Company and in the civil engineering profession as a whole.

An internal memorandum from Gordon Thomas to Thomas Millner, dated 8th January 1916. COURTESY THE FOXTON INCLINED PLANE TRUST This memorandum was written a few weeks before Thomas was accused of embezzlement by his employer, the GJCC. Whilst the subject of the memorandum is rather mundane, take note of the flamboyant signature.

TELEGRAMS,
"ENGINEER, WATERWAY,
ESTRAND, LONDON."

Telephone Gerrard, 1899.

Enclo.

Grand Junction Canal.

Engineer's Department.
21. Surrey Street.
London, W.C.

Jany., 8th. 1916.

MEMO to Mr.T.W.MILLNER.

NORTON JUNCTION STOP.

I have made some amendment in your sketch of the Office desk proposed for the above, which I think it will be advisable to adopt; the dimensions are generally in accord with the desk in our General Office, which is found to be most convenient for working at. Please obtain from Messrs.Harris & Harris a tender for this made in American Oak. With regard to the Office fitment, I should like to consider this on the site.

Engineer.

Gordon Thomas, centre, with Barnabas Thomas on his left and Thomas Holt on his right, circa 1896. COURTESY THE FOXTON INCLINED PLANE TRUST

By January 1916, Gordon Thomas and his family had been relocated from Buckinghamshire to London, so that he could be based at the Company's head office at 21 Surrey Street, near Aldwych in the Strand. The fact that Thomas was highly regarded in his profession was demonstrated by the fact that, as well as being the Engineer to the GJCC, he was, from time to time, acting for various other companies on a consultancy basis. By then, the GJCC had issued Thomas with a car and a chauffeur to find his way about London, and presumably to travel to other locations related to his work.

In January 1916, Gordon Thomas would have been approaching his fiftieth birthday and the world and the engineering profession was seemingly at his feet. His fall from grace from this pinnacle was both rapid and momentous.

★ ★ ★ ★ ★

Interestingly, just three weeks or so prior to the revelations concerning Gordon Thomas' alleged fraudulent behaviour, as referred to in the extract at the top of this chapter, the Minute Book of the Sub-committee records, on 22nd December 1915, that:

'The Chairman brought up the question of the issue of orders and checking of accounts for Materials requisitioned by the Engineer, and after some discussion the Committee agreed to the principle that this work should be transferred from the Engineer's Department to the Clerk to the Company.'

One cannot help connecting this decision, which appears to cast doubts on the legitimacy of the actions of the Engineer's Department with respect to purchasing and using materials, with the action that was soon to take place against Gordon Thomas and some of his subordinates. Perhaps by this time, there were already some suspicions about the honesty of the Engineer.

★ ★ ★ ★ ★

Within two weeks of the meeting on 14th January 1916, at which the alleged fraudulent behaviour was first recorded, the Sub-committee met again and resolved that:

'… an account be prepared against Thomas in respect of the works and monies not accounted for by him … also that any personal belongings of the late Engineer be given up.'

On the 23rd February 1916, the Sub-committee met again with the following record in the Minute Book:

'The Sub-Committee again considered certain irregularities of the Engineer Mr G.C. Thomas referred to in the previous Minutes of the Sub-Committee. A letter was also read from Mrs Thomas, dated 16th inst, asking the Company to accept her husband's resignation.'

At this stage, the Sub-committee decided to recommend that Gordon Thomas be dismissed from the office of Engineer and to write a response to Mabel Thomas accordingly. It was also resolved that Messrs Percy H. Clarke & Son would be engaged to carry out an audit of materials in storage at the Bulbourne Depot.

Just five days later, at yet another special meeting, the Sub-committee:

'… reported that they had held meetings on the 14th and 23rd inst to consider certain irregularities of the Engineer Mr Gordon Cale Thomas, and that their investigations had conclusively proved that money paid to him by Bells United Asbestos Company Limited in the years 1912 and 1913 for work done by the Company's men and plant at the premises of the Asbestos Company at Harefield, which should have been accounted for to the Company, had been appropriated to his own use, and that they had suspended Mr Thomas from the office of Engineer to the Company pending the decision of the Select Committee.'

It was left up to the Chairman to consider the culpability of other members of staff of the Engineer's Department and to take any actions, as appropriate. There was no further record available on this particular issue.

The accusation against Gordon Thomas was that he had failed to pass on to the GJCC payments that had been made to him by the Bells United Asbestos Company.

At the meeting of the Select Committee on 12th April 1916, presumably after careful examination of the evidence, it was unanimously resolved that steps should be taken to prosecute Gordon Thomas. Soon after, Messrs Wantner & Sons, a firm of solicitors, were appointed by the GJCC.

★ ★ ★ ★ ★

Although the misdemeanours were stated to have begun in 1911, there clearly would have been other opportunities for misappropriation of funds in the way suspected by the Board. Apparently, it was not unusual for Gordon Thomas to be hired out by the GJCC to other organisations, to give them the benefit of his engineering expertise. An example of this is revealed by letters between Gordon Thomas and Thomas Millner in 1912, which indicate that, in November of that year, the GJCC Engineer was investigating the condition of the Harecastle Tunnel north of Stoke-on-Trent, presumably for the Trent & Mersey Canal Company. Another example is revealed in the minutes of a meeting of a GJCC Sub-committee, on 24th March 1915:

'Read letter dated the 17th inst from the Regents Canal & Dock Company enquiring whether the Company would be prepared to assist them to undertake the necessary works in connection with the repairs of Grove Road Bridge, Marylebone and landslip adjoining in which Mr. Gordon Thomas had been authorised to report to the Regents Company directors. RESOLVED: That the Board be recommended subject to Agreement to carry out the works required at cost price

plus 12.5% to include the use of any of the Company's plant which may be available, and that Mr Thomas be permitted to accept a fee from the Regents Company for reporting on and superintending the work.'

On 28th July 1915, further details of the agreement with the Regents Canal & Dock Company were recorded:

'... that the Select Committee be recommended to consent to Mr Gordon Thomas acting as Consulting Engineer to the Regents Canal & Dock Co. upon which terms and remuneration as may be agreed between Mr Thomas and that company ... That the consideration for the Company foregoing the claim to Mr Thomas' exclusive services the Regents Company pay to them during the continuance of the above arrangements the sum of £200 per annum and so in proportion for any less period than a year... In view of the difficulty of separating the Engineer's travelling and incidental expenses during the time he is employed as Consulting Engineer ... the Committee recommend an allowance at the rate of £360 a year being made to him to cover all expenses including those in connection with running and repairs to the Company's motor car.'

It is evident from the Minute Books that Gordon Thomas' illustrious career as Engineer to the GJCC was, for all intents and purposes, at an end. The whole matter was considered to be serious enough to warrant the establishment of a Select Committee, under the chairmanship of Rodolph Fane De Salis. In the meantime, with the suspension of Thomas, John Bliss, Clerk of the Canal Company, took over control of the Engineering Department, whilst Thomas Millner, the Manager of the Northern District, was temporarily appointed as replacement Engineer.

★ ★ ★ ★ ★

On 14th June 1916, Wantner & Sons were instructed by the GJCC to:

'... accept a plea of Guilty [from Gordon Thomas] to the charge of embezzling £61.12.6 received of Messrs Willis & Powis so that the case can be dealt with at the Police Court and that the solicitors inform the Court that a number of other sums of money have similarly been misappropriated and the total defalcations amount to a considerable sum, but that having regard to the long and good service of the father of the Prisoner, the long service of Thomas himself, and his present bad state of health the Company do not desire to press the case against him.'

This extract from the Minute Books is the first intimation that Thomas was in poor health, although it is not clear whether this was due to the stress of the situation or whether there was an underlying health problem – perhaps the early stages of the illness that would eventually lead to his death five years later. The extract also refers to Thomas as *'the Prisoner'*, which indicates that, in spite of his ill-health, he had been incarcerated pending a trial.

Wantner & Sons were also instructed to endeavour to obtain agreement from Gordon Thomas to surrender the lease of Gade Cottage, formerly Mill House, at Hunton Bridge, near Kings Langley, and to return all books, papers and plans in his possession connected with the Canal Company.

The GJCC clearly expected Gordon Thomas to plead guilty, thereby avoiding the need to take the matter to a higher court. Although suffering from ill-health, however, he was seemingly not yet ready to capitulate and he instructed a firm of solicitors, Messrs Thomas, Guest & Pearson of Birmingham, to act in his defence. The latter subsequently wrote to the GJCC on 24th June 1916 requesting a meeting, presumably with the intention of dissuading the Canal Company from its proposed course of action. This request, however, was rejected and, at a meeting on 12th July 1916, the GJCC ratified its decision to proceed with the action against Gordon Thomas.

Presumably somewhat to the GJCC's disappointment, Thomas pleaded *'Not Guilty'* at the

Police Court. The minutes of a meeting of the Select Committee on 9th August 1916 reveal that the GJCC was not prepared to accept this plea:

'The Clerk reported that the proceedings taken at Bow Street Police Court against G.C. Thomas late Engineer to the Company had resulted in the defendant being committed to the Central Criminal Court for trial, the defence being reserved.'

At the same meeting, the Select Committee considered a letter received from the Right Honourable Lord Anslow CB, addressed to the Chairman, as follows:

Bangor Park
Iver
Bucks
July 27th 1916

My dear De Salis,
    From what I heard yesterday in Surrey Street I gather that although I have paid all accounts for labour and materials supplied to me by the Grand Junction Canal Company as far as I know, still the money paid by cheques to Mr Gordon Thomas may not have been paid to the Company. Under the circumstances as a Director of the Company, I feel bound to make myself responsible for any such losses,
Yours most sincerely,
Anslow.

Lord Anslow was presumably referring to being a director of the GJCC, which goes some way to explain his feelings of obligation to repay the monies owed by him to the Company that were thought to have been misappropriated by Gordon Thomas. The total amount eventually paid by Lord Anslow in this matter was £185 14s 7d. The GJCC subsequently wrote to him to express their appreciation for his kind gesture.

The trial at the Central Criminal Court at the Old Bailey lasted nine days during October 1916. As recorded in *The Times* newspaper on 19th October:

'The trial of Gordon Cale Thomas, 51, civil engineer, on bail, on the charge of embezzling cheques received by him for the Grand Junction Canal Company, was continued before the Recorder at the Central Criminal Court yesterday. The allegation is that the defendant himself did the work for firms having wharves and mills on the canal banks by using the company's plant and the labour, and retained the cheques forwarded in payment.'

What appears to have been a critical piece of evidence during the trial, that may have had the effect of undermining the case against Gordon Thomas, was given on 18th October by Mr De Salis, Chairman of the GJCC and a witness for the prosecution. *The Times* newspaper, the next day, records that De Salis told the court:

'... that the defendant might have had permission [from the GJCC] to do the work outside and possibly use the company's men and plant, but always on condition that the men were not employed in the company's time.'

T.W. Millner, seen here on his Bradbury motorcycle, who temporarily took over as Engineer to the GJCC on the dismissal of Gordon Thomas.
COURTESY THE FOXTON INCLINED PLANE TRUST
Millner was Manager of the Northern District of the Grand Junction Canal.

Another article in *The Times* of 26th October records Gordon Thomas' defence against the charge of embezzlement:

> *'The defendant gave an emphatic denial to the charge, and said that the contracts for the work were made by him on his own behalf in his private capacity.'*

Perhaps unsurprisingly, therefore, the first part of the trial ended on 25th October with the jury, after two hours of deliberation, being unable to agree upon a verdict. The jury was discharged and the trial adjourned until the next sessions of the court.

The minutes of the Select Committee meeting of the GJCC on 1st November 1916 record that Mr De Salis, Mr Woolley and Mr Butcher KC were authorised to form a sub-committee to meet Mr R.D. Muir, presumably from Wantner & Sons, to decide on the next course of action. The minutes record the outcome of a meeting on 8th November as follows:

> *'... Mr Muir and Mr Travers Humphrey were strongly of the opinion that there was no reasonable likelihood of a conviction being obtained if the case is retried and under these circumstances advised that no further evidence be offered and a plea of 'Not Guilty' accepted.'*

The GJCC evidently agreed to this but most probably with reluctance given its original confidence regarding the strength of the case against their former Engineer. Consequently, when the court sat again on 14th November to reconsider the case, with no further evidence being offered by the prosecution, the Recorder of the court directed the jury to find Gordon Thomas not guilty.

After the unsuccessful trial, one of the main witnesses for the prosecution, J.A. Cann, manager of Bells United Asbestos Co. Ltd, suggested that his expenses associated with attending the trial, amounting to £10 10s 0d, rather than being paid to him, should be donated by the GJCC to the Uxbridge Cottage Hospital. The minutes of the Select Committee on 13th December record that Cann's proposal:

> *'... was agreed to, and a cheque ordered to be drawn for the amount. The Committee at the same time approved the letter of thanks to Mr Cann for the public spirit evinced by him in coming forward as a witness.'*

After having been acquitted, Gordon Thomas was seemingly not yet prepared to let the matter close. Several letters were exchanged between his solicitors and those acting for the GJCC, which related to payment of his outstanding salary. At a meeting on 14th February 1917, however, the GJCC decided that:

> *'... the Company co-operate with the Regents Canal & Dock Company to defend any claims that may be made against either Company by Thomas for salary and otherwise.'*

It would appear that Thomas was unsuccessful in any counterclaim but at least he had the satisfaction of retaining the lease of Gade Cottage against the GJCC's wishes. Soon after, he sublet the house to General Sir Leslie Rundle.

The final contact between Gordon Thomas and his former employers may well have taken place in February 1917 when, according to an internal company memorandum, dated 26th February 1917, he visited the head office of the GJCC in London and asked for the return of a few items of drawing and surveying equipment that had belonged to his deceased father, Hubert Thomas, and which he considered were rightfully his own. It would seem that his request was followed up more formally by his father's executors. Whether or not he was successful in obtaining the items is, however, unclear. With respect to the surveying equipment, the last written record on the matter was in a GJCC inter-office memorandum, dated June 1917, from Thomas Millner at Bulbourne to John Bliss at Surrey Street, that concluded with the sentence:

> 'The Company would be taking a generous view of the matter by handing the level over to Mr H. Thomas, Exors.'

★ ★ ★ ★ ★

Unfortunately, there do not seem to have been any detailed records kept of the Central Criminal Court trial, with the result that the precise reason why the jury were unable to agree on a verdict will probably never be known. Was Gordon Thomas guilty as charged but reprieved due to the lack of substantial evidence or on a technicality, or was he in fact innocent?

A lady, perhaps Mabel Thomas in happier times, laying the keystone in the arch of a new bridge on the Grand Junction Canal at Gayton in 1911.
COURTESY THE FOXTON INCLINED PLANE TRUST
On 16th February 1916, Mabel Thomas wrote a letter to the GJCC asking for the company to accept her husband's offer of resignation, presumably in an attempt to avoid the ignominy of being sacked and then prosecuted. Her valiant attempt failed.

One curious aspect of the affair was the letter that Mabel Thomas, Gordon's wife, wrote on 16th February 1916, asking the GJCC to accept her husband's resignation. Without the text of the letter being available, the first question that comes to mind is why did she write it and not Gordon himself? The obvious and only sensible answer would surely be that Thomas was, at that stage, in such poor health that he was unable to put pen to paper. The second question is what was she hoping to achieve by offering her husband's resignation? Perhaps her letter was an admission of her husband's guilt but it may also just have been an attempt to secure a rapid closure of the issue, thereby protecting her husband from the stresses of any subsequent investigations. Again, we will probably never know.

If he was guilty, however, what drove Gordon Thomas, a man at the height of his career and popularity, to commit such indiscretions? It can be taken that, as the longstanding Engineer to the Grand Junction Canal Company, he would have had a very respectable income which, under normal circumstances, would have supported a good lifestyle for him and his family. So why risk his career and reputation for yet more money? Perhaps he and his wife were living beyond their means or there was some other pressing need for money. Perhaps Thomas was already aware of some underlying ill-health and was accruing monies, albeit by illegal means, to provide for his wife and family in the future should he have to retire early. Again, it seems likely that we will never know the answers.

Innocent or guilty, Gordon Thomas lost heavily, both in reputation and financially. The Thomas dynasty at the GJCC had come to an ignominious end; his father was dead and he had been forced out of his profession.

★ ★ ★ ★ ★

Gordon Thomas' distinguished civil engineering career is worthy of repetition. He began working for the GJCC in around 1885. At the age of 26, in 1891, he was appointed Assistant Engineer to the GJCC when his father Hubert, being the Engineer at the time, also took on the duties of Clerk to the Company. In 1900, Gordon was promoted to the role of Engineer, a decision that was backdated to 1894. He was the driving force behind the Foxton Inclined Plane, a veritable 'Wonder of the Waterways', for which a gold medal and diploma was awarded at the St. Louis Exhibition in 1904. He continued as Engineer to the GJCC for a further twelve years and was obviously highly regarded by the Company and fellow professionals. The accusation of embezzlement in 1916 brought him disgrace and, possibly, ill-health from which he never recovered. Despite being found not guilty, he did

The death certificate for Gordon Cale Thomas. COURTESY THE NATIONAL ARCHIVES
The certificate records that Thomas died on 23rd August 1921 of caries of the spine and an abscess.

not regain his position as Engineer to the Company and apparently failed in his efforts, after the case was dropped, to win any financial compensation for his dismissal and fall from grace.

Gordon Thomas subsequently joined the British Army as a surveyor but, not very long after, died at home in Harborne in west Birmingham on 23rd August 1921, at the age of 56. The death certificate records the cause of death as caries (decay and crumbling) of the spine and an abscess. Fittingly, his wife Mabel was present at his death bed. Perhaps the affair had served only to shorten his life. It is disappointing that such a gifted engineer ended his life in relative ignominy and obscurity.

Not surprisingly, given Thomas' fall from grace, the death of its former Engineer was not recorded, as would otherwise be customary, in the Minute Book of the GJCC.

★ ★ ★ ★ ★

Finally, I would like to express my personal opinion on the whole sorry affair. Being a bit of a romantic, I prefer to think that Gordon Thomas was wrongfully accused of embezzlement and went to his grave an innocent victim. However, the weight of the historical records that remain probably favours the conclusion that he was indeed guilty as charged.

Sources For This Chapter

The Grand Junction Canal Company's minutes books held at the National Archives, Kew
'The Thomas Affair', David Heathcote, *Journal of the Old Union Canals Society*, Jan. 1985
Foxton Locks and Inclined Plane – A Detailed History, compiled by the Foxton Inclined Plane Trust, Department of Planning & Transportation, Leicestershire County Council, circa 1986
The archive of the Foxton Inclined Plane Trust
Copy-books and letters from the Grand Junction Canal Company's Northern Area Engineer's office at Blisworth, held at the Northamptonshire Record Office
Death certificate for Gordon Thomas from the General Register Office

CHAPTER 12
1975 TO 2012
THE REVIVAL OF THE FOXTON INCLINED PLANE

'With the passage of time much of the plane has become overgrown, but a Trust was founded in 1980 to work towards its long-term restoration. A museum has been created in the old [rebuilt] engine house, and further works are planned. The short branch to the Old Union at the bottom of the plane is now used for moorings, but the branch at the top is completely overgrown.'
From The Grand Junction Canal *by Alan Faulkner*

O ver sixty years after being taken out of service and forty years after being dismantled, new life was at last breathed into what then remained of the Foxton Inclined Plane in the 1970s. By that time all the buildings had been demolished and the steelwork sold for scrap. What remained of the site had become overgrown with shrubs and trees. The lower canal basin was being used for mooring residential boats, whilst most of the upper canal arm had become badly silted up and overgrown with reeds and scrub. Onto this somewhat desolate scene, however, came the Campaign for the Protection of Rural England (CPRE), soon to be followed by the Foxton Inclined Plane Society. The latter subsequently changed its name to the Foxton Inclined Plane Trust.

In this chapter, I intend telling the final part of the story of the Foxton Inclined Plane, from the 1970s up to the present. I will then address the future prospects for this historically significant structure, which L.T.C. Rolt described in his book *Narrow Boat* as '*the strangest of the many strange freaks of the mechanical age*'.

★ ★ ★ ★ ★

Restoration work first began on the Foxton Inclined Plane site in the mid-1970s, with working parties, organised by the CPRE, clearing vegetation from the upper section. At that time, the land occupied by this part of the plane was accessible, being in the ownership of British Waterways. The lower canal basin, which apparently included the lower section of the plane, had been leased to Foxton Boat Services in 1968 to be used for moorings. On the basis of maintaining the privacy of the boat owners, the lower section of the plane had been fenced off and was hence inaccessible to the CPRE. It needs to be pointed out, however, that Foxton Boat Services came to Foxton when the inclined plane site was overgrown and relatively neglected; the company did much to keep the part that it occupied in good condition

A working model of the Foxton Inclined Plane with its creator, Peter Cook, on the right, and the Archivist of the Foxton Inclined Plane Trust, Mike Beech, on the left, circa 1982. COURTESY THE FOXTON INCLINED PLANE TRUST *The model is now an exhibit in the Museum of the Foxton Inclined Plane Trust in the rebuilt boiler house at Foxton.*

The lower canal basin, circa 1980. COURTESY THE FOXTON INCLINED PLANE TRUST The lower canal basin when in use by Foxton Boat Services for the mooring of boats.

Re-roofing of the boiler house, part of the refurbishment works carried out by the Foxton Inclined Plane Trust in the winter of 1988. COURTESY THE FOXTON INCLINED PLANE TRUST

and to revive canal-based activity in the area. The office of Foxton Boat Services was in what used to be the bottom lock cottage at Foxton.

Around that time, the CPRE took the necessary steps to protect what was left of the Foxton Inclined Plane by requesting the Department of the Environment to schedule it as an Ancient Monument. Not long after, Peter Gardner and Frank Foden, who were members of the CPRE, wrote *Foxton: Locks and Barge Lift*, the first modern book about the inclined plane, published in 1978. Dr Foden was on the executive committee of the CPRE and was apparently an active member of the early working parties.

The CPRE, however, was not really set up for practical work and it was for this reason that a meeting was held in Leicester to create an organisation to carry out the day-to-day care of the Foxton Inclined Plane site. This resulted in the formation of the Foxton Inclined Plane Society, with Mike Beech as its first chairman. Many of the early members of the Society had been involved with the CPRE working parties and were members of the Old Union Canals Society.

In March 1980, the Foxton Inclined Plane Society took on the status of a charitable trust and changed its name to the Foxton Inclined Plane Trust. The Trust's aims, as set out in its booklet entitled *The Foxton Locks and Inclined Plane – A Detailed History*, were:

'… to carry out remedial restoration works, foster interest in the old boat Lift and help in the education of anyone who takes an interest in our canals.'

Since its origins, the Trust has been run almost entirely by volunteers. The only exception is that, today, Mike Beech is paid to be the Museum Keeper and Company Secretary, and Mike Cooper is the Assistant Keeper. Mike Beech is also the editor of the Trust's regular magazine, the *Plane Informer*.

One of the first tasks carried out by the Trust was the rebuilding of the boiler house, which had been demolished back in the 1920s. To achieve this, the Trust made extensive use of old photographs and drawings of the original building. Apparently, this task was taken on by the Trust as a means of proving that the volunteers actually had the necessary skills and drive to achieve such ambitious projects.

Trust members also continued with the work of clearing the inclined plane site, originally started by the CPRE, with one of its first acts being the creation of paths, so that members of the public could explore what remained of the structure safely. Further site clearance was carried out with the assistance of the Waterways Recovery Group, particularly by members from the Essex Branch.

It was during these early phases of work at Foxton that the Trust's hopes for the restoration of the Foxton Inclined Plane met with a setback – the

Part of the opening ceremony for the Museum of the Foxton Inclined Plane Trust, on 10th June 1989. COURTESY THE FOXTON INCLINED PLANE TRUST

FAR LEFT: Mrs Daisy Dainty and Mr Ken Goodwin about to cut a cake with a model of the rebuilt boiler house on top.

LEFT: Mr Ken Goodwin, with Mrs Daisy Dainty and Mr Trevor Towers, cuts the ribbon at the entrance to the Museum in the rebuilt boiler house. Trevor Towers was Chairman of the Trust at the time.

closure of the Anderton Boat Lift in 1983. Shut due to its poor structural condition, this resulted in the individuals and organisations that mattered in the industry, focussing their attention on the restoration of the boat lift at Anderton, to the detriment of the Foxton Inclined Plane. The Anderton Boat Lift was eventually restored and re-opened on 26th March 2002.

Notwithstanding this, the Trust continued working at Foxton. Its first major success was the completion of the replacement boiler house, which was to be used as a museum. It was opened with much pageantry by Mrs Daisy Dainty and Mr Ken Goodwin on 10th June 1989. In a replication of earlier opening events at Foxton, the ceremony began with the guests arriving by canal boat to the accompaniment of a brass band. The significance of Mrs Dainty was that, as a child, she had helped to raise money for the building of the Baptist Chapel at Husbands Bosworth, the windows of which had subsequently been salvaged by the Trust, with the help of Harborough District Council, for use in the rebuilt boiler house at Foxton. Daisy was the daughter of one of the former lock-keepers at Kibworth, the family having moved there by boat from Husbands Bosworth – a journey that involved coming down the Foxton Inclined Plane. She was one of the last people alive who remembered travelling on the incline. Ken Goodwin was a former Chairman of the Inland Waterways Association.

The boiler house, or museum, was used to house the Trust's rapidly growing collection of artefacts and archive material. Since opening, the museum has been a great success, fulfilling the Trust's secondary aim of educating the public about Britain's inland waterways and, more specifically, the Foxton Inclined Plane. The museum has won awards from Leicestershire Heritage and was highly commended in the national Gulbenkian Awards.

Part of the opening ceremony for the refurbished boiler house, on 10th June 1989. COURTESY THE FOXTON INCLINED PLANE TRUST *A horse-drawn narrowboat, with invited guests, descends the flight of locks at Foxton.*

Work to improve the incline continued but access was still not available to enable the clearance of the lower half, which made it difficult to appreciate the full scale of the structure. Volunteers from the Waterways Recovery Group laid the hedge along the towpath of the upper canal arm and helped clear the channel of vegetation. Members of the Trust cut the grass on the incline, carried out improvements to the museum and continued with fund-raising activities.

Early in 1996, realising that it was unlikely that it could achieve the desired full restoration of the Foxton Inclined Plane on its own, the Trust set up the Foxton Locks Management Group, which, on the initiative of British Waterways, soon after became the Foxton Locks Partnership. The members of the Partnership were British Waterways, the Foxton Inclined Plane Trust, Harborough District Council, Leicestershire County Council, Foxton Parish Council, the Inland Waterways Association and the Old Union Canals Society. British Waterways and the Foxton Inclined Plane Trust were the lead organisations in the Partnership, the first meeting of which took place in November 1996. It was only after the formation of the Partnership that significant momentum for the more complete restoration of the inclined plane was built up.

In November 1999, the Trust contributed £15,000, which enabled British Waterways, on behalf of the Partnership, to commission a study by consultants W.S. Atkins into the viability of full restoration of the inclined plane. The consultants' report, which was submitted in May 2000, concluded that full restoration of the inclined plane was feasible.

Foxton Boat Services' lease on the lower canal basin and the lower part of the plane expired in 2003, which finally gave access to enable vegetation clearance works on this part to start the following year.

On 11th January 2007, an article in the *New Civil Engineer*, under the headline '*Restoration drama – Restoration of one of the man-made wonders of the world is moving closer thanks to works now underway on the Grand Union canal*', announced that work had been started to restore several elements of the Foxton Inclined Plane. This was made possible following a successful bid by the Partnership to the Heritage Lottery Fund, securing £1.78 million towards the £2.9 million project cost. For the record, the contributors that made up the remainder of the funds for the restoration works were the East Midlands Development Agency, with nominally £0.7 million; British Waterways with £0.3 million; Leicestershire County Council with £50,000; Harborough District Council with £20,000; the John Hobley Trust with £20,000; the FIPT with £15,000; and Lafarge with £7,000.

The restoration works on the lower canal basin in spring 2007. AUTHOR
The basin has been dewatered and repair works are ongoing to the left bank, the brick walling on the right bank and the causeway between the entrances to the two caissons.

Contractors working under the supervision of British Waterways carried out refurbishment of the lower canal basin and the re-watering of the upper canal arm, complete with a new working stop lock. The lower canal basin was dewatered and large amounts of silt were removed to make way for repairs to the brick and stone sides of the basin. Locally sourced bricks and stone copings were incorporated to best match the original masonry. The timber causeway that once separated the entrances to the caissons was renewed, using oak timbers, back to its original width. Where possible, the remains of the original timber support structure were re-used.

A short section of upper canal arm, still containing water, was dredged by means of floating equipment, whilst the dry section was cleared of vegetation. Steel sheet piling had to be driven into the eastern bank of the arm, to overcome potential destabilisation of the bank caused by decades of drying-out and a large number of badger sets. After clearing, the arm was re-profiled to its original cross-section. A PVC welded liner was then placed on a concrete bed, with interlocking concrete revetment blocks laid up the banks, containing pockets for marginal plants to establish themselves.

In parallel with the reinstatement of the lower canal basin and the upper canal arm, extensive works were carried out on the plane itself and the general surrounding area. The concrete track support to the plane, which had suffered significant damage over the years due to tree roots and frost, was tidied up and the buried brickwork to the foundations was repaired using lime mortar. With the clearance of the remaining trees and shrubs, the site was made more accessible in keeping with its status as an Ancient Monument. Attractive interpretation was installed as part of the overall project. Paths around the site were resurfaced and re-graded, with 80% of the site made accessible by wheelchair, including the new observation point perched above the incline.

Interestingly the article in the *New Civil Engineer* closes with the statement that:

'*It is hoped funding to reinstall the lift itself will be found in time for a reopening in 2011, 100 years after its closure.*'

More recently, an article in *Waterways World* magazine in the summer of 2009, under the heading '*Major Award For Foxton*', announced that the ongoing restoration works had secured a number of 'wins' in that year's Waterway Renaissance Awards, including the

Outstanding Achievement category. The article went on to say that the award was:

> '... a well-deserved accolade after five years of development of the 20-acre historic site beside the Leicester Section of the Grand Union Canal which has become a key regional tourism destination. The five-year project costing £3.8m was led by British Waterways on behalf of the Foxton Locks Partnership, and involved the installation of new viewing areas and upgrading 3 kilometres of paths. Additional interpretation panels were put in place and there were substantial engineering works too, including refurbishment of the bottom canal basin, clearing and re-profiling of the inclined plane slope, and relining and re-watering of 200 metres of the upper canal arm.'

It should be noted that the article wrongly quoted the cost of the project as £3.8 million; the figure should have been £2.8 million.

Numerous awards have been made with respect to the Foxton Locks site since the opening of the Museum, as summarised in **Table 12.1**. These awards are a worthy testament to the efforts of the various organisations and individuals that have been involved in the opening up of the site and the restoration of the inclined plane.

★ ★ ★ ★ ★

Today, the Trust remains fully committed to the idea of restoring the inclined plane to full working condition. To support this, it raised a quarter of the cost of an £80,000 Master Plan Study, commissioned by British Waterways on behalf of the Foxton Locks Partnership. Assuming there were no insurmountable engineering problems to rebuilding the inclined plane, the study looked instead at the commercial viability of the project, including the necessary visitor facilities.

Restoration works on the upper canal arm, spring 2007. Both Author

Above: The finished upper canal arm, surfaced with concrete revetment blocks, prior to filling with water. The top of the inclined plane is in the middle background. Working in the dry, the many years of vegetation growth in the upper canal arm was cleared and the trapezoidal shape of the channel re-established, prior to placing of the revetment.

Right: The arm has been dewatered, desilted, reprofiled and lined with a PVC welded liner. In the foreground is the restored stop-lock.

TABLE 12.1: List of Awards Made to the Foxton Site 1992-2010			
Date	**Award**	**Category**	**For**
September 2010	Red Wheel Plaque' awarded by the Transport Trust	Preservationist of the Year	Site
October 2009	East Midlands Tourism's Enjoy England Excellence Awards	Bronze winner 'Access for All'	Site
March 2009	BURA national award, finalist in the Design & Construction and the Historic Environment Categories	Winner Outstanding Award Winner HE Commended in D&C	Site
November 2008	Royal Town Planning Institute's East Midlands Regional Award	Joint Winner	Site
July 2008	Leicestershire & Rutland Renaissance Heritage Awards – Inspiration Award for Best Special Project – Foxton Inclined Plane Trust for Foxton Locks Restoration	Highly Commended	Site
September 2008	European Route of Industrial Heritage	Award 'Anchor Point' status for East Midlands	Site
2008	Leicestershire County Council Heritage Awards for Publication 2008 – Foxton Canal Museum	Winner	Museum
February 2008	New Civil Engineer – professional publication	Commendation	
May 2008	Museums Libraries & Archives Council (MLAC) Standards/Accreditation body for museums	Accreditation	Museum
May 2008	English Heritage 'Buildings at Risk Register' – Inclined Plane removed from register in recognition of the restorative work of the Foxton Locks Partnership, 2006-8		Site
October 2008	East Midlands Tourism Enjoy England Excellence Awards – Large Attraction category	Bronze	Site
May 2008	Royal Institution of Chartered Surveyors Regional Awards – upper canal arm shortlisted in Heritage category	Short Listed	Upper Arm
November 2007	Institution of Civil Engineers Historic Bridge & Infrastructure Awards	Special Mention	Site
2007	Visitor Attraction Quality Assurance Scheme (VAQAS)	Accreditation	Site
2007	Leicestershire & Rutland Renaissance East Midlands – Renaissance Heritage Awards – Peoples' Choice Award	Runner-up	Museum
2006	British Urban Regeneration Association (BURA) Waterway Renaissance awards – Foxton Locks Masterplan	Commended	Site
March 2006	Leicester Sound (Radio) Award (by popular vote) – Best Visitor Attraction	Third Place	Museum
2005	Royal Institution of Chartered Surveyors Regional Award, Building Conservation Category	Silver	Top Lock Cottage
2001	Re:source (later renamed MLAC)	Full Registration	Museum
2000	Leicestershire County Council Heritage Award	Best Publication	Museum
1997	Leicestershire County Council Heritage Award	Third Prize	Museum
1996	Leicestershire County Council Heritage Award	Highly Commended	Museum
1995	Gulbenkian Awards – Most Improved Museum	Highly Commended	Museum
1993	Leicestershire County Council Heritage Award	Second Prize	Museum
1992	Leicestershire County Council Heritage Award	Commended	Museum

The winter 2009 edition of the *Plane Informer* advised that the consultants working on the Master Plan, Britton McGrath Associates, had recently submitted three reports; namely the Foxton Locks Masterplan Report, a Business Plan and a Marketing Plan. These indicated that, if the money for full restoration could be obtained at no cost, *e.g.* by grants, the inclined plane could potentially cover its running costs without additional financial input from elsewhere. The consultants advised that the development of the site with new and improved visitor facilities would be likely to attract 30,000 more visitors, whilst a further 20,000 visitors would visit the site if the full restoration of the inclined plane was also carried out. The Foxton Locks site is already the fourth most visited in the East Midlands and

ABOVE: Foxton Locks looking northwards in October 2009. AUTHOR
The side ponds to the locks are clearly visible on the right, as is the
rebuilt boiler house, now the museum and archive of the Foxton Inclined
Plane Trust, opened in 1989.

RIGHT: Looking up the Foxton flight in October 2009. AUTHOR
The white top lock cottage is prominent on the skyline.

*BELOW: The upper staircase of five locks at Foxton as seen in October
2009. AUTHOR*
The side ponds are in the foreground and the top lock cottage in the left
background.

View looking up the plane from the lower canal basin, October 2009. AUTHOR
The two parts of the plane are clearly visible. The brick abutment forming the end of one of the aqueducts can be seen in the left background, at the top of the plane.

second only to Chatsworth House and gardens in the list of 'paid for' attractions.

The estimated cost of restoring the inclined plane to working condition was £11.64 million, whilst the additional cost for the enhanced site facilities increased this to a total of £22 million. Income to support and maintain the site is expected to come from increased car parking charges, 'paid for' visitor attractions – including a living history museum and rides on the inclined plane – higher retail sales, increased catering and on-site accommodation, including camping.

★ ★ ★ ★ ★

In conclusion, I quote from the Waterscape website, accessed on 11th February 2010:

> '*Foxton Locks possesses a redundant inclined plane boat lift, which has been nominated as one of Leicestershire's favourite attractions and one of the East Midlands seven man made wonders. The site is considered to be one of the significant visitor assets within Leicestershire.*'

The upper curved section of the plane as viewed from below, October 2009. AUTHOR
The concrete foundations and the rebates in which the sleepers and rails for the caissons would have been installed are clearly visible. The section of rail and sleepers to the left of the picture were installed by the Foxton Inclined Plane Trust as an example of how it might once have looked. Note that the short timber sleepers placed laterally across the slope are not as original, which made use of 14-foot long sleepers aligned longitudinally down the slope.

Even today, without the full restoration of the Foxton Inclined Plane, visitor numbers to the site can reach as many as 250,000 a year, approximately 20,000 of which also visited the Museum. It must be said that the Foxton Inclined Plane Trust has, over the last thirty years, done a wonderful job in rescuing the Foxton Inclined Plane from obscurity and promoting it to the wider public. The role of the Trust has been key to all the good works that have been carried out on the site to date.

Let us hope that, despite the pending transformation of British Waterways into a so-called 'Third Sector' organisation with all that entails, both the commitment and the investment are forthcoming to enable the final step to be taken in the revival of the Foxton Inclined Plane. Hopefully then, this wonderful engineering structure, as designed

The view of the basin at the bottom of the flight of locks at Foxton, October 2009. AUTHOR

With the buildings on the left now in use as the Foxton Locks Inn and the similarly refurbished lock cottages on the right also now part of the visitor attractions here, it is undoubtedly fair to say that the Foxton Locks site has never looked so good.

THE REVIVAL OF THE THE FOXTON INCLINED PLANE

The upper curved section of the plane today as viewed from above, October 2009. AUTHOR
Timber sleepers have been inset into the concrete foundations and a section of rail fixed on top by the Foxton Inclined Plane Trust to indicate how the arrangement might have been.

and built by Gordon Thomas, can be restored to full operating condition and re-opened to traffic.

Sources For This Chapter

Foxton Locks and Inclined Plane – A Detailed History, compiled by the Foxton Inclined Plane Trust, Department of Planning & Transportation, Leicestershire County Council, circa 1986
The New Civil Engineer, issue for 11th January 2007
Waterways World, No. 224, 229
The Foxton Inclined Plane website available at http://www.fipt.org.uk
Plane Informer (Winter 2009, No. 112), Foxton Inclined Plane Trust
Narrow Boat, L.T.C. Rolt, Eyre Methuen, 1944
The Grand Junction Canal, Alan Faulkner, David & Charles, 1972
The archive of the Foxton Inclined Plane Trust

ABOVE: *One of the main guide pulleys for the wire hauling ropes, now an exhibit at the entrance to the Foxton site from the main car park.*

LEFT: *Three of the original horse-drawn, narrow gauge, side tipping wagons used during the construction, October 2009.* BOTH AUTHOR
The wagons would have been used for moving excavated spoil from the upper and lower basins, and tipping it on the hillside between to make the inclined plane. These examples are now positioned outside the museum of the Foxton Inclined Plane Trust.

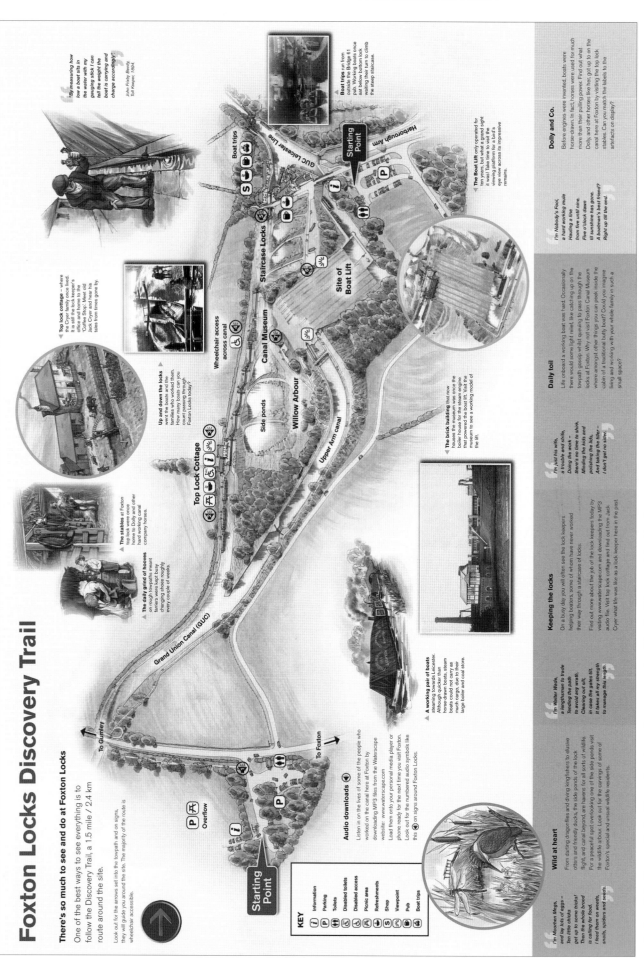

Foxton Locks Discovery Trail

There's so much to see and do at Foxton Locks

One of the best ways to see everything is to follow the Discovery Trail, a 1.5 mile / 2.4 km route around the site.

Look out for the arrows set into the towpath and on signs, they will guide you around the site. The majority of the route is wheelchair accessible.

Audio downloads ⏺

Listen in on the lives of some of the people who worked on the canal here at Foxton by downloading MP3 files from the Waterscape website: www.waterscape.com

Load them onto your personal media player or phone ready for the next time you visit Foxton. Look out for the numbered audio symbols like this ⏺ on signs around Foxton Locks.

KEY

- ⓘ Information
- Ⓟ Parking
- Toilets
- Disabled toilets
- Disabled access
- Picnic area
- Ⓢ Shop
- Refreshments
- Viewpoint
- Pub
- Boat trips

Starting Point

Wild at heart

From darting dragonflies and diving kingfishers to elusive otters and timidly ducks, the side ponds of the lock flight, and canal beyond, are havens for all sorts of wildlife. For a peaceful spot overlooking one of the side ponds visit the wildlife arbour. Look out for the carvings of some of Foxton's special and unusual wildlife residents.

I'm Moorhen Megs, and lay lots of eggs – Ten little chicks get up to some tricks! Then the whole brood is calling for food I feed them on sweets, snails, spiders and seeds!

Keeping the locks

On a busy day you will often see the lock keepers helping boaters, some of whom have never worked their way through a staircase of locks.

Find out more about the job of the lock keepers today by visiting www.waterscape.com and downloading the MP3 audio file. Visit top lock cottage and find out from Jack Cryer what life was like as a lock keeper here in the past.

I'm Walter Wade, a lengthsman to trade Tending the path to avoid any wrath. Clearing out silt, in case the gates silt, it takes all my strength to manage this length.

Daily toil

Life onboard a working boat was hard. Occasionally there would some light relief, like catching up on the towpath gossip whilst queuing to pass through the locks at Foxton. Why not visit Foxton Canal Museum where amongst other things you can peek inside the cabin of a traditional butty boat? Could you imagine living and working with your whole family in such a small space?

I'm just his wife, a trouble and strife, Doing this work – there's no time to shirk. Minding the kids, polishing the lids, And taking the litter – I don't get no sitter.

Dolly and Co.

Before engines were invented, boats were horse-drawn. In fact, horses were used for much more than their pulling power. Find out what Dolly, and other horses like her, got up to on the canal here at Foxton by visiting the top lock stables. Can you match the labels to the artefacts on display?

I'm Nobody's Fool, a hard working mule Hauling a line from five until nine. Five o'clock dawn til sunshine has gone. A boatman's best friend? Right up till the end.

To Gumley

To Foxton

Overflow

Grand Union Canal (GUC)

▲ **A working pair of boats** steaming towards Leicester. Although quicker than horse-drawn boats, steam boats could not carry as much cargo, due to their large boiler and coal store.

Top Lock Cottage

▲ **The stables** at Foxton top lock were once home to Dolly and other hard working canal company horses.

▲ **The daily grind of hooves** on rough towpaths meant farriers were kept busy changing shoes roughly every couple of weeks.

▲ **Top lock cottage** – where the Cryer family once lived. It is still the lock keeper's office and home to the 'Coffee Shop'. Meet old Jack Cryer and hear his tales from times gone by.

▲ **Up and down the locks** went the boats and the families who worked them. How many boats can you count passing through Foxton Locks today?

Side ponds

Willow Arbour

Upper Arm canal

Wheelchair access across canal

Canal Museum

Staircase Locks

Site of Boat Lift

▲ **The brick building** that now houses the museum was once the boiler house for the steam engine that powered the boat lift. Visit the museum to see a working model of the lift.

GUC Leicester Line

Harborough Arm

Boat trips

Starting Point

▲ **Boat trips** run from outside the Bridge 61 pub. Working boats once sat below bottom lock waiting their turn to climb the steep staircase.

◄ **The Boat Lift** only operated for ten years, but what a grand sight it was! Take time to visit the viewing platform for a bird's eye view across its impressive remains.

"By measuring how low a boat sits in the water with my gauging stick I can tell the weight the boat is carrying and charge accordingly."
John Frisby Bennly, Toll Keeper, 1894

A plan of the Foxton Locks Site as it exists today, as reproduced in the Discovery Trail leaflet. COURTESY BRITISH WATERWAYS.

INDEX

ABOUT THE AUTHOR

David Carden was born in April 1952 and, with short exceptions, has lived and still lives at Tonbridge in Kent. He trained as a civil engineer at City University in London, from where he graduated with an honours degree in 1974.

Apart from two brief periods before and after university, when he worked as a farm labourer, David has been employed as a civil engineer, principally in the UK water industry. He started his career with the Southern Water Authority, initially at Maidstone but later held posts at Gravesend, Tonbridge and Chatham. In all, he stayed with the water authority for eleven years, during which time he was principally involved in design and construction works relating to coastal and river flood defences. Several of the projects on which he worked related to the navigable section of the River Medway, and included structural works to locks and sluice gates.

In 1985, David joined Lewin Fryer & Partners, an engineering consultancy based at Hampton, in Middlesex, that specialised in river, canal and coastal engineering. Their main clients included the National Rivers Authority, now the Environment Agency, and British Waterways. It was in 1992 that David first started working on a long term project for British Waterways - North West Region to refurbish and partly modernise the sluices on the Weaver Navigation in Cheshire. Not long after he became fully involved in British Waterways' plans to restore the Anderton Boat Lift, when Lewin, Fryer & Partners were appointed as lead consultants on the project. He currently works for consulting engineers Black & Veatch.

David's first book, *The Anderton Boat Lift*, was published by Black Dwarf Publications in 2000 and a revised second edition was published in 2004. Having sold out again in 2010, a new third edition has been brought out to coincide with the publication of this volume. In conjunction with Neil Parkhouse, David also compiled *A Guide to the Anderton Boat Lift*, first published in 2001 which will shortly reach its seventh edition.

In the autobiographical notes which appeared on the flyleaf of the first edition of *The Anderton Boat Lift*, it was stated that '*David has not written any previous books – and may well not write another!*'. This volume happily disproves the validity of that statement!

WATERWAYS HISTORY TITLES FROM BLACK DWARF LIGHTMOOR

www.lightmoor.co.uk for full details of all our publications

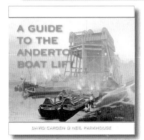
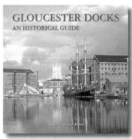
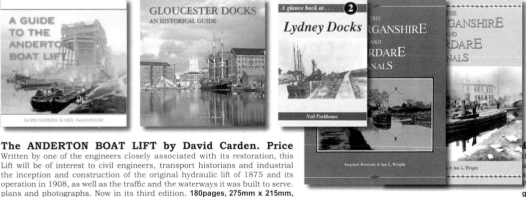